Secret History

Secret History

THE CIA'S CLASSIFIED ACCOUNT
OF ITS OPERATIONS IN
GUATEMALA, 1952-1954

SECOND EDITION

Nick Cullather

with an introduction by the author and
an Afterword by Piero Gleijeses

Stanford University Press
Stanford, California
2006

Stanford University Press
Stanford, California
Preface, Introduction, Afterword, Notes
to Appendixes C and D, and Index
© 1999 and 2006 by the Board of Trustees of
the Leland Stanford Junior University
Printed in the United States of America

Library of Congress Cataloging-in-Publication Data

Cullather, Nick
    Secret history : the CIA's classified account of its operations in
Guatemala, 1952–1954 / Nick Cullather ; with an introduction by
the author and an Afterword by Piero Gleijeses—2nd ed.
        p.   cm.
    Includes bibliographical references and index.
    ISBN-13: 978-0-8047-5467-5 (cloth : alk. paper). —
    ISBN-13: 978-0-8047-5468-2 (pbk. : alk. paper)
    1. Guatemala—History—1945–1985. 2. United States—
Central Intelligence Agency. 3. Guatemala—History—
Revolution, 1954. 4. Arbenz Guzmán, Jacobo, 1913–1971. 5.
United States—Relations—Guatemala. 6. Guatemala—
Relations—United States. I. Title.

F1466.5.A688C85   2006
972.8105'2—dc22   2006010315

This book is printed on acid-free, recycled paper.

Contents

Preface to the Second Edition   vii

Introduction: A Culture of Destruction   xi

Foreword to the CIA Edition   5

Chapter 1: America's Backyard   7
Chapter 2: Reversing the Trend   38
Chapter 3: Sufficient Means   74
Chapter 4: The Sweet Smell of Success   105

Appendix A: PBSUCCESS Timeline   127
Appendix B: Bibliography   133
Appendix C: A Study of Assassination   137
Appendix D: New Documents   143

Afterword: The Culture of Fear, by Piero Gleijeses   xxiii

Index   xxxix

Photographs and Maps

Photographs

Carlos Castillo Armas in exile 13
Jacobo Arbenz addressing a crowd in Guatemala City 21
Allen Dulles 30
John Foster Dulles conferring with President Eisenhower 36

Maps

Invasion plan, 18 June 1954 86
Actual invasion, late June 1954 91

Preface to
the Second Edition

The term had not come into general usage when the first edition
of this book was published in 1999, but what occurred in Guatemala in 1954 would nowadays be referred to as an example of
"regime change." Since 2001, the United States has made clear
that it would resort to this measure in response to threats from
terrorism or mass-destruction weapons and to deal with recalci-
trant or "failed" states. The unspoken assumption is that governments are interchangeable components, easily detached from
the societies and economies over which they preside, and just as
easily replaced. The architects of Operation PBSUCCESS were
equally certain of this point, and sure of their ability to remove
and rebuild a regime. Readers adapt their understandings of history in light of new developments, and so, while this book once
concerned a secretive episode in the cold war in Central America,
today it describes an early precedent for the global "path of action" pursued in the war on terror.[1]

Although the administration has, at least publicly, preferred to
draw analogies to the post–World War II occupations of Germany

[1]George Bush, *The National Security Strategy of the United States* (Washington:
The White House, September 17, 2002), p. ii.

and Japan, and critics have invoked the Viet Nam parallel, there are reasons to consider the civil wars in Central America a more direct antecedent to policies pursued in Iraq and Afghanistan. The U.S. invasion of Afghanistan placed heavy emphasis on the use of surrogate armies backed by airpower, while the Iraq invasion relied on selective violence to produce psychological effects ("shock and awe"), the principal techniques of PBSUCCESS. Since 2003, the Pentagon has modeled its counterinsurgency campaign in Iraq on methods developed in "dirty wars" in El Salvador and Guatemala in the 1980s. In the 1950s, it was axiomatic that proximity justified energetic measures to secure the United States's "backyard" in Central America. Polls show that people in many countries in Asia, the Middle East, and Africa now worry that our backyard has grown to include them.

As I listen to the administration's reassurances about U.S. intentions, I hear echoes of the "facts of life" that CIA operatives tried to impress on the Guatemalan military in 1954: that "the US is the most generous and tolerate taskmaster going, that cooperation is studded with material reward, and that the US permits much more sovereignty and independence in its sphere . . ." This second edition is occasioned by events which lend the story of PBSUCCESS fresh significance for a new generation of nation builders.

Thanks to the release of additional documentation, it is also a richer story. In 2003, the State Department released a volume of declassified materials as part of its *Foreign Relations of the United States* series, a project which since 1861 has upheld a governmental commitment to open diplomacy. FRUS (rhymes with spruce), as it is called by historians, publishes a substantial assortment of the memos and cables on which U.S. foreign policy is based. In 1989, the Organization of American Historians charged that the series had lost its integrity when it issued a volume on Iran containing no CIA documents or indeed any mention of the

---

²On the Central American precedent to counterinsurgency policy, see Peter Maass, "The Way of the Commandos," *New York Times Magazine*, May 1, 2005; Robert Parry, "Iraq: Quicksand and Blood," *In These Times*, December 26, 2003, http://www.inthesetimes.com/comments.php?id=521_0_1_0_C.

1953 covert operation that overthrew Iranian prime minister Mohammad Mossadeq. The long-delayed Guatamala volume signals an effort to return FRUS to its original purpose of permitting the public to gain accurate information on the activities of government agencies. It contains a wide sampling of documents from CIA, State, the National Security Council, and the office of the President.[3] The absence of Defense Department documents related to military advisers, aid, and Operation HARDROCK/BAKER still leaves a large gap in the historical record, but the new volume represents a considerable advance. Additional documentation has come to light as part of the truth and reconciliation process in Guatemala and through the efforts of scholars using the Freedom of Information Act. This new edition includes a new appendix, Appendix D, with some of the more significant new documents.

US Navy blockade of Guatemala

The original text has not been revised. I have been conscious of Robert Shaffer's description of this book as a "secondary source that functions also as a primary source," and so the original text and, equally important, the gaps in the text have remained untouched.[4] I have received more compliments on the eloquence of the gaps than on any of the legible passages. Readers have found they can check their speculations for fit, and search the blank spaces for clues on the aspects of the operation that the agency, even after 50 years, prefers to cloak in "plausible deniability."

Nick Cullather

Bloomington, Indiana
August 2005

[3]Department of State, *Foreign Relations of the United States, 1952–1954, Guatemala* (Washington: USGPO, 2003).
[4]Robert Shaffer, "The 1954 Coup in Guatemala and the Teaching of U.S. Foreign Relations," *Passport* 35 (December 2004) 3: 5–13.

Introduction

A Culture of Destruction

This study is a product of the Central Intelligence Agency's "openness" initiative, which for a short while promised to reveal the agency's history to the public. Director of Central Intelligence Robert Gates apologized to the Oklahoma Press Association in February 1992 for the agency's reflexive secrecy and announced that all documents over thirty years old would be reviewed for declassification. Senator David Boren, a member of the Select Committee on Intelligence, applauded, noting that a new understanding of history would "create a climate in which the wisdom of current operations will be carefully weighed." → *past influences current action*

It seemed a natural, almost predictable announcement, given the history-making events of the early 1990s. Two months earlier, the Soviet Union dissolved, and the new Russian government threw open the archives of the Communist Party in Moscow. *following Russia* The KGB escorted network television crews on tours of its inner sanctum while former spymasters signed book deals in New York. Almost every week newspapers carried revelations from the Soviet files on the Alger Hiss case, the fate of POWs in Vietnam, and other mysteries of the Cold War. If the Communist enemy was going public, how could the United States refuse?

Americans expected not only a "peace dividend" after the Iron

Curtain fell, but a truth dividend as well. Governmental secrecy, at least on the scale that it had been practiced during the Cold War, seemed a relic of the past. Responding to the public mood, Congress passed legislation requiring the release of materials on the assassination of John F. Kennedy and accelerating the declassification and publication of diplomatic records. Oliver Stone's movie *JFK* turned support for declassification into a fashion statement. Shortly before Christmas 1991, I noticed a sales clerk at Marshall Fields in Chicago sporting a stylish pin that read "Free the Files."

Having spent the previous three years requesting, and for the most part being denied, information on U.S. government activities in the Philippines, I cheered the prospect of a more open CIA. The agency destabilizes history, particularly in poorer nations where rumors of dark plots often blend into a kind of surrogate history in which the CIA is the only real actor. When I arrived in Manila just after a military coup attempt had nearly toppled the Aquino government in 1990, I found many people who believed the CIA had both initiated the coup and then engineered its failure. Secrecy prevents such stories from being challenged, and they gradually harden into fact. Picking up the pieces years later, historians can never be entirely sure of themselves as they try to sort reality from illusion. Openness might remove the veil of mystery which keeps intelligence and espionage in the shadows of history.

Shortly after Gates announced the openness program, the CIA began advertising for historians in the newsletters of scholarly associations. In my last year of graduate school and intrigued by this unusual opening, and I telephoned J. Kenneth McDonald, the CIA's chief historian, to ask about the position. He explained that the History Staff would be at the center of the openness effort. Its eight historians would have complete access to the agency's files. They would locate documents, rank the papers in order of importance, and then pass them to the review group that did the declassifying. Major covert actions had first priority, and agency historians would research and write secret, internal histories of operations in Iran, Guatemala, and Indonesia as part of a process that would end with a public conference at which the history and documents would be released. The job was a career posi-

tion; I could stay with the History Staff or, if I wanted, move off into Intelligence, Operations, or one of the other directorates. *granted*
I asked if anyone was working on Guatemala. Operation PBSUC- *clearance*
CESS, which overthrew the Guatemalan government in 1954, was one of the best known and most analyzed covert operations. Richard Immerman wrote in the 1980s that it set a pattern for later agency activities, from the Bay of Pigs to support for the Nicaraguan Contras. Piero Gleijeses had recently attacked the story from the Guatemalan side, revealing the secret of Jacobo Arbenz's ties to the Communists and the military's complicity in the coup that overthrew him. There were still plenty of contested issues—What was the CIA's connection to United Fruit? Was the CIA-sponsored invasion a real threat?—but since this was the most studied covert operation, it could show, better than any other, what CIA documents had to offer. I could see what the agency's files had that was completely new and unavailable in outside sources. McDonald said that the project was mine if I wanted it.

After a security check, polygraph test, and an interview by a psychiatrist, I arrived on July 26, 1992, at the PlayDoh-shaped Old Headquarters Building in Langley, passing under a concrete entrance canopy that ramped skyward in a gesture of early space-age optimism. For three days, I trained with other agency recruits who would be secretaries, scientists, and spies. The program consisted of several hours on personal financial management, instructions on whom to consult about psychological or substance abuse problems, a short course in agency lingo, a rundown on the various departments and subunits that made up the intelligence community, and procedures for classifying documents and disposing of them in special "burn bags."

The following week I began working through boxes of classified material. With Top Secret and compartmentalized clearances, I had access to all of the records I needed. Internal restraints on the flow of documents and ideas seemed to be loosening up. The information control officers who guarded the compartmental boundaries—the firewalls that keep secret information from moving from one part of the agency to another—were renamed "access management officers." The one I dealt with seemed eager to help me find documents on PBSUCCESS. Over 260 boxes of material related to the Guatemala operation had already been found in Job 79-01025A.

The only constraints on my work were time, space, and sloppy record-keeping. There was almost too much material. Allowing a year to complete the project, I would have to read over 500 pages a day just to get through the records already discovered. Security procedures made it difficult to skim the files in a hurry. Archive boxes had to be ordered from a distant location, usually arriving the next day at the vaulted office where between eight and eleven historians worked in cramped cubicles. Only a few boxes at a time could fit into a cubicle or the office safe, and the remainder had to be sent back at the end of the day. Other document collections (called "jobs" in agency parlance) contained some useful information, but finding anything in the trackless storehouse of agency records was uphill work. Indexes listed materials by office of origin, not by topic, and offices frequently took vague titles (like the "Office of Survey Information") to deflect inquiries. Indexes had been destroyed in routine purges, and there was often no way to tell which files had been burned and which preserved. Occasionally a hunch paid off or a cache of valuable files turned up in an unexpected place, but such discoveries depended on having plenty of time and luck.

Ken McDonald, Mary McAuliffe, Gerald Haines, and other historians on the staff were happy to offer suggestions, but decisions about how to shape the project and the final manuscript were left entirely up to me. I first had to decide how to limit the project to a manageable scope. Job 79-01025A contained over 180,000 pages, and to write a concise story in a reasonable amount of time I had to choose what to keep and what to leave out. Early on, I elected not to deal with the question of how much the operation cost. The small price tag was one of the features that drew the Eisenhower administration to covert operations in the first place, but the Kirkpatrick Report on the Bay of Pigs revealed that while operational budgets started small they quickly mushroomed out of control.[1] I suspected

---

[1]Office of the Inspector General, *Survey of the Cuban Operation and Associated Documents* (Washington, D.C.: Central Intelligence Agency, February 16, 1962).

that the same was true of PBSUCCESS, and that the total cost may have been larger than the estimates given to the administration. It was only a guess, but I doubted that Oliver North was the first person to think of diverting money from one operation to another. The cost figures could also be checked: Agency accountants demanded exacting records; every pencil eraser, hotel bill, and bribe was vouchered. There were entire boxes filled with receipts, and expense reports and ledgers interlarded nearly every file. Partly because these sources were so plentiful, I decided to lay them aside. The side tracks and spur lines on the money trail would take months, perhaps years, to chart, and I was not sure I had the expertise to do the job.

Despite a trove of intriguing materials, I also chose not to analyze the content of the radio propaganda effort known as SHERWOOD. Believing the new techniques of advertising and psychology could create a revolution by themselves, agency officers invested SHERWOOD with more effort and creativity than any other aspect of the Guatemala operation, and dozens of boxes of well-preserved materials, including recordings of the actual broadcasts, and scripts in Spanish and English, offered a look at how the agency tried to manipulate culture and opinion. But David Atlee Phillips had described this operation at some length in his book *The Night Watch*, and shortly after beginning my research I came across cables from the Guatemala City station complaining that SHERWOOD's signal was too weak to be heard in the capital. In this, and in many other instances, the elaborateness of the scheme seemed inversely related to its effectiveness.

By omitting the financial and SHERWOOD materials I could set aside a third of the records and concentrate on the question implied by the operation's codename: How does the CIA define success? The book's core audience would be CIA officers and trainees who would want to know how an operation worked from start to finish: How the agency assessed a threat and devised a plan to combat it, what kind of government and society it aimed to create, how the operation played out, and how (or whether) the outcome was measured against the original plans and goals.

As the manuscript took shape, some of the CIA's skilled specialists lent a hand. Mapmakers in the cartography lab used computers to reconstruct Guatemala's road and rail network as it looked in 1954, and then plotted the invasion route from descriptions in cable traffic. Photo researchers tracked down images of the story's characters.

Research occasionally stopped to make room for the office's other duties. Twice a year we offered a course in the history of the agency, a seminar for senior executives, and a lecture course for over 300 junior officers and staff held in the Bubble, the futuristic auditorium adjoining the Old Headquarters Building in Langley. The course itself was classified secret, but nearly all of the materials we used came from outside, "open" sources. Having done so little historical research of its own, the agency had to rely on accounts by historians with no access to classified documents, and its training program suffered from its own efforts to conceal and distort the public record. For Operation PBSUCCESS, for example, we assigned an article that I later learned was based on disinformation the agency itself spread in 1954. The CIA was reabsorbing its own hype. The classified, internal histories that each of us were writing were designed to solve that problem.

Openness had momentum in the fall of 1992. In October, the CIA hosted a conference on the Cuban Missile Crisis, inviting the press to Langley and releasing a 376-page collection of documents. There was talk of opening a reading room where the public could sift through declassified materials. The inauguration of President Clinton, however, cast uncertainty on the future of openness. Although the new director, R. James Woolsey, promised a "warts and all" disclosure of historical material and made covert operations the first priority, the policy was identified with his predecessor. Clinton increased the agency's budget and the specter of a congressional push to eliminate the agency evaporated. Pressure for more releases seemed to slacken. The access managers greeted my requests more skeptically. When the history staff proposed a conference on the détente-era debate over Soviet nuclear strength (an episode known as the Team-A Team-B Experiment), higher echelons turned it down.

The changed political climate was not the only thing holding up openness. The Guatemala papers had been spared routine destruction by the lawsuit described below in chapter 4, but other covert operations had not been so lucky. Virtually all of the documents on an important early covert operation in Iran had been burned in the 1960s when an agency official found them cluttering up his safe. The destruction was unsystematic. Instead of a deliberate effort to obliterate the historical record, the destruction resulted from a careless disregard for the past that is perhaps natural in an agency where the only valuable information is minutes, or at most hours old. There were signs that casual destruction continued to go on. In early 1993 a case officer for Tibet who was retiring after thirty years of service contacted the History Staff. A friend of the Dalai Lama, he had filing cabinets bulging with records on Tibetan operations going back to the early 1960s. When he gave notice, his supervisor dropped off some burn bags and asked him to clean out his cubicle before he left. Desperate, he wanted to know if we would take the papers that constituted his life's work.

Down the hall from our office, declassification continued at a crawl. The agency hired former officers to read and censor documents before release. They were in some ways the poorest possible choice for the task. Steeped in the culture of secrecy, they took a dim view of releasing documents. When Mary McAuliffe submitted her Cuban Missile Crisis compendium, they blacked out over nine-tenths of it. Without pressure from the director's office, there would have been nothing to release at the October conference. Almost as bad was their unhurried pace. Declassifying is hard on the eyes and demands steady attention to detail, not ideal work for men as far past retirement age as many of them were. What's more, agency policy required that they receive salaries equivalent to the highest salary they had while on duty, often twice that of a new recruit or a clerical worker. This assured that funds allotted for declassification served mainly to brighten the golden years of agency pensioners.

I left the agency in July 1993, a year and a day after I started. A week earlier I placed the manuscript of the PBSUCCESS history on McDonald's desk. It would be classified "secret" and published internally by the CIA under the title *Operation PBSUCCESS: The United States and Guatemala, 1952–1954*. Several thousand copies, in hard- and soft-cover editions, were distributed throughout the agency in 1994.

In the following years releases on the VENONA code-breaking operation and CORONA satellite photography grabbed headlines, but historians grew increasingly dissatisfied with the pace of the openness program. The promised disclosures on covert operations failed to materialize. Documents released for publication in the State Department's *Foreign Relations of the United States* series were heavily "redacted," edited often in ways that rendered them useless. When Clinton issued a new executive order on declassification, the agency requested exemption for 106 million pages of pre-1975 documents, almost two-thirds of the total.

Complaints about the program appear to have prodded the CIA into releasing this history. On May 20, 1997, the *New York Times* published the remarks of George C. Herring, a member of the CIA's Historical Review Panel, who called the program "a brilliant public relations snow job" that created "a carefully nurtured myth" of openness. Two days later, one of my former colleagues on the History Staff called to say that the agency was releasing my Guatemala study along with a few other papers on PBSUCCESS. I asked if he could send me a copy in advance of the release, since I had never seen the printed version. Not possible, he replied: "The press conference is going on now."

I never expected my study to be released by itself. From my earliest discussions with McDonald on, I understood that the agency planned to release a significant portion of the papers in Job 79-01025A. A few weeks before leaving the agency, at McDonald's request, I drew up a priority list for the declassification of files on Guatemala. My study was not on it. But the actual release consisted only of the published text along with some supporting documents, less than 1 percent of the total collection. In writing it, I never imagined my study as a full account or as an "official version" of PBSUCCESS. It was meant to stand alone only as a training manual, a cautionary tale for future covert operators.

What follows is that study in the form in which it was released. Although it is redacted, the narrative is substantially intact. Where cuts have occurred they are indicated by brackets, and within the limits of the typographer's art I have tried to reproduce the excisions' relative size in order to allow the reader to speculate on the contents of the missing passage. On a few occasions, the agency censored quotes taken from commonly available materials, books or articles, and in those instances I have restored the missing words in a footnote.

The most sensational disclosure contained in the 1,400 pages of documents released along with this study concerned an aspect of PBSUCCESS that is not discussed in this narrative: agency plans to assassinate Guatemalan officials either in conjunction with the operation or in the event of its failure. Among the released documents is a memorandum entitled "A Study of Assassination." It provides a do-it-yourself guide to political murder. The documents also contain lists of Communists to be "eliminated" after a successful coup. I came across none of the assassination documents during my research, not because they were withheld from me, but probably because of my own oversight. The citations listed by the National Archives indicate that they were dispersed among the 180,000 pages of material in Job 79-01025A. The released copies are heavily redacted (the target lists, for instance, contain no names), and without an adequate context it is difficult to discern how the plots fit into the larger operation. They do, however, reveal the agency's attitude toward the use of violence in what was supposed to be a "psychological" operation, and a sample of these documents is included in Appendix C.

This morning's *New York Times* carries a story headlined "CIA, Breaking Promises, Puts Off Release of Cold War Files." It is an obituary for the openness program. Citing a shortage of money and personnel, the director of central intelligence, George Tenet, has decided to "hold the reviews of these covert actions in abeyance for the time being." Tenet had previously said that as far as he was concerned openness was over. "I would turn our gaze from the past," he told a Senate confirmation committee; "it is dangerous, frankly, to keep looking over our shoulders." The following story, I believe, shows why it is even more dangerous not to.

Nick Cullather

Bloomington, Indiana
July 1998

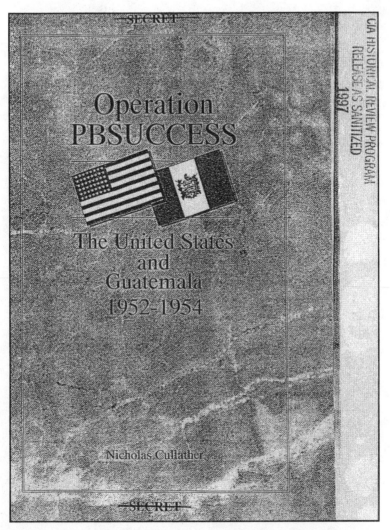

The cover of *Operation PBSUCCESS*, deposited in photocopy in the
National Archives in May 1997.

What follows is the sanitized version of *Operation PBSUCCESS* deposited in the National Archives in May 1997 by the CIA. Every effort has been made to reproduce the redacted version of the text exactly; blank spaces in the text, notes, and appendixes represent excisions of approximately the same length in the sanitized version. Appendix C reproduces, with new explanatory notes, excerpts from related documents released at the same time.

Operation PBSUCCESS

The United States and Guatemala 1952-1954

Nicholas Cullather

History Staff
Center for the Study of Intelligence
Central Intelligence Agency
Washington, DC
1994

All material on this page
is unclassified.

Foreword

This work offers a fast-moving narrative account of CIA's Operation PBSUCCESS, which supported the 1954 *coup d'état* in Guatemala. This early CIA covert action operation delighted both President Eisenhower and the Dulles brothers by ousting President Arbenz and installing Colonel Castillo Armas in his place. In light of Guatemala's unstable and often violent history since the fall of Jacobo Arbenz Guzmán in 1954, we are perhaps less certain today than most Americans were at the time that this operation was a Cold War victory.

It is tempting to find lessons in history, and Allen Dulles's CIA concluded that the apparent triumph in Guatemala, in spite of a long series of blunders in both planning and execution, made PBSUCCESS a sound model for future operations. A major hazard in extracting lessons from history, however, is that such lessons often prove illusory or simply wrong when applied in new and different circumstances. Nick Cullather's study of PBSUCCESS reveals both why CIA thought PBSUCCESS had been a model operation, and why this model later failed so disastrously as a guide for an ambitious attempt to overthrow Fidel Castro at the Bay of Pigs in 1961.

Nick Cullather joined CIA and the History Staff in July 1992, soon after completing his Ph.D. at the University of Virginia. He is author of

Cullather sees as failure

Illusions of Influence: The Political Economy of United States–Philippines Relations, 1942–1960, which Stanford University Press will publish this year. In July 1993 he left the CIA to take an appointment as assistant professor of diplomatic history at Indiana University. This publication is evidence of his impressive historical gifts and of the highly productive year he spent with us.

Finally, I should note that, while this is an official publication of the CIA History Staff, the views expressed—as in all of our other works— are those of the author and do not necessarily represent those of the Central Intelligence Agency.

J. Kenneth McDonald
Chief Historian

CHAPTER I

America's Backyard

They would have overthrown us even if we had grown no bananas.
Manuel Fortuny[1]

The CIA's operation to overthrow the Government of Guatemala in
1954 marked an early zenith in the Agency's long record of covert action. Following closely on successful operations that installed the Shah
as ruler of Iran [   ] the Guatemala operation, known as PBSUCCESS, was both more ambitious
and more thoroughly successful than either precedent. Rather than
helping a prominent contender gain power with a few inducements,
PBSUCCESS used an intensive paramilitary and psychological campaign to replace a popular, elected government with a political nonen-
tity. In method, scale, and conception it had no antecedent, and its triumph confirmed the belief of many in the Eisenhower administration
that covert operations offered a safe, inexpensive substitute for armed
force in resisting Communist inroads in the Third World. This and
other "lessons" of PBSUCCESS lulled Agency and administration officials into a complacency that proved fatal at the Bay of Pigs seven
years later.

Scholars have criticized the agency for failing to recognize the

[1] Quoted in Piero Gleijeses, *Shattered Hope: The Guatemalan Revolution and
the United States, 1944–1954* (Princeton: Princeton University Press, 1991), p. 7.

unique circumstances that had led to success in Guatemala and failing to adapt to different conditions in Cuba. Students of the 1954 coup also question the nature of the "success" in Guatemala. The overthrown Arbenz government was not, many contend, a Communist regime but a reformist government that offered perhaps the last chance for progressive, democratic change in the region. Some accuse the Eisenhower administration and the Agency of acting at the behest of self-interested American investors, particularly the United Fruit Company. Others argue that anti-Communist paranoia and not economic interest dictated policy, but with equally regrettable results.[2]

CIA records can answer these questions only indirectly. They cannot document the intentions of Guatemalan leaders, but only how Agency analysts perceived them. CIA officials participated in the process that led to the approval of PBSUCCESS, but as their papers show, they often had little understanding of or interest in the motives of those in the Department of State, the Pentagon, and the White House who made the final decision. Agency records, however, do document the conduct of the operation, the [

] how Agency operatives construed the problem, what methods and objectives they pursued, and what aspects of the operations they believed led to success. They permit speculation on [

] whether misperceptions about PBSUCCESS led overconfident operatives to plan the Bay of Pigs. Chiefly, however, they offer a view other historical accounts lack—the view from inside the CIA.

Agency officials had only a dim idea of what had occurred in Guatemala before Jacobo Arbenz Guzmán came to power in 1950. Historians regard the events of the 1940s and 1950s as following a centuries-old cycle of progressive change and conservative reaction, but officers in the Directorate of Plans believed they were witnessing something new. For the first time, Communists had targeted a country "in

---

[2]The principal books on the Guatemalan Revolution of 1954 are Stephen Schlesinger and Stephen Kinzer, *Bitter Fruit: The Untold Story of the American Coup in Guatemala* (Garden City: Doubleday and Co., 1982); Richard Immerman, *The CIA in Guatemala: The Foreign Policy of Intervention* (Austin: University of Texas Press, 1982); and Gleijeses, *Shattered Hope*.

America's backyard" for subversion and transformation into a "denied area." When comparing what they saw to past experience, they were more apt to draw parallels to Korea, Russia, or Eastern Europe than to Central America. They saw events not in a Guatemalan context but as part of a global pattern of Communist activity. PBSUCCESS, nonetheless, interrupted a revolutionary process that had been in motion for over a decade, and the actions of Guatemalan officials can only be understood in the context of the history of the region.

[The Revolution of 1944]

Once the center of Mayan civilization, Guatemala had been reduced by centuries of Spanish rule to an impoverished outback when, at the turn of the 20th century, a coffee boom drew investors, marketers, and railroad builders to the tiny Caribbean nation. The descendants of Spanish colonizers planted coffee on large estates, *fincas*, worked by Indian laborers. Coffee linked Guatemala to a world market in which Latin American, African, and Indonesian producers competed to supply buyers in Europe and the United States with low-priced beans. Success depended on the availability of low-paid or unpaid labor, and after 1900 Guatemala's rulers structured society to secure *finqueros* a cheap supply of Indian workers. The Army enforced vagrancy laws, debt bondage, and other forms of involuntary servitude and became the guarantor of social peace. To maintain the uneasy truce between the Indian majority and the Spanish-speaking *ladino* shopkeepers, labor contractors, and landlords, soldiers garrisoned towns in the populous regions on the Pacific coast and along the rail line between Guatemala City and the Atlantic port of Puerto Barrios.[3]

When the coffee market collapsed in 1930, *ladinos* needed a strong leader to prevent restive, unemployed laborers from gaining an upper hand, and they chose a ruthless, efficient provincial governor, Jorge Ubico, to lead the country. Ubico suppressed dissent, legalized the killing of Indians by landlords, enlarged the Army, and organized a

[3]Jim Handy, "'A Sea of Indians': Ethnic Conflict and the Guatemalan Revolution," *The Americas* 46 (October 1989): 190–192.

Ubico wanted investment

personal gestapo. Generals presided over provincial governments; officers staffed state farms, factories, and schools. The Guatemalan Army's social structure resembled that of the *finca*. Eight hundred *ladino* officers lorded over five thousand Indian soldiers who slept on the ground, wore ragged uniforms, seldom received pay, and were whipped or shot for small infractions. Urban shopkeepers and rural landlords tolerated the regime out of fear of both Ubico and the Indian masses.[4]

Ubico regarded the *ladino* elite with contempt, reserving his admiration for American investors who found in Guatemala a congenial business climate. He welcomed W. R. Grace and Company, Pan American Airways, and other firms, making Guatemala the principal Central American destination for United States trade and capital. The Boston-based United Fruit Company became one of his closest allies. Its huge banana estates at Tiquisate and Bananera occupied hundreds of square miles and employed as many as 40,000 Guatemalans. These lands were a gift from Ubico, who allowed the company a free hand on its property. United Fruit responded by pouring investment into the country, buying controlling shares of the railroad, electric utility, and telegraph. It administered the nation's only port and controlled passenger and freight lines. With interests in every significant enterprise, it earned its sobriquet, *El Pulpo*, the Octopus. Company executives could determine prices, taxes, and the treatment of workers without interference from the government. The United States Embassy approved and until the regime's final years gave Ubico unstinting support.[5]

As World War II drew to a close, dictators who ruled Central America through the Depression years fell on hard times, and authoritarian regimes in Venezuela, Cuba, and El Salvador yielded to popular pressure. Inspired by their neighbors' success, Guatemalan university students and teachers resisted military drills they were required to perform by the Army. Unrest spread, and, in June 1944, the government was beset by petitions, public demonstrations, and strikes. When a

---

[4]Gleijeses, *Shattered Hope*, pp. 11–19.
[5]*Ibid.*, pp. 21–22; Immerman, *CIA in Guatemala*, p. 83.

Ubico overthrown
in Depression

soldier killed a young schoolteacher, a general strike paralyzed the country, and the aged, ailing dictator surrendered power to his generals. Teachers continued to agitate for elections, and in October younger officers led by Capt. Jacobo Arbenz Guzmán and Maj. Francisco Arana deposed the junta. The officers stepped aside to allow the election of a civilian president, a sacrifice that earned popular acclaim for both them and the Army. The Revolution of 1944 culminated in December with the election of a university professor, Juan José Arévalo, as President of Guatemala.[6]

Arévalo's regime allowed substantially greater freedoms, but remained essentially conservative. Political parties proliferated, but most were controlled by the ruling coalition party, the Partido Acción Revolucionaria (PAR). Unions organized teachers, railroad workers, and the few factory workers, but national laws restricted the right to strike and to organize *campesinos*, farm laborers and tenants. The Army remained in control of much of the administration, the schools, and the national radio. Modest reforms satisfied Guatemalans, and the revolutionary regime was highly popular. Most expected one of the revolution's military heroes, Arbenz or Arana, to succeed Arévalo in 1951.[7]

So sure was Arana of taking power that he laid plans to hasten the process. In July 1949, with the backing of conservative *finqueros*, he presented Arévalo an ultimatum demanding that he surrender power to the Army and fill out the remainder of his term as a civilian figurehead for a military regime. The President asked for time, and along with Arbenz and a few loyal officers tried to have Arana arrested on a remote *finca*. Caught alone crossing a bridge, Arana resisted and was killed in a gunfight. When news reached the capital, Aranista officers rebelled, but labor unions and loyal Army units defended the government and quashed the uprising. In a move they later regretted, Arbenz and Arévalo hid the truth about Arana's death, claiming it was the work of unknown assassins. Arbenz had saved democracy a second time, and his election to the presidency was ensured, but rumors of his

[6] *Ibid.*, pp. 38–49.
[7] *Ibid.*, pp. 31–49; Immerman, *CIA in Guatemala*, pp. 48–57.

role in the killing led conservative Guatemalans, and eventually the CIA, to conclude that his rise to power marked the success of a conspiracy.[8]

After the July uprising, Arbenz and Arévalo purged the military of *Aranista* officers and placed it under loyal commanders who enjoyed, according to the US Embassy, "an unusual reputation for incorruptibility." Unions enthusiastically supported Arbenz's candidacy, expecting him to be more progressive than Arévalo. The candidate of the right, Miguel Ydígoras Fuentes, lagged behind in the polls, and Arbenz would win in a landslide. Rightists made a final bid to usurp power in the days before the election. Along with a few followers, a purged *Aranista* lieutenant, Carlos Castillo Armas, mounted a quixotic attack on a military base in Guatemala City. He believed Army officers, inspired by the spectacle of his bravery, would overthrow the government and install him as president. Instead, they threw him in jail.[9]

Castillo Armas came to the attention of the Agency [   ] in January of 1950, when he was planning his raid. A protégé of Arana's, he had risen fast in the military, joining the general staff and becoming director of the military academy until early 1949, when he was assigned to command the remote garrison of Mazatenango. He was there when his patron was assassinated on 18 July, but he did not hear of the *Aranista* revolt until four days later when he received orders relieving him of his post. Arbenz had him arrested in August and held on a trumped-up charge until December. When a CIA agent interviewed him a month later, he was trying to obtain arms from Nicaraguan dictator Anastasio Somoza and Dominican dictator Rafael Trujillo. The interviewer described him as "a quiet, soft-spoken officer who does not seem to be given to exaggeration." He claimed to have the support of the Guardia Civil, the Quezaltenango garrison, and the commander of the capital's largest fortress, Matamoros. He met with a CIA informer in

[8]Gleijeses, "The Death of Francisco Arana," *Journal of Latin American Studies* 22 (October 1990): 527–551.
[9]Gleijeses, *Shattered Hope*, pp. 81–83.

Carlos Castillo Armas in exile. Collection of the Library of Congress.

August and again in November, just a few days before he and
handful of adventurers mounted a futile assault on Matamoros. A
year later, Castillo Armas bribed his way out of prison and fled to
Honduras where he thrilled rightist exiles with stories of his rebellion and escape. He planned another uprising, telling supporters he
had secret backers in the Army. This was delusion. After the July
uprising, Arbenz was the Army's undisputed leader, and he took
steps to keep it that way.[10]

---

[10][   ] "Col. Carlos Castillo Armas in Initial Stage of Organizing

Partisan and union activity had grown amid the freedom of the Arévalo years, creating new political formations that later affected the Arbenz regime. The PAR remained the ruling party, but rival parties were tolerated. The federation of labor unions, the Confederación General de Trabajadores de Guatemala (CGTG), headed by Víctor Manuel Gutiérrez, claimed some 90,000 members. An infant union of *campesinos* led by Leonardo Castillo Flores, the Confederación Nacional Campesina de Guatemala (CNCG), began shortly after the July uprising to form chapters in the countryside. Toward the end of Arévalo's term, Communist activity came into the open. Exiled Salvadoran Communists had opened a labor school, the Escuela Claridad, in 1947 and though harassed by Arévalo's police, gathered a few influential converts, among them Gutiérrez and a onetime president of the PAR, José Manuel Fortuny. In 1948, Fortuny and a few sympathizers attempted to lead the PAR toward more radical positions, but a centrist majority defeated them. Shortly before Arbenz took office, they resigned from the PAR, announcing plans to form "a vanguard party, a party of the proletariat based on Marxism-Leninism." They called it the Partido Guatemalteco del Trabajo (PGT).[11]

American Apprehensions

United States officials' concern about Communism in Guatemala grew as Cold War tensions increased. Preoccupied by events in Europe and Asia, Truman paid scant attention to the Caribbean in his first years in office. The State Department welcomed the demise of dictatorships and found the new Guatemalan Government willing to cooperate on military aid programs and the Pan-American Highway. The FBI gathered dossiers on Fortuny and Gutiérrez in 1946 but found lit-

---

Armed Coup Against Guatemalan Government," 19 January 1950, Job 80R-01731R, Box 38; [   ] "Plans of Col. Carlos Castillo Armas for Armed Revolt Against the Government," 24 August 1950, Job 80R-01731R, Box 38; [

] "Plans of Col. Carlos Castillo Armas to Overthrow Guatemalan Government," 3 November 1950, Job 80R-01731R, Box 38; Gleijeses, *Shattered Hope*, pp. 219–220.

[11] *Ibid.*, pp. 76–78.

tle of interest. Officers from the newly created Central Intelligence Group arrived in March 1947 to take over the FBI's job of monitoring Perónist and Communist activities, but Guatemala remained a low priority. [   ][12]

The Berlin crisis, the fall of China, and the Soviet acquisition of nuclear weapons in 1948 and 1949 made Agency and State Department officials apprehensive about Soviet designs on the Western Hemisphere. They reevaluated Arévalo's government and found disturbing evidence of Communist penetration. Guatemala's relative openness made it a haven for Communists and leftists from Latin America and the Caribbean.[13] The number of homegrown Communists remained small, but they held influential positions in the labor movement and the PAR. The State Department complained, listing the names of persons to be watched and removed from high positions, but Arévalo refused to act, revealing a defiance Embassy officials found inappropriate in a Latin leader. "We would have been concerned with any tendency toward excessive nationalism in Guatemala," department officials told the NSC, "but we are the more deeply concerned because the Communists have been able to distort this spirit to serve their own ends." They saw other signs that Arévalo's nationalism had grown excessive in his treatment of American companies, particularly United Fruit.[14]

United Fruit executives regarded any trespass on the prerogatives they enjoyed under Ubico as an assault on free enterprise. The company continued to report only a fraction of the value of its land and exports for tax purposes and initially found Arévalo cooperative and respectful. But United Fruit soon grew concerned about the new government's sympathy for labor. In 1947, Arévalo passed a labor code giving industrial workers the right to organize and classifying estates

[12][   ]
[13]As J. C. King later explained, "Generally speaking, when a Communist in a Central American country gets into difficulties at home, he can find refuge, a well-paid job, and often a public post of major responsibility in Guatemala." King to Allen Dulles," Background Information on Guatemala," Job 78-01228A, Box 13.

[14]Department of State, "Guatemala," 2 May 1951, *Foreign Relations of the United States,* 1951, 2: 1415–1426.

employing 500 or more as industries. The law affected many of the larger *fincas* as well as state farms, but United Fruit contended—and the Embassy agreed—that the law targeted the company in a discriminatory manner. Workers at Bananera and Tiquisate struck, demanding higher wages and better treatment. The company had never asked for or needed official support from the United States before, but now it sought to enlist the Embassy and the State Department to do its negotiating.[15]

The State Department placed the Embassy at the service of the company. "If the Guatemalans want to handle a Guatemalan company roughly that is none of our business," the first secretary explained, "but if they handle an American company roughly it is our business." When Embassy pressure proved insufficient, the company found lobbyists who could take its case to the Truman administration. Edward L. Bernays, the "father of modern public relations," [   ] directed a campaign to persuade Congress and administration officials that attacks on the company were proof of Communist complicity. "Whenever you read 'United Fruit' in Communist propaganda," United Fruit's public relations director told audiences, "you may readily substitute 'United States.'" Thomas G. Corcoran was the company's main conduit to the sources of power. Described by *Fortune* as a "purveyor of concentrated influence," Corcoran had a network of well-placed friends in business and government. [

] calming bureaucratic waters when an occasional regulator found peculiarities in the airline's activities. United Fruit officials were impressed by his quick grasp of the situation. "Your problem is not with bananas," he told them. "You've got to handle your political problem."[16]

[15]Gleijeses, *Shattered Hope*, pp. 91–94. United Fruit customarily underreported its production by 700 percent of value. The company appraised its Tiquisate land at $19 million, but its assessed value for tax purposes was just over $1 million.

[16]Jim Handy, "'The Most Precious Fruit of the Revolution': The Guatemalan Agrarian Reform, 1952–54," *Hispanic American Historical Review* 68

Corcoran met in May 1950 with the head of the State Department's office on Central America, Thomas C. Mann, to discuss ways to secure the election of a centrist candidate. Mann considered special action unnecessary. His colleagues saw Arbenz as conservative, "an opportunist" concerned primarily with his own interests. They expected him to "steer more nearly a middle course" because his country's economic and military dependence on the United States required it. His ties to the military augured well. The Army received weapons and training from the United States, and although Embassy officials had only vague notions of its internal politics, they considered it free of Communist influence. The department had a low opinion of Arévalo's policies, but in 1950 it watched for signs of improvement in the new administration.[17] Corcoran searched for other officials who might be more sympathetic—meeting with the Agency's Deputy Director, Allen Dulles, on 9 May—but without approval from State, CIA evinced little interest.[18]

Despite Dulles's procedural correctness, Agency officials were, in fact, more apprehensive about Guatemala than their counterparts at State. Officials in the Office of Policy Coordination (OPC) grew concerned in August 1950 about "the rapid growth of Communist activity in Guatemala and the probability that Guatemala may become a central point for the dissemination of anti-US propaganda." Technically part of CIA, OPC operated under the direction of Frank Wisner, who reported to the Secretary of State. The office had undertaken covert propaganda and antisubversive operations in Europe in 1948 and later expanded its operations to include Latin America and Asia. [   ] of OPC's Latin America Division included Guatemala in [   ] a program to counter propaganda and subversion in areas where Communist agents might strike in wartime.

(1988): 699; Thomas P. McCann, *An American Company* (New York: Crown Publishers, 1976), pp. 50–54; Schlesinger and Kinzer, *Bitter Fruit*, pp. 91–93; [   ] to Allen Dulles, "Current US position with regard to Government loan requested by Guatemala," 22 October 1954, Job 79-01228A, Box 23.

[17] State Department, "Guatemala," 2 May 1951, *Foreign Relations of the United States, 1951*, 2: 1489.

[18] [   ]

They received authorization to send an agent to enroll in Guatemala City's Institut de Anthrópólogia y História where he would try to find "suitable indigenous Guatemalan personnel" to carry out projects devised by LA Division. [   ] was a global program that included [   ] and Alaska. While Guatemala's inclusion indicated heightened interest in the potential for subversion there, it did not mark the beginning of a sustained effort to deal with it by covert means. The project had a budget of only $6,000 and it produced few results.[19]

Even without official help, United Fruit could put Guatemala's feet to the fire. Bernays laid down a PR barrage that sent correspondents from *Time*, *Newsweek*, the *New York Times*, and *Chicago Tribune* to report on Communist activities in Guatemala. Company officials encouraged Castillo Armas with money and arms, and the rebel leader began seeking support from Central American leaders and the United States. A CIA official interviewed him in Mexico City in early 1950 and judged his expectation of Army support fanciful, but admitted that "if any man in Guatemala can lead a successful revolt against the present regime, it will be he who will do it." United Fruit threatened Guatemalan unions and the government, warning that any increase in labor costs would cause it to withdraw from the country. When a hurricane flattened part of the Tiquisate plantation in September 1951, the company suspended 4,000 workers without pay and announced it would not reopen until it completed a study of the business climate. Courts ordered the workers reinstated, but Walter Turnbull, the company vice president, ignored the order and presented Arbenz with an ultimatum. Unless the government guaranteed no wage increases for three years and exempted the company from the labor code, United Fruit would halt operations. To prove his earnestness, he suspended passenger shipping to the United States.[20]

[19][   ] "Project Outline [   ] Guatemala," 23 August 1950, Job 78-865 (DO), Box 1. [   ] went to Guatemala City in November 1951.

[20][   ] "Guatemala," 13 January 1950, Job 80R-01731R, Box 17, Folder 688; [   ] "Plans of Col. Carlos Castillo Armas for Armed Revolt Against the Government," 23 August 1950, *ibid.*; NIE 62, "Present Political

The administration's concern about the Arbenz regime had increased in mid-1951, and there is evidence that the Truman administration encouraged the company to take a hard line. United Fruit's vast holdings and monopolies on communications and transit in Central America attracted the attention of lawyers in the Justice Department's antitrust division as early as 1919. In May 1951, they were preparing for court action to force United Fruit to divest itself of railroads and utilities in Guatemala when the State Department intervened. In a National Security Council session, Department representatives argued that a legal attack on United Fruit's Guatemalan holdings would have "serious foreign policy implications," weakening the company at a time when the United States needed it. The action was suspended until the situation in Guatemala had improved. It is often asserted that the United States acted at the company's behest in Guatemala, but this incident suggests the opposite may have been true: the administration wanted to use United Fruit to contain Communism in the hemisphere.[21]

The State Department remained ambivalent about how far it should go in putting pressure on Guatemala. In June 1951, three months into Arbenz's term, the Department had seen no improvement. The President showed few indications of extremism in matters of policy, but he appointed several leftists to key positions. The state newspaper and radio criticized United States involvement in Korea and ran stories copied from Czech newspapers. American companies got little help from the government in dealing with labor. The "ascending curve of Communist influence" had not leveled off under Arbenz, but tilted more steeply upward.[22]

Department officials were increasingly concerned, but they wanted to avoid big stick tactics that could prove counterproductive. Guate-

Situation in Guatemala and Possible Developments During 1952," *Foreign Relations of the United States, 1952–1954*, 4: 1035–1036.

[21] Memorandum of Conversation, "Possible anti-trust suit by the Department of Justice Against the United Fruit Company," 22 May 1953, Records of the Office of Middle American Affairs, Lot 58D78, NARA, RG 59, Box 3.

[22] Notes of the Under Secretary's Meeting, 15 June 1951, *Foreign Relations of the United States, 1951*, 2: 1440–1442.

mala might obstruct United States military and development programs in the area or charge the United States with violating the Non-
Intervention Agreement, an accusation that would arouse sympathy
throughout Latin America. The Department decided to discourage
loans and drag its feet on aid and construction programs for Guatemala, steps it considered subtle but unmistakable signs of Washington's displeasure. If Arbenz were an opportunist, such moves might
have induced cooperation, but the department's analysts misjudged
the new President. Twice he had risked his life and career for democracy. His plans for development and agricultural reform were modest,
but he was determined to carry them out. Stiffening resistance from
the United States and United Fruit led him to reassess his assumptions,
adopt a more radical program, and find friends who shared his new
opinions.

Arbenz, the PGT, and Land Reform

Agency reports described Arbenz as "brilliant, . . . cultured." The
son of a Swiss pharmacist and a *ladino* woman, he planned a career
as a scientist or engineer before his father's suicide impoverished the
family and left him no alternative apart from the military academy.
His intelligence and personal magnetism earned him the admiration
of cadets and teachers alike, and he rose quickly to high rank in the
officer corps. At 26 he married María Villanova, an American-
educated Salvadoran from a prominent landed family. The intellectual, socially concerned couple studied and discussed Guatemala's
chronic economic and social problems, and in 1944 they joined the
Revolution on the side of the teachers. As Defense Minister under
Arévalo, Arbenz advocated progressive reforms, unionization, and
forced rental of unused land. He and María became friends with the
reformers, labor organizers, and officers who made up the intellectual
elite of Guatemala City. Arbenz remained close with friends from the
academy, Alfonso Martínez and Carlos Enrique Díaz, and increasingly associated with members of the PGT, Carlos Pellecer, Gutiérrez,
and Fortuny. He had particular regard for the latter, whose intellect

Jacobo Arbenz addressing a crowd in Guatemala City. Collection of the Library of Congress

and wit he put to work in the election campaign of 1950, writing speeches and slogans.[23]

The PGT contributed little to Arbenz's victory in 1950, but it gained influence under the new regime. Total party membership never exceeded 4,000 in a nation of almost three million, a fact reflected in the party's weakness at the polls. Only four Communists held seats in the 61-member congress, a body dominated by moderates. Arbenz did not appoint any Communists to the Cabinet, and only six or seven held

[23] Gleijeses, *Shattered Hope*, pp. 134–142.

significant sub-Cabinet posts. Those few, however, occupied positions that made them highly visible to United States officials, controlling the state radio and newspaper and holding high posts in the agrarian department and the social security administration. The party's principal influence came from Fortuny's friendship with the President. Arbenz's coalition disintegrated after election day into disputatious factions that offered no help amid the struggles with United Fruit and increasing tensions with the United States.

The President admired the undemanding, socially concerned members of the PGT and relied increasingly on Fortuny's political skill. Their relationship grew closer as the two men worked toward a common goal—land reform. At Arbenz's direction, Fortuny, Pellecer, and Gutiérrez drafted a proposal in 1951 for a major restructuring of property ownership in Guatemala. The PGT leadership's close ties to the President gave the party influence in Guatemala entirely out of proportion to its electoral strength. The land reform initiative enhanced that influence and drew the President even closer to Fortuny.[24]

Arbenz's attempt at land reform established his regime's radical credentials in the eyes of domestic and foreign opponents. Unable to obtain funding from the United States or the World Bank, he hesitated for a year, then on 17 June 1952 released Decree 900, an ambitious program to remake rural Guatemala. US aid officials considered it moderate, "constructive and democratic in its aims," similar to agrarian programs the United States was sponsoring in Japan and Formosa. It expropriated idle land on private and government estates and redistributed it in plots of 8 to 33 acres to peasants who would pay the government 3 to 5 percent of the assessed value annually. The government compensated the previous owners with 3 percent bonds maturing in 25 years. The proposal aimed not to create Stalinist collectives but a rural yeomanry free of the tyranny of the *finca*. For Central America it was a radical plan, and Guatemalan landowners joined Nicaraguan dictator Anastasio Somoza in denouncing it. Conserva-

[24]Schlesinger and Kinzer, *Bitter Fruit*, p. 59; Memorandum of Conversation, Dr. Robert Alexander and Mr. William L. Krieg, 1 April 1954, Job 79-01025A, Box 99; Gleijeses, *Shattered Hope*, pp. 145–147.

tives feared the program would release the Indians' suppressed hunger for land, with unpredictable consequences for *ladinos*. Historians have recently described Decree 900 as a moderate, capitalist reform, but in 1952 few local observers saw it as anything other than an attack on the wealth and power of Guatemala's propertied elite, and by example, on the social order of the region.[25]

The reform intensified conflict between the regime and United Fruit, drawing the United States into confrontation with Arbenz. The company's plantations contained huge tracts of idle land valued on the tax rolls at a fraction of their actual worth. In December 1952, workers at Tiquisate filed for expropriation of 55,000 acres. Other claims followed, and in February 1953 the government confiscated a quarter of a million acres of company land appraised at just over $1 million. United Fruit claimed the actual value was near $20 million. The company and the US Embassy charged the government with discrimination, and the State Department pressed Guatemala to submit the matter to arbitration. The Department was concerned about more than the company. Officials saw Decree 900 as a potential opening for the radicalization of Guatemala. Communists would use land redistribution "to mobilize the hitherto inert mass of rural workers," destroy the political effectiveness of large landholders, and spread disorder throughout the countryside. The Department discerned that the law had originated in the PGT and had "strong political motivation and significance."[26]

Land reform stirred up conflict within Guatemala as well. Within weeks of passage, peasants organized to seize land on idle estates. Vagueness in the law and poor enforcement led to illegal seizures, conflicts with landlords, and fighting between rival peasant claimants. Pellecer, the PGT's peasant organizer, encouraged tenants to take land by force. *Finqueros* organized to resist and brought suit against the

[25] Immerman, *The CIA in Guatemala*, pp. 64–67; Gleijeses, *Shattered Hope*, pp. 149–164; Schlesinger and Kinzer, *Bitter Fruit*, pp. 54–56; Handy, "Most Precious Fruit," pp. 683–686.

[26] Gleijeses, *Shattered Hope*, p. 164; NIE 84, "Probable Developments in Guatemala," 19 May 1953, *Foreign Relations of the United States, 1952–1954*, 4: 1064, 1070.

government. In February 1953 as disorder reigned in the countryside, entrenched landed interests and peasant unions waged a bureaucratic duel in the capital. Acting on the landlords' suit, the Supreme Court declared Decree 900 unconstitutional and ordered a halt to expropriations. Arbenz fired the justices, and after 39 hours of debate, Congress upheld the President. Peasant leaders claimed victory. "One can live without tribunals," Gutiérrez declared, "but one can't live without land." The decisive shift of power to Arbenz and *campesino* unions aroused the animosity of powerful groups. Left without recourse, landowners struck directly at peasant organizations, shooting, hanging, or beating suspected agitators. Leaders of the Catholic Church criticized the disruption of the social order. The Army felt threatened by rural unrest and peasant organizers who petitioned for the removal of uncooperative local commanders. The opposition remained leaderless and divided, but escalating conflict over land reform left the populace exhausted and bitter.[27]

The Agency Assessment

Even before implementation of land reform, the CIA saw Guatemala as a threat sufficient to warrant action. In early 1952, analysts found that increasing Communist influence made the Arbenz government "a potential threat to US security." The failure of sanctions to produce improvement in the Arbenz government disturbed State Department officials, who began to contemplate sterner action. Agency officials had stronger views. They saw a determined Communist effort to neutralize Guatemala and remove it from the Western camp. They regarded sanctions as insufficient, possibly counterproductive, and saw direct, covert action as the only remedy to Communist takeover.[28]

Agency analysts saw no immediate danger of a Communist seizure of power in 1952, but regarded the PGT as enjoying substantial and increasing influence. The party had fewer than 200 active members

[27]Handy, "Most Precious Fruit," pp. 687–703.
[28]NIE 62, "Present Political Situation in Guatemala and Possible Developments During 1952," 11 March 1952, *Foreign Relations of the United States, 1942–1954,* 4: 1031.

and had failed to infiltrate the Army, railroad and teachers' unions, and student organizations. Analysts saw the party as disciplined and in "open communication with international communism." It would seek to increase its control through the "coordinated activity of individual Communists," and by using the state media to appropriate the slogans and aims of the 1944 Revolution. It had powerful opponents—the Army, United Fruit, large landholders, the Church—but anti-Communists had failed to coalesce into a united opposition. Analysts predicted the PGT would be able to keep its opponents divided and stigmatized, gradually eroding the potential for effective anti-Communist action.[29]

Neither the United States nor United Fruit, Agency officials agreed, could undermine Communist influence with diplomatic and economic pressure. If the company surrendered to Arbenz's demands, it would hand a victory to the PGT and the unions, who would then target other US interests. If the company left Guatemala, it would injure the economy, but not critically. Arbenz would recover and in the process strengthen his ties to unions and the PGT. Analysts held that the United States was trapped in a similar dilemma: economic and diplomatic sanctions would hurt the economy, but not enough to prevent Communists from exploiting the resulting disruption. State Department observers were less pessimistic, believing a crisis triggered by United Fruit's withdrawal or US pressure could induce Arbenz to align with the right. Pentagon officials sided with the Agency, and an NIE-approved 11 March 1952 predicted a slow, inevitable deterioration of the situation in Guatemala.[30]

To CIA observers, land reform seemed a powerful weapon for the expansion of Communist influence. Decree 900 would weaken the power of conservative landowners while radicalizing the peasant majority and solidifying its support for Arbenz and the PGT activists who led groups of *campesinos* in land seizures. If land reform succeeded, thousands of small farmers would owe their land and livelihood to the influence of the PGT. Ironically, the CIA supported the objectives of the Guatemalan reform—the breakup of large estates into small free-

---

[29] *Ibid.*, pp. 1033–1035.
[30] *Ibid.*, pp. 1035–1036. [NIE = national intelligence estimate—NC.]

holds—in some of its own programs. The Agency, worried that feudal agriculture would allow Communists in the Third World to ride to power on a wave of reform, had tried for some years to change traditional rural social structures that it considered vulnerable to subversion. [   ] had supported a non-Communist farm cooperative movement. In 1952, the Directorate of Plans undertook a global program, [   ] to encourage small, independent landowners. In the [   ] the program organized 15,000 peasants into 75 study groups, each of which formed a credit union to help its members buy land.[31] Just as Agency officials saw [   ] as a way to enlarge US influence, they regarded Decree 900 as a menacing instrument of Communist penetration. Control made all the difference.

Agency officials considered Guatemala a potential Soviet beachhead in the Western Hemisphere. In 1947 and 1948, the Truman administration developed a subtle understanding of the likely consequences of the Communist takeover of a government outside of the Eastern Bloc. Officials recognized that indigenous revolutionary parties received scant support and often had little contact with Moscow. Even so, they reasoned, Communist governments would likely take actions—such as closing bases or restricting trade—that would shift power away from the United States and toward the Soviet Union. By the onset of the Korean war this analysis lost nuance. Officials in the State Department, the CIA, and the Pentagon regarded all Communists as Soviet agents. John Peurifoy, who became Ambassador to Guatemala in 1953, expressed the consensus when he observed that "Communism is directed by the Kremlin all over the world, and anyone who thinks differently doesn't know what he is talking about."[32]

Agency officials assumed the existence of links between the PGT and Moscow. They scrutinized the travel records of Guatemalan officials for signs of enemy contact and attempted to uncover the workings of an imaginary courier network. These were not manifestations

[31] See [   ] file, Job 79-01025A, Box 81.
[32] House Select Committee on Communist Aggression, *Communist Aggression in Latin America*, 83rd Cong., 2d sess., 1954, p. 125.

of McCarthyite paranoia but of a fear shared by liberals and conservatives, academics, journalists, and government officials, that a Soviet conspiracy aimed to strike at America in its own backyard.[33]

Agency analysts saw the Guatemalan threat as sufficiently grave by 1952 to warrant covert action. They began to look for State Department officials who shared their pessimism about overt remedies and to find assets in Central America around which to build a covert program. The Truman administration, however, remained divided over whether Arbenz posed a threat dire enough to warrant such strong action. In 1952 and 1953, indecision led to a fumbling paramilitary program that came close to destroying the anti-Communist movement in Guatemala.

The Agency and the Opposition

As Arbenz completed his land reform plans, the CIA began to explore the possibility of supporting his opponents. Agency officials believed that Guatemala was headed for eventual Communist takeover, and that the opportunity to act was rapidly passing. Without help, the Guatemalan opposition would remain divided and inert, enabling the PGT to consolidate its power. Early in 1952, [

] the Director of Central Intelligence, Walter [

] Smith asked the chief of the Western Hemisphere Division, J. C. King, to find out whether Guatemalan dissidents with help from Central American dictators could overthrow the Arbenz regime. King sent an agent to Guatemala City in March to search for an organized

[33]Ronald Schneider searched PGT records seized by CIA in 1954 and found no evidence of funds transfers or correspondence with Moscow. Gleijeses, who examined the same records and interviewed former Agency and Communist officials, concludes that CIA and State Department fears about Soviet links were grossly exaggerated. The Soviets made one contact with the Arbenz government, an attempt to buy bananas. The deal fell through when the Guatemalans could not arrange transport without help from United Fruit Company. Ronald M. Schneider, *Communism in Guatemala, 1944–1954* (New York: Praeger, 1958), p. 41; Gleijeses, *Shattered Hope*, pp. 187–188.

opposition and find out whether CIA could buy support, "particularly Army, Guardia Civil, and key government figures."[34] King had lived in Latin America in the 1930s [

]^35

In April 1952, State Department officials welcomed Nicaraguan President Anastasio Somoza to Washington on his first state visit. American officials had regarded Somoza as a pariah throughout the 1940s, but now the dictator received a state dinner and was escorted to meetings by Maj. Gen. Harry Vaughan, Truman's personal military adviser. Somoza told State Department officials that, if they provided arms, he and Castillo Armas would take care of Arbenz. At Vaughan's urging, Truman instructed DCI Smith to follow up. Smith dispatched [   ] a Spanish-speaking engineer who joined the Agency in 1951, to make contact with Castillo Armas and other dissidents in Honduras and Guatemala. [   ] arrived in Guatemala City on 16 June, the day before Arbenz enacted the agrarian reform, [

]^36

[   ] learned that Castillo Armas's rebels had financial backing from [   ] Somoza, and Dominican dictator Rafael Trujillo and claimed support from Army units inside Guatemala. At the request of [   ] Castillo Armas produced a battle plan calling for invasions from Mexico, Honduras, and El Salvador. The incursions would be coordinated with internal uprisings led by [

[34]J. C. King [   ] 22 March 1952, Job 79-01025A, Box 7.
[35][   ]
[36]Paul Coe Clark, *The United States and Somoza, 1933–1956: A Revisionist Look* (Westport: Praeger, 1992), pp. 187–188; [   ] to Dulles, "Conference with SEEKFORD," 4 August 1952, Job 79-01025A, Box 69; [
]

] The plotters needed money,
arms, aircraft, and boats, but [   ] considered their plans serious
and likely to proceed whether they received additional help or not.[37]
Agency officials sought approval from the State Department before
finishing plans to aid the rebels. King located arms and transport, and
on 9 July, he gave Dulles a proposal for supplying [   ] and Castillo Armas with weapons and $225,000. He recommended that So-
moza and Honduran President Juan Manuel Gálvez be encouraged to
furnish air support and other assistance. The proposal emphasized the
Agency's minor role in the plot. The rebellion would proceed in any
case, King warned, but without CIA help it might fail and lead to a
crackdown that would eliminate anti-Communist resistance in Guatemala. Allen Dulles, the Deputy Director of Central Intelligence, met
the following day with Thomas Mann of the State Department and the
Assistant Secretary of State for Inter-American Affairs, Edward G.
Miller, who told him they wanted a new government in Guatemala
imposed by force if necessary, but avoided direct answers when Dulles
asked if they wanted the CIA to take steps to bring about that outcome. Dulles accepted the officials' vagueness as implying approval,
but Smith wanted firmer backing. The DCI contacted Under Secretary
of State David Bruce and got explicit approval before signing the order
on 9 September 1952 to proceed with operation PBFORTUNE.[38]
King proceeded with plans to supply arms to Castillo Armas. He
acquired a shipment of contraband weapons confiscated by port authorities in New York: 250 rifles, 380 pistols, 64 machine guns, and

[37][   ] to Dulles, "Guatemalan Situation," 9 July 1952, Job 79-
01025A, Box 69; J. C. King, "Memorandum of Conversation with [
]" 5 May 1952, Job 79-01025A, Box 69; [
] to Dulles, "Conference with [   ]" 4 August 1952, Job 79-
01025A, Box 69. [   ] is sometimes referred to in the documents as "[
]" Agency sources revealed that Castillo Armas received $136,000 in aid [
] Contact Report 32, 1 December 1953, Job 79-01025A, Box 69.
[38][   ] "Chronology of Meetings Leading to Approval of Project A," 8 October 1952, Job 79-01025A, Box 69; [   ] to [   ] "Guatemala,"
8 October 1952, Job 79-01025A, Box 69; [   ] to Dulles, "Guatemala Situation," 9 July 1952, Job 79-01025A, Box 69.

Allen Dulles. Courtesy
of the Dwight D. Eisen-
hower Library/U.S.
Navy.

4,500 grenades. Repackaged as farm machinery, they were scheduled
to leave New Orleans [   ] in early October. CIA officials encouraged Somoza and Gálvez to lend additional aid, but soon
regretted doing so. Somoza spread word of the Agency's role in the rebellion among government officials in Central America, and the State
Department learned that the operation's cover was blown. During a
meeting with Miller in Panama, Somoza's son, Tacho, casually asked
if the "machinery" was on its way. Other diplomats caught wind of

the operation, and Secretary Dean Acheson summoned Smith on 8 October to call it off.[39]

State Department officials had reason to hesitate. President Truman had announced in March that he would not seek another term of office, turning the last 10 months of his presidency into what Acheson called a "virtual interregnum."[40] Acheson feared a blown operation would destroy the remnants of the Good Neighbor policy carefully constructed by President Franklin D. Roosevelt. The United States had pledged not to intervene in the domestic affairs of any American state and had attempted to foster Pan-American unity throughout the 1940s. Truman wanted to build on these policies in order to shield the hemisphere from subversion and to marshal support for the United States' global policies in the United Nations. The 1947 Rio Pact created an Organization of American States (OAS) that recognized the obligation of each member to meet an armed attack on any other. With US support, the United Nations had given the OAS jurisdiction over disputes within the hemisphere. Latin American leaders cooperated with these initiatives and followed the United States' lead in the UN, but criticized the Truman administration for failing to support economic development. They also remained alert for signs of backsliding on the nonintervention pledge. The appearance that the United States was supporting the invasion of an OAS member state in retaliation for expropriating American property would set US policy back 20 years. Once PBFORTUNE was blown, Miller wasted no time in terminating it.[41]

PBFORTUNE's demise took the Agency by surprise, and Colonel King scrambled to salvage part of the operation and allow Castillo Armas to save face. He arranged for the arms shipment to proceed as

[39]Packing list, [undated], Job 79-01025A, Box 150; [   ] Memorandum for the Record, 9 October 1952, Job 79-01025A, Box 69;[   ] Memorandum for the Record, 10 October 1952, Job 79-01025A, Box 69.

[40]Douglas Brinkley, *Dean Acheson: The Cold War Years, 1953–71* (New Haven: Yale University Press, 1992), p. 6.

[41]Immerman, *CIA in Guatemala*, pp. 11–12; Robert Ferrell, *American Diplomacy: A History*, 3rd ed., (New York: W. W. Norton and Co., 1975), pp. 766–771.

far as [   ] the Canal Zone and to remain there in case the project was revived. Castillo Armas was kept on a retainer of $3,000 a week, allowing him to hang on to a small force. Through the winter of 1952–53, the operation led a twilight existence, neither dead nor alive. King remained in contact with Castillo Armas through [   ] and continued to finance the rebels as a precaution in case rebellion broke out in Guatemala.[42]

Meanwhile, he began to test how far he could go without State Department approval. In November, he asked DCI Smith to allow him to build a pier at the arms storage site in Panama, buy a boat, and fly a portion of the arms to Managua "to test our ability to move supplies clandestinely by air." Smith approved the pier and the boat, but not the flight. On a slim budget, King tried to develop means to transport arms to sites in Nicaragua and Honduras, with nearly disastrous results. The aged World War II transport he acquired left port only twice. On the first trip, its crew reconnoitered a supposedly deserted island in Nicaragua for use as a supply drop, only to discover several hundred inhabitants and a suspicious policeman. On the second, the boat's four engines expired in high seas, and the US Navy had to send a destroyer to the rescue. In the end the boat was left to rust at its newly built pier.[43]

Smith and King hoped that the new administration of President Dwight D. Eisenhower would breathe new life into the project. Early signs indicated that the new President would be receptive to plans for covert operations. Eisenhower had promised during the campaign to retake the initiative in the Cold War while reducing Federal spending, goals that made covert action seem a likely recourse. On 5 March, the Assistant Secretary of State, John Cabot, asked Wisner about the possibility of stepping up psychological warfare against Arbenz, but other

[42][   ] to King, "Arrangements to receive certain items in the Canal Zone," 10 October 1952, Job 79-01025A, Box 69; King to [   ] "Central American Situation," 10 October 1952, Job 79-01025A, Box 69.

[43]King to Dulles, 20 October 1952, Job 79-01025A, Box 69; King to Smith, "PBFORTUNE," 25 November 1952, Job 79-01025A, Box 69. See also [   ]] file, Job 79-01025A, Box 81.

members of the Department hesitated.⁴⁴ Mann predicted that Guatemalan radicalism would soon be countered by a conservative reaction. If the United States allowed events to take their course, he said, "the pendulum in Guatemala would swing back." Paul Nitze, head of the Department's Policy Planning Staff, worried that Guatemalan Communism would be difficult to contain and might spill over into neighboring states.⁴⁵ With no certain mandate, Smith and King worked to keep the Guatemala operation alive until the new administration decided what to do with it.

Despite [   ] prediction, Castillo Armas showed little inclination to launch his revolution without Agency support, King approved of his restraint. His greatest fear was that a rebellion would erupt before the Agency could lend it sufficient help. If the rebels failed, the Agency could lose its assets in Guatemala. Smith urged State Department officials to approve a covert aid program before there was no one left to aid. He stressed the imminence of revolt and the sympathy of Central American rulers for the rebel cause. He exaggerated only partly. Somoza and Castillo Armas had no immediate plans, but Guatemala was rife with talk of impending invasion. The meager amounts of aid funneled in by the Agency persuaded some rebels that they had powerful friends and led them to take precisely the kind of risk King wanted to avoid.

Failure at Salamá

King's fears were realized on 29 March 1953 when Carlos Simmons launched a futile attack on the garrison at Salamá and provoked a backlash that cost the Agency and Castillo Armas most of their usable assets in Guatemala. Two hundred raiders from nearby banana plantations seized the remote town of Salamá and held it for 17 hours [   ] While the raid's planners escaped abroad, the rebels went

⁴⁴[   ] Acting Chief, Western Hemisphere Division, to Wisner, "Conversation Regarding Guatemala," 10 March 1953, Job 79-01228A, Box 13.

⁴⁵Memorandum of Conversation, Thomas C. Mann, Paul H. Nitze, 3 March 1953. Job 79-01228A, Box 13.

to jail, and the Guatemalan Government launched a dragnet to round up other suspected subversives. The failed rebellion [

] severely impaired Castillo Armas's potential. The latter's principal ally inside Guatemala was Córdova Cerna, leader of the most prominent anti-Communist organization, the Comité Civico Nacional. Despite his ties to United Fruit, Córdova Cerna's reputation as a principled opponent of Ubico (he had resigned the justice ministry in protest) lent respectability to his resistance against Arbenz. After Salamá, police raids crushed his organization and he fled to Honduras, where he began intriguing to gain control of Castillo Armas's following. PBFORTUNE suffered a severe blow. The Agency lost all its assets inside the country and was left to deal with contentious and fragmented exile groups.[46]

In the wake of Salamá, Agency analysts regarded Guatemalan developments with even deeper pessimism. Opposition within the country, according to an NIE of 19 May 1953, had been reduced to scattered "urban elements" who were unlikely to join United Fruit and landholders in a resistance movement. El Salvador, Honduras, and Nicaragua wanted new leadership in Guatemala, but analysts considered outside intervention "highly unlikely." The "only organized element in Guatemala capable of decisively altering the political situation," the Army, showed no inclination toward revolutionary action. Arbenz still had the power to break free of Communist influence, but the trend seemed in the opposite direction. "As long as President Arbenz remains in power the Arbenz-Communist alliance will probably continue to dominate Guatemalan politics." "Any increase in political tension in Guatemala," the Estimate concluded, "would tend to increase Arbenz's political dependence on this alliance."[47]As the State Department's apprehensions grew during the summer of 1953, it became increasingly receptive to proposals for bold action against Arbenz. In May, the desk officer for Central America, John M. Leddy, noted that "the trend toward increased Communist strength is unin-

[46]Schlesinger and Kinzer, *Bitter Fruit*, p. 103.
[47]NIE 84, "Probable Developments in Guatemala," 19 May 1953, *Foreign Relations of the United States, 1952–1954*, 4: 1061–1070.

terrupted," and that Salamá had furnished a pretext for a thorough crackdown on the opposition. Three months later the Bureau of Inter-American Affairs painted a bleak picture for the National Security Council. The Communists were using land reform—a program "designed to produce social upheaval"—to gain control of Guatemalan politics. The situation was progressively deteriorating. "Communist strength grows, while opposition forces are disintegrating.... Ultimate Communist control of the country and elimination of American economic interests is the logical outcome, and unless the trend is reversed, is merely a question of time."[48]

State Department analysts saw few good options. US military intervention or overt economic sanctions would violate treaty commitments and enrage other American republics. Covert intervention posed the same danger, if it were discovered. The policy of "firm persuasion" had produced few results so far, and there seemed little chance that continuing or escalating official pressure would help. "This situation," officials concluded, "tests our ability to combat the eruption and spread of Communist influence in Latin America without causing serious harm to our hemisphere relations." In the minds of Eisenhower's aides, Guatemala put the new administration on trial. It represented "in miniature all of the social cleavages, tensions, and dilemmas of modern Western society under attack by the Communist virus," explained a member of the NSC staff. "We should regard Guatemala as a prototype area for testing means and methods of combating Communism."[49]

The administration was ready to meet the challenge. In the summer of 1953, the new President encouraged his advisers to revise their strategies for fighting the Cold War. In a series of discussions, known as the Solarium talks, administration officials explored ways to fulfill

[48]Leddy to Cabot, "Relations with Guatemala," 21 May 1953, *Foreign Relations of the United States, 1952–1954,* 4: 1071–1073; NSC Guatemala, 19 August 1953, *ibid.,* 4: 1074–1086.

[49]Leddy to Cabot, "Relations with Guatemala," 21 May 1953, *Foreign Relations of the United States, 1952–1954,* 4: 1071–1073; NSC Guatemala, 19 August 1953, *ibid.,* 4: 1074–1086.

John Foster Dulles conferring with President Eisenhower. Courtesy of the Dwight D. Eisenhower Library/National Park Service.

[handwritten marginalia: Eisenhower Promoted covert action]

Eisenhower's promises to seize the initiative in the global struggle against Communism while restraining the growth of the Federal budget. The result was NSC 162/2, a policy known to the public as the "New Look." It stressed the need for a cheaper, more effective military striking force that would rely more on mobility, nuclear intimidation, and allied armies. The new policy placed a greater emphasis on covert action. Eisenhower saw clandestine operations as an inexpensive alternative to military intervention. He believed that the Cold War was entering a period of protracted, low-level conflict. Relying too much on the military would exhaust the economy and leave the United States vulnerable. In his mind, finding creative responses to Communist penetration of peripheral areas like Guatemala posed one of the critical tests of his ability as a leader.[50]

The new administration's Cabinet stood ready to put the "New Look" into effect. Eisenhower had elevated Allen Dulles to the directorship, placing the Agency under the charge of its chief covert operator. The new DCI's brother, John Foster Dulles, had become Secretary of State, a development that promised unprecedentedly smooth cooperation with the State Department, as did the appointment of Bedell Smith as Under Secretary of State. Under the new administration, key departments and agencies were headed by officials predisposed to seek active, covert remedies to the Guatemala problem.

By mid-1953, the administration stood poised to take action against Arbenz. Faltering policies late in the Truman administration—aggravated by the State Department's indecision and the Agency's poor security—accelerated the deterioration of the situation in Guatemala and left the United States with fewer options. Guatemala no longer had an organized opposition that could moderate Arbenz's behavior or offer the United States the possibility of peaceful change. American commercial interests, particularly United Fruit, intensified conflict between the United States and the Arbenz regime and precipitated the disaster at Salamá, but played only a contributing role in shaping policy. Truman and Eisenhower saw Guatemala as succumbing to Communist pressures emanating ultimately from Moscow. The threat to American business was a minor part of the larger danger to the United States' overall security. The failure of PBFORTUNE, in fact, led CIA officials to reconsider [
                                                    ] in later ventures against Arbenz.

[50]Leddy to Cabot, "Relations with Guatemala," 21 May 1953, *Foreign Relations of the United States, 1952–1954*, 4: 1071–1073; NSC Guatemala, 19 August 1953, *ibid.*, 4: 1074–1086.

CHAPTER 2

Reversing the Trend

A policy of non-action would be suicidal, since the Communist movement, under Moscow tutelage, will not falter nor abandon its goals.
National Security Council, 19 August 1953[1]

Reviewing the situation in Guatemala on 12 August 1953, the staff of the National Security Council determined that the Arbenz government posed a threat to the national security sufficient to warrant covert action against it. Eisenhower's "New Look" policy and the success of TPAJAX, an operation that overthrew Prime Minister Mohammed Mossadeq of Iran, elevated the Agency's reputation to unprecedented heights, and the new administration gave CIA primary responsibility for the action while allowing it to call on other departments for support as needed. The Operations Coordinating Board cautioned against relying on [   ] noting that [   ] was "to be used only to the extent deemed desirable by CIA, and is to be kept informed on a strict need-to-know basis."[2] The plans CIA developed in the following weeks reflected the Agency's confidence in the tactics it had developed in the first six years of its existence. Despite the lack of hard information on Guatemalan politics and society, planners

[1] Draft NSC Policy Paper, 19 August 1953, *Foreign Relations of the United States, 1952–1954*, 4: 1083.

]

were sure Guatemalans would respond to stratagems proven in Europe, the Middle East, and Asia. What made the new operation truly appealing was that covert action tactics would be applied on a grander scale, over a longer period, and for higher stakes than ever before.

J. C. King's Western Hemisphere Division staff began developing plans immediately after the NSC decision. The operation's optimistic title—PBSUCCESS—reflected the high hopes of its planners. [

] Hans Tofte, and [

] drafted an outline of the Guatemala operation during the dramatic denouement of TPAJAX. The covert operation shattered Mossadeq's Tudeh Party and gave the pro-American Shah unchallenged authority. The Iranian operation's chief officer found Secretary of State John Foster Dulles "almost alarmingly enthusiastic" about the outcome.[3] The Eisenhower administration saw this success as proof that covert action could be a potent, flexible weapon in the Cold War. King's aides were anxious to prove it again in Guatemala. They brought considerable experience to the task. [   ] had been an intelligence officer in [   ] during the war and had joined the Agency as soon as it was established in 1947. He served as [

]⁴ Tofte had fled his native Denmark in 1941 and joined the [   ] serving in Burma and China before quitting to join the OSS. Impressed by his credentials, William Donovan placed him in charge of an operation to resupply Yugoslav partisans from a secret base in [

]. He eventually came to command a force of over 600 guerillas.[5] After the war he joined CIA and earned a reputation [   ] for mounting behind-the-lines operations. In 1953 he was a member of the Psychological and Paramilitary Operations Staff in the Directorate of Plans (DDP). [   ] who served with Army intelligence

[3]Kermit Roosevelt, *Countercoup: The Struggle for Control of Iran* (New York: McGraw Hill, 1979), p. 209.

[4][   ]

[5]William J. Donovan to Adjutant General, "Recommendation for Award of Legion of Merit to Major Hans V. Tofte," 19 September 1945, Job 57-102, Box 162.

in Chile during the war and afterward as a US military adviser in Latin America, was chief of the DDP's Central America branch.[6]

The Plan

The planners decided to employ simultaneously all of the tactics that had proved useful in previous covert operations. PBSUCCESS would combine psychological, economic, diplomatic, and paramilitary actions. Operations in Europe, [   ] and Iran had demonstrated the potency of propaganda—"psychological warfare"—aimed at discrediting an enemy and building support for allies. Like many Americans, US officials placed tremendous faith in the new science of advertising. Touted as the answer to underconsumption, economic recession, and social ills, advertising, many thought, could be used to cure Communism as well. In 1951, the Truman administration tripled the budget for propaganda and appointed a Psychological Strategy Board to coordinate activities.[7] The CIA required "psywar" training for new agents, who studied Paul Linebarger's text, *Psychological Warfare*, and grifter novels like *The Big Con* for disinformation tactics.[8] PBSUCCESS's designers planned to supplement overt diplomatic initiatives—such as an OAS conference convened to discredit Guatemala—with "black operations using contacts within the press, radio, church, army, and other organized elements susceptible to rumor, pamphleteering, poster campaigns, and other subversive action."[9] They were particularly impressed with the potential for radio

[6]Thomas Powers, *The Man Who Kept the Secrets: Richard Helms and the CIA* (New York: Alfred A. Knopf, 1979), p. 323; [
], Job 78-06607R, Box 2, Folder 7.
[7]Ludwell Montague, *General Walter Bedell Smith as Director of Central Intelligence* (University Park: Pennsylvania State University Press, 1992), pp. 203–215.
[8]Paul Linebarger, *Psychological Warfare* (Washington: Infantry Journal Press, 1948). For details of Agency instruction in psywar, see Joseph Burkholder Smith, *Portrait of a Cold Warrior* (New York: G. P. Putnam's Sons, 1976), pp. 85–95.
[9]King to Dulles, "Guatemala—General Plan of Action," 11 September 1953, Job 83-00739R, Box 5.

propaganda, which had turned the tide at a critical moment in the Iran operation.[10]

The planners' faith in radio as a propaganda weapon derived from their experience in other areas of the world, and it ignored local conditions that limited the strategy's usefulness in Guatemala. Only one Guatemalan in 50 owned a radio, and the vast majority of the nation's 71,000 sets were concentrated in the vicinity of the capital, in the homes and offices of the wealthy and professional classes. Agency analysts noted that "radio does not constitute an effective means of approach to the masses of agricultural workers and apparently reaches only a small number of urban workers." Communist organizations eschewed radio and exercised influence through personal contact and persuasion. Radio, nonetheless, became a central feature of the operational plan. Although Guatemalans were "not habituated" to radio, an analyst observed, they "probably consider it an authoritative source, and they may give wide word-of-mouth circulation to interesting rumors" contained in broadcasts.[11]

[   ] Tofte, and [   ] considered Guatemala's economy vulnerable to economic pressure, and they planned to target oil supplies, shipping, and coffee exports. An "already cleared group of top-ranking American businessmen in New York City" would be assigned to put covert economic pressure on Guatemala by creating shortages of vital imports and cutting export earnings. The program would be supplemented by overt multilateral action, possibly by the OAS, against Guatemalan coffee exports. The planners believed economic pressures could be used surgically to "damage the Arbenz government and its supporters without seriously affecting anti-Communist elements."[12]

Planners had only sketchy ideas about the potential of two crucial parts of the program: political and paramilitary action. King's aides believed that to succeed the opposition would need to win over Army

[10]Roosevelt, *Countercoup*, p. 191.

[11][

]

[12]King to Dulles, "Guatemala—General Plan of Action," 11 September 1953, Job 83-00739R, Box 5.

leaders and key government officials. They considered the Army "the only organized element in Guatemala capable of rapidly and decisively altering the political situation." In Iran, cooperative army officers had tilted the political balance in favor of the Shah. Planners felt PBSUC-CESS needed similar support, but they had few ideas on how to foment opposition. Arbenz, a former officer, remained popular among military leaders. Castillo Armas had little appeal among his former colleagues, and his guerillas were no match for the 5,000-man Army. Rebel forces suffered from desertion and low morale, and agents in Honduras reported that without help, the organized opposition would disintegrate by the end of 1953.[13]

PBSUCCESS planners were disturbed by the shortage of assets around which to build a covert program. The Catholic Church opposed land reform and Arbenz, but was handicapped by its meager resources and the shortage of native priests. Foreigners were subject to deportation, and most priests avoided challenging authority. Resistance among landowners was declining "due to general discouragement" after the failure of the Salamá raid. The planners noted widespread discontent in both the capital and the countryside, but saw little prospect of stimulating disgruntled elements to take political action. The estimated 100,000 passive opponents included property owners, laborers, and *campesinos* who shared few common goals. Castillo Armas's organization, "a group of revolutionary activists, numbering a few hundred, led by an exiled Guatemalan army officer, and located in Honduras," remained the Agency's principal operational asset. In addition, some fifty Guatemalan students belonging to the Comité Estudiantes Universitarios Anti-Comunistas (CEUA) had [

][14] The group published a newspaper, *El Rebelde*. Members who fled the country after Salamá formed an exile group and published a weekly paper, *El Combate*, which was smuggled over

[13] *Ibid.*
[14] [   ] "Report on Stage One PBSUCCESS, Annex B, Friendly Assets and Potential," 15 December 1953, Job 79-01025A, Box 1.

the border. These assets, the planners reported, did "not even remotely match the 1,500–3,000 trained Communists."[15]

While TPAJAX achieved victory in less than six weeks, PBSUCCESS planners warned that Guatemala would require more effort and patience. The Agency would have to develop from scratch assets of the sort that it had used in Iran, a process that might take a year or more. [   ] foresaw a preparation period followed by a buildup of diplomatic and economic pressure on the Arbenz regime. When pressure reached its maximum point, political agitation, sabotage, and rumor campaigns would undermine the government and encourage active opposition. During this crisis, Castillo Armas would establish a revolutionary government and invade Guatemala. The plan was silent about what would happen next.[16]

Trusting the Agency's proven tactics to generate results, planners saw no problem in their inability to predict how the operation would play out. Reviewing their work, Deputy Director for Plans Frank Wisner remarked that "the plan is stated in such broad terms that it is not possible to know exactly what it contemplates, particularly in the latter phases." He added that he did "not regard this as a particular drawback" since adjustments could be made as the operation unfolded. King expected a long assessment phase during which specific goals and plans would be set, with periodic reassessments throughout the life of the operation.[17]

King and Tracy Barnes, Chief of the DDP's Political and Psychological Staff, presented the plan on 9 September to Raymond Leddy, head of the State Department's Office of Middle American Affairs, and James Lampton Berry, the Department's liaison to the Agency. Department officials had given up on the policy of gradually escalating pressure. Leddy admitted that "prospects do not appear very bright" adding that "some organizational work and some fundamental chan-

[15]King to Dulles, "Guatemala—General Plan of Action," 11 September 1953, Job 83-00739R, Box 5 (also in Job 81-00206R, Box 1).
[16]Ibid.
[17]Wisner to Dulles, "Program for PBSUCCESS," 16 November 1953. Job 83-00739R, Box 5.

ges in the situation will have to occur" before a revolt could succeed. He and Berry reviewed King's plan in detail and agreed to go ahead.[18]
  PBSUCCESS relied on the State and Defense Departments to isolate Guatemala diplomatically, militarily, and economically. In King's plan, the State Department would mount a diplomatic offensive in the OAS to declare Guatemala a pariah state and cripple its economy. State and Defense would work together to enforce an arms embargo and build up the military potential of neighboring states. The US Navy and Air Force would provide essential logistical support, maintenance, expertise, and training for paramilitary forces. Overt initiatives would create an atmosphere of fearful expectancy, which would enhance the effectiveness of covert action. PBSUCCESS would be a government-wide operation led by CIA.[19]

On 9 December 1953, Allen Dulles authorized $3 million for the project and placed Wisner in charge. Wisner's Directorate of Plans assumed exclusive control of PBSUCCESS, neither seeking nor receiving aid from other directorates. Robert Amory, Deputy Director for Intelligence (DDI) was never briefed, and Guatemala Station excluded references to PBSUCCESS in its reports to the DDI. The DDP carefully segregated the operation from its other activities, giving it a separate chain of command, communications facilities, logistics, and funds. Wisner ran the operation in Washington, with Tracy Barnes serving as a liaison to [   ] headquarters in Florida. King, who had nurtured the operation from its beginning, was pushed aside to give Wisner a free hand. "King was very upset," Richard Bissell, the Assistant DDP, recalled later. "PBSUCCESS became Wisner's project."[20]

The State Department fulfilled its assigned duties, increasing aid to industrial and road building projects in Honduras, El Salvador, and Nicaragua, and assembling a special team of diplomats to assist PB-

[18]King to Dulles, "Guatemala—General Plan of Action," 11 September 1953, Job 83-00739R, Box 5; William L. Krieg to Raymond G. Leddy, 10 November 1953, Department of State Decimal Files [hereafter DSDF], 714.00/11-1053, RG 59. US National Archives.
[19]King to Dulles, "Guatemala—General Plan of Action," 11 September 1953, Job 83-00739R, Box 5.
[20]Gleijeses, *Shattered Hope*, pp. 243–244.

SUCCESS from Central American embassies.[21] The group's leader, John Peurifoy, took over as Ambassador in Guatemala City in October 1953. He was in a familiar rôle. As Ambassador to Greece during its civil war, he coordinated State [   ] activities on behalf of the royalists. An admirer of Joseph McCarthy, he shared the Senator's taste in politics. Whiting Willauer and Thomas Whelan arrived at their ambassadorial posts in Honduras and Nicaragua in early 1954. Willauer also had a long association with CIA. As one of the founders of Civil Air Transport, he had arranged the airline's secret sale to the Agency in 1950.[22] Whelan had developed strong ties to Somoza and was considered part of the team even without an intelligence background. The ambassadors reported to the CIA through former DCI Walter Bedell Smith, whom Eisenhower had appointed Under Secretary of State.[23]

Meanwhile, [   ] established PBSUCCESS headquarters in a [   ] The [   ] offered facilities for offices, storage, and aircraft maintenance, and two days before Christmas, the operation moved [
], Florida, under the cover name [
] If asked, officers were to explain that they were part of a unit that did [   ]. Code named LINCOLN, the headquarters soon became the center of feverish activity as over a hundred case officers and support personnel began the operation's assessment phase. [   ] under his new title, Special Deputy for PBSUCCESS, issued orders from a desk facing a 40-foot wall chart detailing the operation's phases and categories of action: political, paramilitary, psychological, logistics.[24]

Gruff and s[   ] enjoyed the loyalty of

[21]Raymond G. Leddy to Ambassador Michael McDermott, 30 December 1953, Records of the Office of Middle American Affairs, Lot 57D95, RG 59, Box 5, US National Archives.

[22]William M. Leary, *Perilous Missions: Civil Air Transport and CIA Covert Operations in Asia* (University, AL: University of Alabama Press, 1984), pp. 110–112.

[23]For a discussion of the ambassadorial team, see Gleijeses, *Shattered Hope*, pp. 289–292; and Immerman, *CIA in Guatemala*, pp. 140–141.

[24]Schlesinger and Kinzer, *Bitter Fruit*, p. 113.

his officers, who regarded him with a mixture of respect [   ]
While [most of the LINCOLN staff moved into new suburban tract
houses in [   ] and enjoyed the recreational advantages
of one of America's post-war boomtowns, [   ] spent long
hours in [   ] and retired late in the evening to his room at
the [   ]. He planned the operation,
guided it through its early stages, and managed its crises. While Wisner
was officially in charge, his decisions consisted of selecting among al-
ternatives developed by [   ] More than any other official, [
] placed his personal stamp on PBSUCCESS.

*[Richard Bissell describes PBSUCCESS's project director as "a for-
mer army officer named Albert Haney.... He was young, bold, and
enthusiastic about the possibilities of covert action.... He set himself
up in charge of what was by CIA standards a rather large headquarters. Located outside of Miami, on the Opa Locka air base, it was the
site from which the operational direction and control of PBSUCCESS
was exercised and from which Haney also managed personnel
throughout Latin America. When the thirty people in the Miami
headquarters were combined with the forty or more Americans in the
field, the result was a sizeable operation by agency standards." Richard M. Bissell, Jr.,* Reflections of a Cold Warrior *(New Haven: Yale
University Press, 1996), p. 83.—N.C.]*

The Assessment

A shortage of reliable information, rivalries among Guatemalan
oppositionists, and failures of security hampered [   ] initial efforts. Case officers participating in the assessment phase bemoaned
the lack of intelligence on Guatemalan Government and society. [
] was shocked to learn that Guatemala Station had "no penetra-
tions of the PGT, government agencies, armed forces, or labor unions."[25] Kermit Roosevelt, who directed TPAJAX had warned that if
the Agency was "ever going to try something like this again, we must

[25] [   ] "Report on Stage One PBSUCCESS," 15 December 1953, Job 79-
01025A, Box 1.

be absolutely sure that people and army want what we want."[26] In Guatemala there was no way to tell. Without sources inside the PGT, [   ] could only speculate on its tactics and vulnerabilities, and PBSUCCESS planners increasingly fell back on analogies to other Communist parties and revolutions, particularly the Russian revolution, in analyzing enemy behavior.[27] But in its opening phases, the operation suffered more from the lack of information on its potential allies: the Army, regional leaders, and rebel factions.

Considering the Army critical to PBSUCCESS, [   ] needed to know the chances of a complete or partial defection by the officer corps, but he lacked sources. The US military advisory group in Guatemala, which had daily contact with officers, could come up with no information on the personalities and politics of its advisees.[28] The military appeared unshakably loyal to Arbenz, who rarely trespassed on its prestige or prerogatives. The elite Guardia Civil, passionately devoted to the President, included 2,500 of the country's best-trained and -equipped soldiers.[29] [   ] urged his officers to learn more, and in December, George Tranger, [   ] found a retired major, [   ] who

---

[26]Roosevelt, *Countercoup*, p. 210.

[27]Attempts to penetrate the PGT were unsuccessful until very late in the operation and then at a very low level. [   ] "Penetration of the PGT," HUL-A-844, 19 May 1954, Job 79-01025A, Box 103. "All Communist Parties, acting under the direction of the Soviet Union, follow the same general pattern in seeking to capture free social institutions and democratic governments," [   ] observed. "Some operate openly and others clandestinely, but all are integral parts of the world wide Communist effort." [   ] to King, "Communist Activities in Central America," HUL-A-544, 21 April 1954, Job 79-01025A, Box 102.

[28][   ] to Frank Wisner, "Performance of the US Army Mission and Military Attache in Guatemala," 9 September 1954, Job 79-01025A, Box 23. Wisner thought the Army might have refused to cooperate on principle or out of reluctance to violate the military assistance agreement, but [   ] explained that the advisers wanted to help but didn't know anything because they didn't socialize with Guatemalan officers.

[29][   ] "Report on Stage One PBSUCCESS," 15 December 1953, Job 79-01025A, Box 1.

claimed to know of a disgruntled faction in the officer corps.[30] By
January, hopes settled on Col. Elfego Monzón, who purportedly
talked of staging a mutiny and boasted of a wide following.[31] But since
the Station had no source close to Monzón, [   ] could not determine how to proceed.

[   ] also needed to know how to gain the support of Central American leaders, and his staff struggled to decipher the byzantine
politics of the region. The largest and best armed of the Central American states, Guatemala had traditionally sought to reestablish a united
Central American federation under Guatemalan leadership. Neighboring states feared these ambitions, but disagreed over whether Guatemala posed a greater threat with a dictatorial or an antidictatorial
regime in power. Somoza resented Guatemala's antidictatorial stance
and eagerly supported Castillo Armas, whom he considered pliable.
[

                                                                            ] Somo-
za's support became essential to PBSUCCESS, and in early January
1954, the United States granted him a long-sought security treaty, en-
titling Nicaragua to substantial military aid. Honduras and El Salvador enjoyed close ties to the United States but, unlike Nicaragua, they
shared a border with Guatemala. President Oscar Osorio of El Salvador and Juan Manuel Gálvez of Honduras had more ambivalent feel-
ings about inciting a rebellion in a neighboring state. Both felt threatened by Arbenz's land reform decree—which might spread rural and
labor unrest throughout the region—and had good reasons to support
Castillo Armas. Both, however, also worried about the risks of supporting the rebellion. Guatemalan forces might invade Honduras or El
Salvador in pursuit of a defeated Castillo Armas. In victory, the rebels
might be equally dangerous, particularly if allied to Somoza. Rumors
circulated that Castillo Armas had agreed to turn his rebellion into a
war of conquest after the fall of Guatemala City. [   ] emis-

---

[30]Tranger to King, "Psychological Barometer Report," 23 December 1953,
Job 79-01025A, Box 98.
[31]Andrew B. Wardlaw (First Secretary of the Embassy) to Mr. William L.
Krieg (Embassy Counselor), 26 January 1954, Job 79-01025A, Box 98, Folder
8.

saries found Gálvez and Osorio demanded a high price for cooperating with PBSUCCESS. They wanted US security guarantees, military aid, and promises to restrain Somoza.[32]

Since 1944, Mexico had taken a paternal interest in Guatemalan democracy, and PBSUCCESS planners feared that the government of Adolfo Ruíz Cortínes, if sufficiently aroused, would come to the aid of its neighbor. In May of 1953, Ruíz Cortínes awarded Arbenz the highest honor given to a foreign dignitary, the Great Necklace of the Aztec Eagle. Mexico responded to US pressure to cut arms supplies to the Arbenz government, but US diplomats estimated that the Mexicans would react strongly against further efforts to coerce or intimidate Guatemala. This Mexican attitude limited measures that could be taken overtly by the United States and intensified the need to maintain cover and deniability.[33]

[   ] case officers also had to learn the politics of the anti-Communist opposition. News of the Agency's interest spread quickly among Guatemalan oppositionists, and LINCOLN was soon inundated with appeals for support. Córdova Cerna, Castillo Armas, and Miguel Ydígoras Fuentes, Arbenz's opponent in the 1950 election, vied with one another for leadership of the Agency-sponsored rebellion. [   ] sought to consolidate all rebel movements into a united opposition, but had difficulty reconciling the pretensions of the three contenders. Despite flaws, Castillo Armas seemed the best suited to lead the rebellion. The leader of the largest rebel group—the only one with substantial paramilitary and intelligence assets—he had an "above average" military record and enjoyed the support of Somoza and Gálvez.[34] Agency officials regretted his lack of combat experience

[32]Gleijeses, *Shattered Hope*, pp. 223–225; [   ] to PBSUCCESS Headquarters, "Position of Anastasio Somoza," HUL-A-646, 5 May 1954, Job 79-01025A, Box 103; LINCOLN to DCI, 23 March 1954, Job 79-01025A, Box 2; LINCOLN to DCI, LINC 3169, 26 May 1954, Job 79-01025A, Box 5; LINCOLN to Director, LINC 4078, 19 June 1954, Job 79-01025A, Box 6.

[33]John Stephen Zunes, "Decisions on Intervention: United States Response to Third World Nationalist Governments, 1950–1957" (Ph.D. dissertation, Cornell University, 1990), pp. 66–67.

[34]J. C. King to Allen Dulles, "Guatemala—General Plan of Action," 11 September 1953, Job 79-01025A, Box 1; [   ] "Guate-

but observed a "readiness to take the fullest advantage of future CIA aid and assistance."[35] With the help of [   ] who had been his liaison since PBFORTUNE, Castillo Armas moved his rebels to two bases in Nicaragua—[

                                        ]—and drafted plans for an invasion.[36]

Castillo Armas's failure to articulate a political philosophy occasionally worried [   ] and he instructed his agents to find out "just what ideas" the rebel leader had "along the lines of a political-economic concept."[37] All they had to go on was the "Plan de Tegucigalpa." This manifesto, issued by Castillo Armas on 23 December 1953, was a vague summons to arms that denounced the "Sovietization of Guatemala" and pledged the rebels to form a government that would respect human rights, protect property and foreign capital, accept the recommendations of United Nations economic experts, and explore for oil.[38] When pressed, Castillo Armas confessed an attraction to "justicialismo," a political program advocated by Juan Perón of Argentina, but he seldom spoke of how he would govern in practice.[39] He believed Guatemala's main problems would be financial, but he was reluctant to speculate further until he knew in what fiscal condition he would find the treasury. Case officers remained confused but drew reassurance from his unassuming receptiveness to advice. One interviewer was amazed at his common sense, middle of the road views; this is no Latin American Dictator with a whip."[40]

---

malan Situation," 17 March 1952, Job 80R-01731R, Box 17, Folder 688. Castillo Armas also received material support from President Tiburcio Carías Andino of Honduras.

[35] Allen Dulles to [   ] and Tofte, "Program PBSUCCESS General Plan of Action," 9 December 1953, Job 83-00739R, Box 5.

[36] [   ]

[37] [   ] HUL-A-662, 5 May 1954, Job 79-01025A, Box 103.

[38] [   ] "El Plan de Tegucigalpa," HUL-A-470, 14 April 1954, Job 79-01025A, Box 102.

[39] For Perón's philosophy, see F. J. McLynn, "Perón's Ideology and its Relation to Political Thought and Action," *Review of International Studies* 9 (1983) 1: 1–15.

                                        ] HUL-A-662, 5 May 1954, Job

Physically unimposing and with marked *mestizo* features, Castillo Armas had none of the aspect of a *caudillo*, but Agency officials regarded this as an advantage, especially in comparison with the leonine demeanor of Castillo Armas's rival, Miguel Ydígoras Fuentes. As a general in Ubico's army, Ydígoras gained a reputation as a ruthless enforcer of the vagrancy laws, on at least one occasion ordering his troops to rape Indian women and imprison their children.[41] With his aristocrat's mien and contempt for the Indian majority, most PBSUC-CESS officers saw Ydígoras as a public relations liability, "ambitious, opportunistic, and unscrupulous."[42] [

] disagreed, passing on to Headquarters *Ydígorista* rumors charging Castillo Armas with being an agent of Arbenz.[43] [   ] summoned [   ] to LINCOLN for reeducation and assigned a new liaison to the Ydígoras group. After February 1954, Ydígoras was excluded from PBSUCCESS plans but remained an operational and security hazard requiring continual observation.

PBSUCCESS [   ] officers had good relations with [

] and pushed him to assume greater prominence in the rebel leadership. A former [   ] and [

], he was one of the few centrist politicians of stature who had taken a principled stand against the growth of Communist influence in Guatemala. PBSUCCESS officers believed his reputation could compensate for Castillo Armas's inexperience, although age, ill-health, and old ties to United Fruit disqualified him for supreme command. Without followers of his own, [

79-01025A, Box 103; "Fisherman" to Chief of Station Guatemala, HGG-A-732, 28 January 1954, Job 79-01025A, Box 99.

[41] Immerman, *The CIA in Guatemala*, p. 61.

[42] "Miguel Ydígoras Fuentes," [undated], Ydígoras file, Job 79-01025A, Box 81.

[43] [   ] to Chief, LINCOLN, "Debriefings of [

] March 1954, Job 79-01025A, Box [

]

]⁴⁴ In early February, [   ] brought Castillo Armas to LIN-
COLN to sign an accord with [   ] creating a provi-
sional revolutionary committee known as "the junta" and formaliz-
ing the rebels' relationship to the Agency. CIA would funnel aid to the
junta through a fictional organization of American businessmen called
"the group."⁴⁵

As the Agency organized and assessed its assets in Central America,
the State Department's diplomatic offensive began to take effect. By
the end of January 1954, [   ] had established a training base [
                    ] in the Canal Zone, recruited pilots for black
flights, and made preliminary arrangements to set up a clandestine radio station in [   ]⁴⁶ John Foster Dulles, meanwhile, arranged for Venezuela to host a special session of the OAS in March to
discuss the Guatemalan situation.⁴⁷ He failed, however, to orchestrate
an embargo on Guatemalan coffee. Company executives told State
Department officials that the sale of Guatemalan beans in highly com-
petitive global markets could not be limited without drastic action that
would inflate coffee prices for American consumers. Dulles had more
luck controlling the trade in arms and ammunition, in which the
United States enjoyed a dominant position. The US had restricted its
own sale of arms to Guatemala in 1951, and in 1953 the State Department intervened aggressively to thwart all arms transfers, foiling
deals with Canada, Germany, and Rhodesia.⁴⁹ By December, the Ar-

⁴⁴ [   ]
⁴⁵[   ] to Chief of Station Guatemala, [   ] HUL-A-
1230, 9 July 1954, Job 79-01025A, Box 104.
⁴⁶[   ], Job 79-
01025A, Box 69; "Meeting with RUFUS and RAMON," 29 January 1954,
January chrono file, Job 79-01025A, Box 69.
⁴⁷Peurifoy to Department of State, 23 December 1953, *Foreign Relations of
the United States, 1952–1954*, 4: 1093.
⁴⁸Edward G. Cale, "Memorandum of Conversation: Guatemalan Coffee,"
25 November 1953, *Foreign Relations of the United States, 1952–1954*, 4:
1088–1090.
⁴⁹Sharon I. Meers, "The British Connection: How the United States Covered
its Tracks in the 1954 Coup in Guatemala," *Diplomatic History* 16 (Summer
1992) 3: 414.

benz government could not purchase guns or ammunition of any kind, and the Army grew increasingly alarmed about the quantities of military hardware arriving in Nicaragua and Honduras.[50]

Arbenz became acutely aware of the threat posed by the arms embargo in late 1953 and prepared to take bold, desperate action to lift it. Conflict touched off by the land reform decree drained the Army's small arsenal and jeopardized the military's ability to fulfill its traditional role as preserver of order in the countryside.[51] As the officer corps grew resentful and apprehensive, Arbenz learned of a second, more dire threat. In September 1953, a Panamanian commercial attaché in Managua, Jorge Isaac Delgado, approached an aide to Arbenz and offered to supply information on a rebel movement led by Castillo Armas and secretly supported by the United States. Delgado carried messages between Mexico City and training bases in Nicaragua and enjoyed the trust of CIA field agents. He owned an apartment in Managua rented to [   ] Few people knew more about the inside working of PBSUCCESS. For the next four months he worked as a double agent, ferrying messages for [   ] and passing their contents on to Arbenz.[52]

what would've happened without US intervention

At a fashionable Guatemala City restaurant on 19 January 1954, the lunchtime crowd enjoyed the spectacle of a heated argument between Arbenz and his agricultural minister, Alfonso Martínez. The only non-Communist prominent in the land reform movement, Martínez was a close friend of the President. The scene touched off rumors that the two men had quarreled over land reform and the growing influence of the PGT. The next day, Martínez fled Guate-

[50][   ] (Guatemala Station) to WH Chief, "Guatemalan Procurement of Arms in Mexico," 21 December 1953, Job 79-01025A, Box 98.

[51]Chief of Station Guatemala to Chief, WH, HGG-A-643, 13 January 1954, Job 79-01025A, Box 98. This was, of course, the embargo's intended effect. Internal conflict intensified the sense of crisis and isolation the embargo was meant to convey, and [   ] gleefully reported the Army's growing desperation.

[52]Delgado worked for Somoza as well. Gleijeses, *Shattered Hope*, p. 258; Director to LINCOLN, DIR 39727, 24 February 1954, Job 79-01025A, Box 7; [   ] "Second Interim Report on Stage Two, PBSUCCESS," 15 March 1954, Job 79-01025A, Box 1.

mala, purportedly for Switzerland. The CIA Station chalked up the incident as a demonstration of growing dissension within the government, but Headquarters suspected there was more to the story. Agents in Europe tracked Martínez from Amsterdam to Berne—where he opened large bank accounts for Arbenz—then to Prague. It soon became clear that the purported flight was actually a secret mission to buy Czech arms. Unknown to CIA, PGT chairman Manuel Fortuny had met in Prague in November with Antonín Novotoný, first secretary of the Czech Communist Party, to negotiate the purchase of 2,000 tons of captured Nazi weapons. Novotoný had delayed, keeping him in Prague through most of December. "I decided," Fortuny remembered later, "that the Czechs must be consulting the Soviets." Finally, he was allowed to return to Guatemala with a favorable response. Now Martínez had arrived to complete the deal.[53]

Over the next few weeks, [   ] staff learned of Delgado's betrayal and witnessed its results. Shortly after Martínez "fled," the largest police dragnet since Salamá rounded up scores of oppositionists, including [   ] virtually the Station's only source close to the military. The Foreign Ministry expelled Sydney Gruson, a correspondent for the *New York Times*; Marshall Bannell, a CBS correspondent; and an American priest.[54] On Thursday, 29 January, [   ] learned that [   ] had been hospitalized for a stomach ulcer and that secret cables kept in his room contrary to security procedures had fallen into the hands of Delgado. Over a frantic weekend, [   ] discovered that the compromise had been extensive, giving Arbenz "intimate knowledge" of rebel training bases, "intelligence operations and a fairly accurate concept of the modus operandi of

[53]Gleijeses, *Shattered Hope*, pp. 280–283; Walter Bedell Smith to American Embassy, Berne, "Maj. Daniel Alfonso Martínez Estévez," 11 February 1954, Martínez file, Job 79-01025A, Box 81; Tranger to [   ] "Psychological Barometer Report," 26 January 1954, Job 79-01025A, Box 98; Director to [   ] DIR 38198, 12 February 1954, Job 79-01025A, Box 7.

[54]Tranger to Lincoln, "Psychological Barometer Report," 10 February 1954, Job 79-01025A, Box 99; [   ] "Reporting on Guatemala by *New York Times* Correspondent Sydney Gruson," 27 May 1954, Job 79-01228A, Box 23.

PBSUCCESS."[55] On Monday morning, [   ] Wisner, and King met to discuss the damage and decide whether to go on with the operation or abort it. Despite [   ]'s conclusion that the security breach "unquestionably has provided the enemy with adequate information to deduce the official support of the US Government in Castillo Armas's operations plus considerable details concerned therewith," the officers decided to continue anyway.[56] PBSUCCESS had crossed the Rubicon. To Wisner and [   ] the United States was too firmly committed to turn back.

Ironically, Guatemala's disclosure of the international plot against it reinforced the decision to continue with PBSUCCESS. On 29 and 30 January, screaming headlines denounced the "counterrevolutionary plot" exposed by the government. Arbenz released copies of documents implicating Somoza and a "Northern government" and spelling out PBSUCCESS plans in detail. Reporters learned the location of training bases [

]"[57] Fearing the Guatemalans would take their charges before the United Nations, [   ] staff glumly watched the flap unfold. As soon as [   ] could walk, they ordered him to Washington for three days of polygraphing.[58] Reports from Guatemala Station, meanwhile, indicated they had less to worry about than they originally supposed. The government, knowing the gist of PBSUCCESS messages but not possessing the originals, had forged letterheads crudely enough to arouse journalists' suspicions. The international press and a skeptical public dismissed

---

[55][   ] "Second Interim Report on Stage Two, PBSUC-CESS," 15 March 1954, Job 79-01025A, Box 1.

[56]*Ibid.*; Director to LINCOLN, DIR 36511, 30 January 1954, Job 79-01025A, Box 7.

[57]V. P. Martin, Air Attaché, "Alleged International Plot Against Guatemala," 1 February 1954, Job 79-01025A, Box 82.

[58]Director to LINCOLN, DIR 39727, 24 February 1954, Job 79-01025A, Box 7. [

] 5," 15 April 1954, Job 79-01025A, Box 70.

Arbenz's accusations as a political ploy. The Guatemalan public, the
Station Chief reported, considered the charges "pure fantasy," a manifestation "of the fear and uncertainty prevailing in government circles."[59] The American press took the same view, unanimously accept-
ing the State Department's characterization of the charges as a propaganda ploy designed to disrupt the Caracas conference.[60]

The January revelations revealed how much the "plausible deniability" of PBSUCCESS relied on the uncritical acceptance by the
American press of the assumptions behind United States policy.
Newspaper and broadcast media, for example, accepted the official
view of the Communist nature of the Guatemalan regime. In the
spring of 1954, NBC News aired a television documentary, "Red Rule
in Guatemala," revealing the threat the Arbenz regime posed to the
Panama Canal.[61] Articles in *Reader's Digest*, the *Chicago Tribune*,
and the *Saturday Evening Post* drew a frightening picture of the danger in America's backyard. Less conservative papers like the *New
York Times* depicted the growing menace in only slightly less alarming
terms. The Eisenhower administration's Guatemala policy did not get
a free ride in press or in Congress. In early 1954, a number of editorials
attacked the President's failure to act against Arbenz, citing the continued presence of US military advisers as evidence of official complacency. Walter Winchell broadcast stories of Guatemalan spies infiltrating other Latin American countries and urged the CIA to "get ac-
quainted with these people."[62] This line of criticism led reporters to
hunt for signs of inertia, not for a secret conspiracy. When Arbenz revealed the plot, American newspapers dismissed it as a Communist
ploy, another provocation to which the administration responded far
too passively.[63]

[59]Tranger to LINCOLN, "Psychological Barometer Report," HGG-A-714,
8 February 1954, Job 79-01025A, Box 99.
[60]Gleijeses, *Shattered Hope*, pp. 260–262.
[61][   ] to Chief, Graphics Register, "Guatemala Red Rule News
Documentary Film Request," 18 May 1954, Job 79-01025A, Box 70.
[62]J. C. King to Dulles, "Walter Winchell Broadcast of 3 January 1954," 7
January 1954, Job 79-01228A, Box 23.
[63]Gleijeses, *Shattered Hope*, pp. 260–263; Immerman, *The CIA in Guatemala*, pp. 7–8.

Assessing the damage, [   ] estimated that the operation had lost a month through confusion and the delays involved in reassigning cryptonyms and shuffling personnel.[64] He rallied his dispirited troops with a reminder that "the morale of the Nazis in the winter of 1932, just before their seizure of power in Spring 1933, was at all-time low ebb. The same thing was true of the French revolutionaries and of the Soviet revolutionaries, on the eve of their success."[65] His psywar staff tried to regain the initiative by leveling a countercharge supported by an elaborate fabrication. On 19 February, they planted a cache of Soviet-made arms on the Nicaraguan coast to be "discovered" weeks later by fishermen in the pay of Somoza. The story was appropriately embroidered with allegations about Soviet submarines and Guatemalan assassination squads.[66] As [   ] should have predicted, the press and public greeted the new allegations as skeptically as they had Arbenz's. The story "did not receive much, if any, publicity in the Guatemalan press."[67] The deception simply left an impression that the region's leaders had carried their intriguing to dangerous lengths.

Despite good intelligence and decisive action, Arbenz failed to capitalize on the opposition's setback. Instead of rallying support for his regime, his January allegations only intensified public anxiety and raised suspicions that he was creating a pretext for seizing dictatorial powers. A more critical failure was his inability to turn the charges of an international plot into a successful diplomatic initiative. Any hopes Foreign Minister Guillermo Toriello may have entertained of bringing

[64]LINCOLN to [   ] "Operational LINCOLN Sitrep," HUL-A-93, 23 February 1954, Job 79-01025A, Box 101.
[65][   ] to Chief of Station Guatemala, HUL-A-374, 31 March 1954, Job 79-01025A, Box 101.
[66]PBSUCCESS History, Job 85-00664R, Box 5, Folder 13; [   ] to Chief of Station Guatemala, "KUGOWN/WASHTUB Publicity in Guatemalan Press," HUL-A-827, 19 May 1954, Job 79-01025A, Box 103. The deception, called operation WASHTUB, culminated with a press conference by Somoza on 7 May at which reporters were told that the Soviet submarine had been photographed, but that no prints or negatives were available. Gleijeses, *Shattered Hope*, p. 294.
[67][   ] to Chief Station Guatemala, "Publicity in Guatemalan Press," 19 May 1954, WASHTUB file, Job 79-01025A, Box 82. See other items in file for the sometimes bizarre details of the WASHTUB plot.

charges before the Organization of American States were dashed by John Foster Dulles's preparations for the Caracas conference. Faced with negative growth for three straight years, Latin American governments needed trade concessions and credit from the United States and they were ready to yield on the issue of Guatemala. The Secretary of State recognized that the "major interest of the Latin American countries at this conference would concern economics whereas the chief United States interest is to secure a strong anti-Communist resolution" against Guatemala, but he recognized that Guatemala's underdog status and the nationalistic pride of Latin diplomats would blunt this diplomatic advantage.[68] The 1–13 March conference proved a mixed success. Dulles got his resolution, but only after Toriello's denunciations received loud, sustained applause. The Guatemalan foreign minister condemned the United States for encouraging boycotts and unleashing a propaganda campaign intended to tar his reformist regime with the epithet "Communist." He presented documents that "unquestionably show that the foreign conspirators and monopolistic interests that inspired and financed them sought to permit armed intervention against our country as 'a noble undertaking against Communism.'" He accused Dulles of using Pan-Americanism and anti-Communism as instruments to suppress the growth of democracy and industry in Latin America.[69] "He said many of the things some of the rest of us would like to say if we dared," one delegate explained.[70] The pride Toriello's speech stirred in Guatemala City, the Station reported, was little consolation for the sense of gloom that followed.[71] After Caracas, Arbenz and the PGT realized international opinion would not rescue them from the United States. Guatemala was alone. "Caracas had exposed her isolation," according to one historian, "and the messages of support that poured in from politicians, intellectuals, and

[68]Immerman, *The CIA in Guatemala*, p. 145.
[69]"Address by His Excellency Guillermo Toriello Garrido, Minister of Foreign Affairs of Guatemala, in the Third Plenary Session, Tenth Inter-American Conference," 5 March 1954, Toriello file, Job 79-01025A, Box 81.
⸺Gleijeses. *Shattered Hope*, p. 273.
⸺LINCOLN, "Weekly Psych Intelligence Report," HGG-A-919, ,, Job 79-01025A, Box 99.

trade unionists of several Latin American countries were of little solace."[72]

PBSUCCESS continued to be plagued by breaches of security, but the operation had acquired a relentless momentum. In early April, security investigators discovered telephone bugs "similar to the jobs the Russians used" in the Embassy in Guatemala City, a microphone concealed in a chandelier in Willauer's residence, and a tap on the telephone of one of Peurifoy's assistants.[73] Castillo Armas refused to sever ties to a number of his assistants who flunked polygraph tests.[74] [
] admitted that members of Castillo Armas's organization had taken classified papers giving conclusive proof of official US involvement. A Nicaraguan immigration officer who helped arrange black flights took asylum in the Guatemalan Embassy in Managua. Jacob Esterline, a senior Agency official, estimated that "the Guatemalan government is well into the details of PBSUCCESS and that they have decided to let the operation proceed undisturbed until they have prepared and documented a brief for presentation to the OAS."[75] PBSUCCESS "in its present form appears to be rather naked," Wisner admitted. "Several categories of people—hostile, friendly, and 'neutral'—either know or suspect or believe that the United States is directly behind this one and, assuming that it proceeds to a conclusion, would be able to tell a very convincing story."[76] Henry F. Holland, the new Assistant Secretary of State Inter-American Affairs, frightened by the revelations, asked that the operation be held up pending a top-level review. Wisner suspended all black flights on 15 and 16 April while

---

[72] Gleijeses, *Shattered Hope*, p. 284.

[73] "Audio Counter Surveillance Check," April 1954, Job 79-01025A, Box 70.

[74] [   ] a spy in Castillo Armas's organization, may have passed on the locations of the paramilitary and communications training bases. Juan [
] suspected of being [   ] confederate, was expelled from the training program but remained in the organization.

[75] Esterline to [   ] "Items for Inclusion in CE Repc   ..]
1954, Job 79-01025A, Box 70.

[76] "Ways and Means of Improving Cover and Deception for
eration," 28 April 1954, Job 79-01025A, Box 70.

the Dulles brothers consulted.[77] On the 17th [   ] once again received the green light.

Preparing for Action

By early April, [   ] team had completed its assessments
and developed an operational plan. LINCOLN case officers now felt
they understood the preparations necessary to mount a successful
coup and the situation likely to prevail in Guatemala after the operation's completion. Rejecting tactics aimed at merely severing Arbenz's
tie to international Communism, they aimed to produce a radical, revolutionary change in Guatemalan politics. They sought the reversal of
the Revolution of 1944, the termination of land reform, and the replacement of Arbenz with a liberal, authoritarian leader. Afterwards,
they foresaw a prolonged period of dictatorial rule during which the
regime would depend on United States aid and arms. [   ] felt a
military coup offered the surest means to this outcome, and he directed
his psychological, political, and paramilitary efforts at intimidating
the Army and inciting it to mutiny.

The final plans for PBSUCCESS called for drastic change. The program and rhetoric of the Revolution of 1944 retained their appeal for
many Guatemalans, and LINCOLN had briefly considered appropri-
ating its themes. But by April they rejected the idea "that a genuinely
fervent and lasting revolutionary movement can be based on the principal program of the incumbent regime." It would be difficult to
loosen Arbenz's identification with the revolution, [   ]
thought, and it might not be worth the effort. Claiming that Arbenz
had betrayed the ideals of 1944 weakened the argument for action
"because we are only pleading for 'reform' of the present system and
there is a world of difference between reform and revolution." Case
officers also felt they needed more conservative themes to appeal to the
groups in Guatemala most likely to take action against the regime: the
Army, conservative students, and landowners. Attacks on land reform

[77]Esterline to [   ] "Things to Do," 15 April 1954, Job 79-01025A,
Box 70.

and other progressive measures would produce the best results with these groups. "Our recommendation," [   ] cabled agents in the field, is "that the revolution of 1944 be declared dead."[78]

[   ] initially considered incorporating Arbenz's agrarian reform "as originally conceived as part of our political program," but he soon came to regard it as an instrument of subversion and instructed case officers to make it a target of disruptive propaganda.[79] "The Agrarian Reform program had provided the communists with weapons which may be useful as their struggle for domination continues," he told King.[80] He urged field officers to use "all means at hand" to spread "slogans like 'Communist land is temporary land,' or something similar," to promote the belief that "parcels of land received from the present government would constitute a proof of guilt in the future."[81] PBSUCCESS propagandists also spread rumors that land reform was simply a prelude to collectivized agriculture, state farms, and forced labor.[82] [   ] believed that the post-Arbenz regime should avoid land redistribution as a solution to rural poverty, and instead should foster the growth of light industry "to provide additional purchasing power to the residents of rural areas" and "make goods avail-

[78] [   ] to Chief of Station Guatemala, "Materials for Transmittal to Eliot P. Razmara," HUL-A-237, 17 March 1954, Job 79-01025A, Box 101. In the September plan, [   ] left open the possibility that Arbenz could be coerced into expelling Communists from government. Schlesinger and Kinzer claim he attempted a bribe but was rebuffed by Arbenz's aides. There is no record of this in Agency archives, but it is not inconsistent with [   ] thinking in early January. By late March, however, the LINCOLN case officers saw no room for Arbenz in the post-PBSUCCESS government. *Bitter Fruit*, p. 113.

[79] [   ] objections to Decree 900 were purely tactical. He thought Castillo Armas could win support among *campesinos* by backing land reform. The key was to obtain the defection of Alfonso Martínez, the reform's non-Communist director. When this appeared impossible in late March, [   ] decided the land reform had to be destroyed. [   ] "Agrarian Reform," 8 March 1954, Job 79-01025A, Box 147.

[80] [   ] to King, "Communist Activities in Central America," HUL-A-544, 21 April 1954, Job 79-01025A, Box 102.

[81] [   ] to King, "Communist Activities in Central America," HUL-A-544, 21 April 1954, Job 79-01025A, Box 102.

[82] [   ] to Tranger, "Economic Propaganda Themes," HUL-A-596, 1 May 1954, Job 79-01025A, Box 102.

able to them at more reasonable prices." "It is well known," he observed, that "raising the level of consumer consumption, the expansion of productive facilities and the general augmentation of prosperity is not only a good deterrent toward Communism, but also an effective method of producing general political stability."[83]

Before deciding on methods and strategies, [   ] case officers carefully listed the goals of PBSUCCESS, beginning with the replacement of Arbenz with a moderate, authoritarian regime. [   ] considered democracy an "unrealistic" alternative for Guatemala. "Premature extension of democratic privileges and responsibilities to a people still accustomed to patriarchal methods can only be harmful," he warned. A "judicious combination of authority and liberty will have to govern the political system." Concentrating authority in the person of a dictator also involved dangers, and [   ] advised against setting up a Somoza-style dictatorship.

> The executive power, without being paralized [sic], must be sufficiently divided in order to provide inner balance. While this at first sight may seem to be a factor making for instability, it actually has a protective aspect, because it prevents the capture of the center of power by a single hostile blow.[84]

A ruling committee, or junta, seemed to be the answer. [   ] foresaw a six-month period of emergency rule followed by a milder authoritarianism of indefinite duration. The principal duties of the new regime were to provide stability, raise living standards, and ensure protection for American business.[85]

As [   ] envisioned it, United Fruit would receive greater protection under the new regime, but it would have to offer concessions in return. United Fruit and other American investments, he conceded, "represent a part of the American national interest and will be protected by the United States as such." But the "United States does not expect American companies to enjoy abroad immunities and privi-

[83][   ] to Tranger, "Political-Economic Views to be Expressed During the K-Program," HUL-A-514, 21 April 1954, Job 79-01025A, Box 102.
[84]*Ibid.*
[85]*Ibid.*

leges that would make for political instability or social injustice in other countries, because such a condition of course would be harmful to the over-riding American political interest." Above all, [   ] wanted the new regime to avoid the embarrassment of retreating from victories won by Arbenz. United Fruit executives would have to understand that there would be no return to the status quo ante. They would have to pay taxes and submit to competition from Guatemalan companies. Labor unions, purged of Communists, would be protected. Since [   ] saw American capital as necessary for the new regime's stability, he saw "no real reason why a legitimate accord, satisfying the interests of both, cannot be found between American companies in Guatemala and the Guatemalan government."[86]

[   ] could see few details of the future regime clearly, but one feature was obvious: it would need American money. "Shortly after the Communists were defeated in Iran, the Iranian Government received generous assistance," he recalled. "Undoubtedly, the disappearance of the Communist regime from Guatemala will leave behind a certain economic and financial chaos which must be rectified by American aid." The new regime should build its reputation by industrializing Guatemala and raising its standard of living. The World Bank had devised a development program that should be pursued, but not in the tightfisted way of the past. "There is increasing recognition in American and other banking circles that the economic development of countries such as Guatemala cannot be undertaken and financed under strictly economic criteria," he explained. "We realize that there must necessarily be a certain wastage of funds because of local political conditions. We are prepared to underwrite this wastage."[87] But before PBSUCCESS could usher in the new dependent, undemocratic regime, it would have to mobilize Guatemalan activists, strengthen Castillo Armas, and coax the Army to commit treason.

[   ] final plans included three areas of action: propaganda (or "PP"), paramilitary, and political. Early in 1954, the Agency began a sustained effort to intimidate the government and convince Guate-

[86] *Ibid.*
[87] *Ibid.*

malans that an active underground resistance existed. The CEUA student group, which [   ]" had been active since late 1953.[88] Headed by a young activist, [   ] the group counted 50 members in the capital and a nationwide network of sympathetic students ready to risk arrest for the cause.[89] The exuberant anti-Communism of the CEUA students elated [   ] tired of the cynical politics of Ydígoras and Castillo Armas [

                                                                    ] a close

friend and adviser of [   ]
who first met members [

                                                               ].[90] This tenuous
pipeline conveyed all of the plans, publications, and schemes LIN-COLN officers could devise.[91]

The students' propagandizing met with immediate and well-publicized success. In their opening salvo on 15 September 1953, they had pasted 106,000 anti-Communist stickers on buses and trains. They leafleted public gatherings, sent fake funeral notices to Arbenz and Fortuny, and covered walls with antigovernment graffiti. Their "32" campaign in March and April 1954 drew wide newspaper coverage. Students painted the number 32—for Article 32 of the Constitu-

(margin, handwritten: would this have happened anyway)

[88][   ] "Report on Stage One PBSUCCESS, Annex B, Friendly Assets and Potential," 15 December 1953, Job 79-01025A, Box 1. [
                    ]
[89][   ] "Report on Stage One PBSUCCESS," 15 December 1953, Job 79-01025A, Box 1.
[90]Tranger to LINCOLN, "Psychological Barometer Report," HGG-A-682, 27 January 1954, Job 79-01025A, Box 98; [   ] Job 63-00545R, Box 274, Folder 35.
[91]*Ibid.*

tion, which forbade international political parties—on walls in the city center. Newspapers recognized it as an anti-Communist slogan and described the constabulary's frustrated attempts to identify the culprits. The students sponsored an "Anti-Communist Hour" on Radio Internacional, an independent station, until 21 April, when armed thugs burst into the station during the airing of the program, beat several broadcasters, and destroyed their equipment.[9] In some of their activities, CEUA received help from an organization of anti-Communist market women, the Comité Anticomunista de Locatorias de los Mercados de Guatemala, who spread rumors and passed leaflets among shoppers. The two groups distributed thousands of copies of a pastoral letter by Archbishop Mariano Rossell y Arrellana calling for a national crusade against Communism.[93] Case officers judged the outraged reaction of Arbenz's officials as indicators of success.

Encouraged by these victories, LINCOLN staffers spent hours inventing schemes for the CEUA students to carry out. The fake funeral notices were their idea, meant to harass and frighten top PGT officials. Throughout March and April, they bombarded [   ] with suggestions for campaigns and themes, some useful others whimsical. After the pastoral letter, they attempted to arouse Catholics with mailings from a phony "Organization of the Militant Godless," purportedly headed by members of the PGT.[94] They printed stickers reading "A Communist Lives Here" for the students to put on houses.[95] Fake

[92]Paul P. Kennedy, "Guatemalans Get Appeal to Revolt," *New York Times*, 5 May 1954.

[93][   ] to LINCOLN, "Weekly Psych Intelligence Report," HGG-A-919, 16 April 1954, Job 79-01025A, Box 99. The pastoral letter was the Church's most useful contribution to PBSUCCESS. The Agency did not have a strong tie to the Catholic hierarchy in Guatemala [

        ] to King, "Roman Catholic Church in Guatemala," HUL-A-30, 2 February 1954, Job 79-01025A, Box 101.

[94][   ] to Tranger, "Black Letter from the 'Preparatory Committee for an Organization of the Militant Godless,'" HUL-A-875, 23 May 1954, Job 79-01025A, Box 103.

[95][   ] to Tranger, HUL-A-516, 21 April 1954, Job 79-01025A, Box 102.

newspaper clippings and articles from International Communist publications were a favorite ploy. [   ] and the Station Chief [   ] Guatemala resented these suggestions because of the burdens they placed on field officers and the goodwill of the CEUA. Mailings had to be posted from outlying towns to avoid detection. Each new scheme involved risks and cost time that could be spent on successful ongoing operations. [   ] complained that overwork and "ravaging amoebae" kept him from spending more than two hours on his cover assignment in the last two weeks of March. He started holding meetings with [   ] in his bathroom.[96]

Field officers also felt LINCOLN's schemes aimed at the wrong audience, targeting intellectuals, a constituency unlikely to be of much help. [   ] aimed to "attack the theoretical foundations of the enemy" on the grounds that "the present state of things in the country is largely determined by intellectuals." Tranger disparaged such appeals. The objective, he told [   ] was to scare the Communists, not debate them. Propaganda "should be designed to (1) intensify anti-Communist, anti-government sentiment and create a disposition to act; and (2) create dissension, confusion, and FEAR in the enemy camp." With the backing off of [   ] and [   ] Tranger won his point. Abandoning the "lofty, lengthy tomes that appeal to the intellectual minority," psychological efforts aimed, in his words, at "the heart, the stomach and the liver (fear)."[97]

As the psychological campaign wore on, CEUA activists grew dissatisfied with the risks involved and the content of the materials they were asked to distribute. Some students considered the group's slogans too harsh and divisive, a feeling for which [   ] had little sympathy. "We are not running a popularity contest but an uprising," he fumed. The students' concerns also, perhaps, stemmed from a suspicion that they were being used. Field officers admitted they were using

[96][   ] to LINCOLN, [   ] 19 March 1954, Job 79-01025A, Box 100.

[97]Tranger to [   ] "KUGOWN/[   ] Activities," 31 March 1954, Job 79-01025A, Box 99.

the students as bait, in Tranger's words, to "invite complete suppression of overt anti-Communist, anti-government units and then use
such suppression to demonstrate to the people here and abroad the nature and seriousness of the menace and refute claims of 'democratic
freedoms.' " In May 1954, as CEUA began to suffer attrition through
the arrest of its members, students became increasingly unhappy with
the sacrifices they were asked to make. By 26 May, field officers reported that 10 students were in jail, the others were afraid to work,
and recruiting had fallen to zero. By then a clandestine radio station
had been operating for three weeks and Castillo Armas was leafleting
the capital from aircraft. PBSUCCESS had moved from its propaganda to its paramilitary phase.[98]

Agency propaganda operations succeeded in making Guatemala
into the type of repressive regime the United States liked to portray it
as. By late April, freedoms of speech and assembly had all but been re-
voked by official decrees and unofficial goon squads, which intimidated independent newspapers and radio stations into silence. Radio
Universal, the only openly anti-Communist radio station, closed after
its offices were raided by goons and its owner placed under arrest. Opposition elements remained active owing largely to the failure of Guatemalan police to make systematic arrests. Guatemala Station reported that the government's behavior demonstrated a "desire to
crush opposition activity together with what appeared to be a lack of
knowledge as to how to proceed most effectively."[99] In the ensuing
weeks, the police would cast scruples aside and move decisively to
suppress the remnants of the opposition.

Despite the intensive effort put into propaganda, [   ] considered it secondary to the political, or "K" program, which aimed to undermine the Army's loyalty to Arbenz and bring it over, whole or in
part, to the side of the rebellion. CEUA publications, *El Rebelde* and
El Combate, carried articles aimed at a military audience. A series of

[98]Playdon to PBSUCCESS Headquarters, "Report on ESSENCE Activities,"
HUL-A-929, 26 May 1954, Job 79-01025A, Box 103.
[99][   ] to LINCOLN, "Weekly Psych Intelligence Report, 19–26
April 1954," HGG-A-969, Job 79-01025A, Box 99.

editorials drafted by LINCOLN in March for *El Rebelde* communicated the sense of intensifying pressure case officers wanted the Army to feel. The first, entitled "A Time to Doubt," raised questions about whether the Army should continue its political neutrality. The second, "A Time to Think," threatened the Army with "a terrible fate if it continues on its present collaborationist path." The series ended with "A Time to Choose," urging officers to break their ties with the government and offer their services to the rebellion "if they wish to share in the triumph over Communism."[100] Egged on by [   ] student activists stepped up the pressure on Army officers and their families with telephone harassment and minor acts of sabotage.[101] US military advisers and Embassy officials joined the effort to spread fear and dissension among the officer corps, telling military leaders in unguarded terms that the United States could no longer tolerate Arbenz and would take drastic steps if the Army failed to act. "We were under enormous pressure," one Guatemalan officer remembered. "The US military mission even hinted that the United States would invade."[102] [   ] used all available means to impress on Army officers "the facts of life as far as they are concerned":

    a. They are in the United States sphere of influence.

    b. If they think that a people of 3,000,000 is going to win in a showdown with 160,000,000 they need psychiatric help.

    c. If they think that the US will never come to a showdown, they don't understand gringos. It might be useful to explain gringos in the way that foreigners see them and point out that force is the follower of reason, in the American pattern.

    d. If they think that the Soviet Union can bail them out of this predicament, they once more require psychiatric help.

    e. If they think that the Soviet Union *will* or even *wants* to bail them out, it should be perfectly clear to them that the Soviet Union is exploiting them only to create a diversion in the US backyard while

[100] [   ] to Frances R. Hegarty, 23 February 1954, "Letter of Instructions," Job 79-01025A, Box 101.

[101] LINCOLN to Chief of Station Guatemala, "Telephone Team for Rumor Propagation," HUL-A-134, 2 March 1954, Job 79-01025A, Box 101.

[102] Gleijeses, *Shattered Hope*, p. 305.

Indochina is hot, and that the Soviets will drop them in a hurry when the going gets tough.

f. If they are unhappy about being in the US sphere of influence, they might be reminded that the US is the most generous and tolerant taskmaster going, that cooperation with it is studded with material reward, and that the US permits much more sovereignty and independence in its sphere than the Soviets, and so forth. PRESSURE

Although [   ] had too few sources close to the Army to know it, these facts already weighed on the minds of Guatemala's military leaders. Deteriorating relations with the United States exacted a price on the Army's effectiveness and prestige. Successive shocks—Peurifoy's denunciations, the arms embargo, and Caracas—filled the officer corps with dread and suspicion. Officers could not tell who among their peers could be trusted, who would betray. "A great number of the officers are extremely unhappy about the Communists in the government and the poor US-Guatemalan relations," a US adviser reported, but "none dares to speak out for fear of jeopardizing his personal security."[103]

[   ] efforts to find and recruit disgruntled officers continued to come up short. An attempt to bribe Carlos Enrique Díaz, chief of the Guatemalan armed forces, failed.[104] [   ] was particularly frustrated by his inability to place an agent close to [   ] In April, LINCOLN case officers obtained the help of [

] who agreed to return to Guatemala and attempt to recruit [   ] and others. [   ] had been popular among the officer corps and appeared "highly knowledgeable regarding key military personnel targeted under K-Program." [

], he arrived in Guatemala City and had no trouble mixing with

---

[103] *Ibid.*

[104] Díaz was to be approached while visiting Caracas and offered a $200,000 bribe to "act decisively to change the present Guatemalan problem." The attempt failed, possibly because Díaz was surprised to be recognized while traveling with his mistress. [   ] to King, "Col. Carlos Enrique Díaz," 14 May 1954, Job 79-01025A, Box 70; King to Wisner, "Approach to Col. Carlos Enrique Díaz," 6 May 1954, Job 79-01025A, Box 70.

his old friends, but the results proved disappointing. Officers were happy to reminisce about happier times but unwilling to discuss current politics. The genial [   ] hesitated to pry, and he returned to Miami a week later with nothing to report.¹⁰⁵

By May, [   ] political program was in crisis. Case officers continued to believe the Army held the key to the operation's success and that [   ] could lead an Army rebellion. [   ] had no way to guide or predict [   ] actions, and he realized that an abortive or mistimed coup could ruin all of his careful preparations. Reluctantly, he instructed [   ] (who replaced Tranger as Chief of Station in Guatemala in April) to look for an opportunity to make a cold approach. The stakes were high. [   ] could alienate or endanger [   ]. But [   ] was ready to take the risk. He felt that the psychological campaign against the Army had reached such intensity that if [   ] could make the approach discreetly, [   ] could be cajoled or bullied into cooperating.¹⁰⁶

[   ] never intended for Castillo Armas's force to challenge the Guatemalan Army. Instead, it was to be used as another psychological weapon in the campaign to intimidate Arbenz and incite an Army revolt. He trained and supplied the small force to accentuate its propaganda (rather than military) value, stressing sabotage and air operations. In March, he began assembling a fleet that came to comprise a dozen aircraft at an abandoned airstrip near Puerto Cabezas, Nicaragua (a base later used by the Bay of Pigs invaders).¹⁰⁷ Somoza

---

¹⁰⁵[   ] to King, HUL-A-449, 9 April 1954, Job 79-01025A, Box 102; [   ] to Chief of Station Guatemala, "SOCCER debriefing," HUL-A-410, 7 April 1954, Job 79-01025A, Box 102; LINCOLN to DCI, LINC 1535, 2 April 1954, Job 79-01025A, Box 3.

¹⁰⁶[   ] "K Program," HUL-A-614, 2 May 1954, Job 79-01025A, Box 103; Guatemala Station to Director, GUAT 866, 16 June 1954, Job 79-01025A, Box 11. See Guatemala cables to LINCOLN for June 1954 in Box 11.

¹⁰⁷LINCOLN to SHERWOOD, LINC 4562, 30 June 1954, Job 79-01025A, Box 6. The aircraft used in PBSUCCESS totaled 12: three C-47 (DC-3) cargo planes, six F-47 Thunderbolt fighter-bombers, one P-38 Lightning fighter, one Cessna 180, and one Cessna 140. In May, the rebel air force moved to a Nicaraguan base adjoining the Managua airport.

purchased some of the planes [   ] and received others under the military assistance agreement. They were then loaned to Castillo Armas and registered to [

                ] in St. Petersburg, Florida.[108] For [   ] aircraft linked the paramilitary and propaganda sides of the operation, enabling the rebels to strike directly at the government in full view of the entire city.

Since Castillo Armas could not furnish pilots, the Agency hired some on contract and transferred others from its proprietary airline in the Far East, Civil Air Transport. Offering $2,000 a month and a $250 bonus for each successful mission, Willauer rounded up a motley assortment of bush pilots, ex-military fliers, and expatriate barnstormers with names like [

          ][109] The group leader was [

worried
not into
not safety

          ][110] and King constantly worried about security and cover for the pilots, who might be downed at any time, or, in the case of [   ] "be bought by the highest bidder."[111] Explaining the presence of pilots from China was tricky, and the cover story King developed nearly ended in disaster. The pilots, on annual leave, were to whoop it up in Miami and Havana "making the usual rounds of clubs and gambling establishments," lose all their money, and fortuitously run into a "Latin businessman" who promised quick money for flying a few loads of farm equipment in Central America. Embassy officials

[108][Unsigned], "Questions arising from Study of LINC 3057 re Purchase of Aircraft," 24 May 1954, Job 79-01025A, Box 70. [   ] "Unauthorized Landing of C-47 in Honduras," 11 May 1954, Job 79-01025A, Box 70.

[109]Debriefing Report, [   ] Assistant Air Operations Officer, [undated], Job 79-01025A, Box 167.

[110]LINCOLN to Director, LINC 4093, 20 JUNE 1954, Job 79-01025A, Box 6.

[111]Contact Report, HUL-A-70, 8 February 1954 [   ] office, LINCOLN, present: Mr. Barnes, [   ] King and [   ] Messrs. [   ] King and [   ] Job 79-01025A, Box 101.

had to intervene when suspicious FBI agents in Havana hauled the pilots in for questioning.[112]

Meanwhile, Castillo Armas completed preparations for the invasion. Training programs at [   ] and the two Nicaraguan bases graduated 37 saboteurs in March, 30 field officers in mid-April, and a handful of communications specialists by mid-May. The friendly, taciturn American instructors, one trainee remembered, were known only by their first names, which were either Pepe or José.[113] Delays in the training program—particularly for radio operators— pushed the scheduled invasion from mid-May into June. Most of the rebel recruits could not read, and communications instructors complained of difficulties in getting across technical concepts.[114]

At least one historian had made the claim that Castillo Armas's force was more fearsome than has generally been reported. Frederick Marks refers to them as small in number but "highly trained and exceedingly well-equipped," and notes that they had "twenty-two thousand rockets, forty-five thousand rifles, four hundred mortars, and pieces of heavy artillery."[115] From Agency records, it is clear that the rebels possessed neither rockets nor artillery. Moreover, it is unlikely Castillo Armas's troops would have carried more than a single rifle apiece, since they were obliged to carry all their food and supplies with them. The rebel army never impressed officials at CIA Headquarters (Bissell later remembered it as "extremely small and ill-trained") and in the months before the invasion some in the PBSUCCESS hierarchy were beginning to have doubts about Castillo Armas's suitability for command.[116] Guatemalan officers' low opinion of him hampered the political program. Tracey Barnes considered him a "bold but incom-

[112]Chief, WHD, to LINCOLN, "Operational Air Support Plan," HUL-A-157, 6 March 1954, Job 79-01025A, Box 101.

[113]Gleijeses, *Shattered Hope*, p. 293.

[114][   ] "Final Report on Stage Two PBSUCCESS" [undated], Job 79-01025A, Box 167.

[115]Frederick W. Marks III, "The CIA and Castillo Armas in Guatemala, 1954: New Clues to an Old Puzzle," *Diplomatic History* 14 (Winter 1990) 1: 69.

[116]Interview with Richard M. Bissell, Jr., 5 June 1967, Dwight D. Eisenhower Library, Job 85-0664R, Box 5.

petent man" who fantasized about rebellion but lacked the leadership to follow through on plans.[117] [   ] however, strongly defended him. Castillo Armas "is the man and there will be no deviation from that," he told his case officers. "Any criticisms or doubts of him pale before the fact that he now has both the manpower and the materiel to accomplish the job." He reminded critics that Castillo Armas would have "considerable technical assistance. He has the humility and decency to rely on advice, and his present advisers have his respect and confidence to a sufficient degree that he would no doubt rely on them for counsel when it comes to the question of whom he shall associate himself with both before and after victory."[118]

As the preparation phase drew to a close at the end of April 1954, LINCOLN staffers felt a mixed sense of elation and apprehension. Their propaganda efforts had shaken the Arbenz regime and heartened the opposition, but the government's crackdown and the fatigue of the CEUA students made it clear the effort could not be sustained much longer. Paramilitary training had made great strides, but Castillo Armas's feeble forces and mercenary air force were still no match for the 5,000-strong Guatemalan Army, if the Army stood by Arbenz. [   ] plans to seduce the officer corps remained as tantalizingly promising but as far from consummation as they were in January. The psychological pressure on the Guatemalan government was reaching its maximum point. The time to act had arrived, yet it was still unclear how and whether success could be attained.

[117]PBSUCCESS History, Job 85-0664R, Box 5, Folder 13.
[118][   ] to Chief of Station Guatemala, "Political-Economic Views to be Expressed During K-Program," HUL-A-514, 21 April 1954, Job 79-01025A, Box 102.

CHAPTER 3

Sufficient Means

I think we tend to overlook simply the massiveness of US power viewed from Arbenz's position. . . . We knew how difficult it was even to get two more aircraft down there and in action. . . . I think it was easy for us to forget that Arbenz felt himself up against the might of the United States, and quite possibly the impact on him of specific events was that it may simply have persuaded him that the US was in earnest, and if these means proved to be insufficient, then other stronger means would be used.

Richard Bissell[1]

PBSUCCESS was ready by the beginning of May to place maximum pressure on the Arbenz regime. [   ] had a variety of instruments at his disposal: propaganda, sabotage, aircraft, an army of insurrectionists, and the implicit threat of US military power. He used all of them to intensify the psychological distress of Arbenz and his officials. Even the paramilitary program—Castillo Armas and his *liberacionistas*—served a psychological rather than a military function. As an Agency memo prepared for Eisenhower explained, the operation relied "on psychological impact rather than actual military strength, although it is upon the ability of the Castillo Armas effort to create and maintain the *impression* of very substantial military strength, that the success of this particular effort primarily depends."[2] Dealing in the insubstantial stuff of impressions and degrees of intimidation, [

] could not always measure progress, and it was difficult for even those close to PBSUCCESS to know what was happening, whether they were succeeding or failing, and why.

---

[1]Interview with Richard M. Bissell, Jr., 5 June 1967, Dwight D. Eisenhower Library, Job 85-0664R, Box 5.
[2]Immerman, *CIA in Guatemala*, p. 161.

The Voice of Liberation

As Guatemalans turned on their short-wave radios on the morning of 1 May 1954, they found a new station weakly audible on a part of the dial that had been silent before. Calling itself *La Voz de la Liberación*, it broadcast a combination of popular recordings, bawdy humor, and antigovernment propaganda. The announcers, claiming to be speaking from "deep in the jungle," exhorted Guatemalans to resist Communism and the Arbenz regime and support the forces of liberation led by Col. Carlos Castillo Armas. The two-hour broadcast was repeated four times. For the next week the station broadcast an hour-long program at 7:00 A.M. and 9:00 P.M. daily.[3] Although only faintly and intermittently heard in the capital, the station electrified a city where open criticism of the regime had become dangerous for journalists and private citizens alike. Government spokesmen denounced the broadcasts as a fraud, originating not in Guatemala but over the border in Mexico or Honduras. Most listeners, however, preferred to believe that brave radiomen, hidden in a remote outpost, were defying official censors and the police. → worked

So began an operation [   ] later called the "finest example PP/Radio effort and effectiveness on the books."[4] The voices heard in Guatemala originated not in the jungle, or even Honduras, but in a Miami [   ] where a team of four Guatemalan men and two women mixed announcements and editorials with canned music. The broadcasts reminded soldiers of their duty to protect the country from foreign ideologies, warned women to keep their husbands away from Communist party meetings and labor unions, and threatened government officials with reprisals.[5] Couriers carried the tapes via Pan American Airways to [   ] where they were beamed into Guatemala from a mobile transmitter. When the traffic in tapes aroused the suspicions of Panamanian customs officials, the announc-

---

[3]LINCOLN to Guatemala Station, LINC 2212, 29 April 1954, Job 79-01025A, Box 4.

[4]LINCOLN to SHERWOOD, LINC 4607, 2 July 1954, Job 79-01025A, Box 6.

[5]Phillips, *The Night Watch* (New York: Ballantine Books, 1977), p. 53.

ers moved to [   ] and began broadcasting live from a dairy farm [   ] a site known as SHER-WOOD. At about the same time, the SHERWOOD operation improved its reception in Guatemala by boosting its signal strength.[6] By mid-May the rebel broadcasts were heard loud and clear in Guatemala City, and SHERWOOD announcers were responding quickly to developments in the enemy capital.

To direct the SHERWOOD operation, Tracy Barnes selected a clever and enterprising contract employee, David Atlee Phillips, a onetime actor and newspaper editor in Chile. When Phillips arrived in [   ] in March, one of the Guatemalan announcers explained that the target audience was mixed. "Two percent are hardcore Marxists; 13 percent are officials and others in sympathy with the Arbenz regime.... Two percent are militant anti-Communists, some of them in exile." The remainder was neutral, apathetic, or frustrated, "a soap opera audience." The objective, the announcer continued, was to intimidate the Communists and their sympathizers and stimulate the apathetic majority to act.[7] Initial broadcasts would establish the station's credibility, setting the stage for an "Orson Welles type 'panic broadcast'" to coincide with Castillo Armas's invasion. The program would follow the lead of earlier PP efforts, combining intimidating misinformation with pithy slogans, and targeting "men of action," particularly the Army.[8] The Station's slogan became *Trabajo, Pan y Patria*, work, bread, and country.

In Phillips's account of the operation, SHERWOOD was singularly responsible for the triumph of PBSUCCESS. "When the campaign started," he observes, "the Guatemalan capital and countryside had been quiet. Within a week there was unrest everywhere."[9] Scholars

[6]Guatemala Station complained of poor reception until 22 May. LINCOLN to SHERWOOD, LINC 3002, 22 May 1954, Job 79-01025A, Box 5.

[7]Phillips, *Night Watch*, pp. 50–51.

[8][   ] to Chief of Station Guatemala, "SHERWOOD: Comment on Broadcasts," HUL-A-756, 12 May 1954, Job 79-01025A, Box 103.

[9]Phillips, *Night Watch*, p. 53. Guatemala Station's weekly "Psych Barometer Reports" were also at odds with Phillips's version, claiming that the initial sensation caused by the appearance of the clandestine radio quickly wore off. [   ] "Psych Inteligence Report," 10–16 May 1954," HGG-A-

have generally given similar credit to *La Voz de la Liberación*, but were it not for a fortuitous turn of events the rebel broadcasters might have made only a muffled impact. Two weeks into the operation Guatemala's state-run radio station, TGW, disappeared from the air. Perplexed, [   ] and Phillips soon learned from Guatemala Station that TGW was scheduled to receive a new antenna and that the government's only broadcast medium would be out of commission for three weeks.[10] Through an accident of timing SHERWOOD acquired a virtual propaganda monopoly during the most critical phase of operation PBSUCCESS. In late May, as Guatemalans witnessed a startling series of dark and portentous events, the largely illiterate populace turned to *La Voz de la Liberación* for news.

(handwritten: ❨not CIA work)

The Voyage of the Alfhem

But if SHERWOOD represented a master stroke for PBSUCCESS, Arbenz riposted with an even bolder countermove long anticipated by CIA but a complete surprise to the public in Guatemala and the United States. On 15 May, the Swedish freighter *Alfhem* arrived at Puerto Barrios carrying thousands of tons of Czech arms. By clever deception, the ship had evaded efforts by the State Department and the CIA to stop or delay it. Following the Martínez mission, the Agency had carefully monitored international arms flows and the traffic in Guatemala's ports. On 8 April, Wisner met with State Department and Navy officials to coordinate intelligence gathering. They agreed to "take no action at this stage to deter or interfere with the shipment, but rather allow events to take their course at least to the point when exposure would be most compromising to the Guatemalans."[11] The following day, Wisner learned from [   ] that the Bank of Guatemala had telegraphically transferred $4,860,000 through the Union Bank of Switzerland and Stabank, Prague, to the account of In-

121, 18 May 1954, Job 79-01025A, Box 101.
[10][   ] "Guatemalan Radio Silence," 28 May 1954, Job 79-01025A, Box 70.
[11] Wisner to King, "Guatemalan Acquisition of Iron Curtain Arms," 8 April 1954, Job 79-01228A, Box 24.

vesta, a Czech firm.[12] No Agency official said so at the time, but the payment revealed the limits of the Communist Bloc's willingness to aid an ally in the Western Hemisphere. The Czechs would provide arms, but on a cash and carry basis.[13] On 17 April, the *Alfhem*, a freighter registered to the Swedish subsidiary of a Czech shipping firm, departed the Polish port of Szczecin bound for Dakar, West Africa, en route to Central America.[14]

The State Department and the Agency worked frantically to stop the shipment, which they mistakenly believed was carried in another ship, the *Wulfsbrook*, registered to a West German firm. Department officials tried to persuade the German Government to order the *Wulfsbrook* into port and sought help in canceling its insurance.[15] The *Alfhem* meanwhile plied a circuitous route to Central America. After a week at sea, the captain received radio orders to proceed to Curaçao in the Dutch West Indies. In the mid-Atlantic, new orders arrived diverting him to Puerto Cortés, Honduras. On 13 May, just two days out of port, he learned his real destination and steered for Guatemala. The Agency had not relied completely on the State Department to thwart the shipment. On 7 May, Wisner sent limpet mines to the sabotage training bases in Nicaragua. By the time the *Alfhem* arrived off Puerto Barrios, however, its destruction posed a ticklish diplomatic problem. The State Department's fevered activity had alerted several European governments, shipping lines, and insurance underwriters of

---

[12][

], LINCOLN to Chief, WH, "Financial Position of Guatemala," 493, 14 June 1954, Job 79-01025A, Box 97.

[13]The Guatemalan Government was fully capable of paying cash. Its foreign currency reserves in 1954 topped $42 million. LINCOLN to Chief, WH, "Financial Position of Guatemala," 493, 14 June 1954, Job 79-01025A, Box 97.

[14]Schlesinger and Kinzer, *Bitter Fruit*, p. 149.

[15]R. G. Leddy to J. F. Dulles, "Action to prevent delivery of Czech Arms to Guatemala," 18 May 1954, Records of the Office of Middle American Affairs, General Records of the Dept. of State, Lot 58D78, Box 2, RG 59; Wisner to Lampton Berry, Policy Planning Staff, "Proposed Diversion of SS *Wulfsbrook*," 6 May 1954, Job 79-01228A, Box 24.

official US interest. If the ship were sunk, it would be impossible to deny involvement.[16]

The arms purchase handed PBSUCCESS a propaganda bonanza. On 17 May, the State Department declared that the shipment revealed Guatemala's complicity in a Soviet plan for Communist conquest in the Americas. John Foster Dulles exaggerated the size of the cargo, hinting that it would enable Guatemala to triple the size of its Army and overwhelm neighboring states. The press and Congress responded on cue. "The threat of Communist imperialism is no longer academic," proclaimed the *Washington Post*; "it has arrived." The *New York Times* warned that Communist arms would soon make their way along "secret jungle paths" to guerrilla armies throughout the Hemisphere. "If Paul Revere were living today," Representative Paul Lantaff imagined, "he would view the landing of Red arms in Guatemala as a signal to ride." House Speaker John McCormack spluttered that "this cargo of arms is like an atom bomb planted in the rear of our backyard."[17] These fulminations intensified the fears of many Guatemalans that the incident would provide a convenient pretext for US intervention.

The *Alfhem* incident helped break down Honduran objections to aiding PBSUCCESS. The Gálvez government viewed the shipment as connected to a major labor conflict that had broken out on United Fruit plantations on 5 May and spread throughout the country. CIA officials suspected Guatemalan involvement, noting "an unusual amount of discipline" and the presence of Guatemalan labor organizers. They admitted, however, that the strikers had the sympathy of most Hondurans while the company had "practically no friends."[18] Honduran officials needed no proof of Guatemalan complicity, believing all labor strife to be Communist inspired. On 23 May, Gálvez

[16]Kermit Roosevelt to [   ] DIR 49642, 7 May 1954, Job 79-01025A, Box 8.

[17]Gleijeses, *Shattered Hope*, p. 299.

[18][   ] to Chief WHD, "Honduran Communist Activities," HHT-34, 7 July 1954, Job 79-01025A, Box 107; [   ] "Honduran Public Opinion Favors Strikers," HUL-012, 22 May 1954, Job 79-01025A, Box 107.

asked the United States to prepare to land Marines if the situation should spin out of control. The Navy placed two warships in the Gulf of Honduras.[19] Castillo Armas helped by sending some of his men to provide muscle for the company.[20] The strike and the arms shipment persuaded Gálvez that he had little to lose by helping PBSUCCESS.

In Guatemala, [   ] propagandists worked to accentuate confusion caused by the landing of the Czech arms. The *Alfhem*'s arrival intensified tensions in the capital. "The man on the street," Guatemala Station reported, "[was] rapidly becoming convinced that 'something' will soon happen." Rightist and centrist members of the government party, PAR, called for the resignation of party leaders. CEUA students predicted a Communist coup. Fearing the new weapons would close the rift between Arbenz and the military, SHERWOOD broadcast rumors that the arms were intended not for the Army but for labor unions and peasant cadres.

This rumor turned out to be true. Arbenz and the PGT had intended the *Alfhem* shipment to remain a secret, enabling them to divert some of the arms to workers' militias before giving the remainder to the Army. The Army, however, learned of the Martínez mission and closely watched shipping traffic at Puerto Barrios for signs of the arms's arrival.[21] Army units sealed off the pier as soon as the *Alfhem* docked, setting up a security cordon around the port area. José Angel Sánchez, the minister of defense, took personal charge of security and transportation arrangements. The President had to give up his plans for arming militias. The weapons belonged to the Army now, and taking them away would only enrage the officer corps. Soldiers loaded the crates, marked "optical equipment," on 123 flatcars for the trip to

[19] Gleijeses, *Shattered Hope*, p. 301.

[20] LINCOLN to [   ] LINC 2960, 21 May 1954, Job 79-01025A, Box 4.

[21] Gleijeses suggests the United States alerted the Army, but this is unlikely. Agency officials were themselves confused about the arrival of the shipment, believing until the last minute that it could be prevented. They also placed no trust in the Army, considering it penetrated by Communists. Finally, the establishment of workers' militias would have substantially helped the K-Program break the military's allegiance to the government. Gleijeses, *Shattered Hope*, p. 304.

Guatemala City.[22] The shipment consisted of large numbers of rifles, machine guns, antitank guns, 100 howitzers, mortars, grenades, and antitank mines. Some of the weapons had been used, and many bore a swastika stamp on the metal parts. The antiquated artillery pieces had wooden wheels. American military advisers, who received the first reliable reports, estimated that there was enough ammunition to last the Guatemalan Army 10 to 15 years in peacetime.[23]

[   ] ordered sabotage teams to destroy the *Alfhem* arms en route, and the mission provided the first test of Castillo Armas's forces. Three four-man teams were dispatched to dynamite railroad trestles between Puerto Barrios and Guatemala City as military trains passed over them.[24] Freshly graduated from training programs at [   ] they carried maps [   ] identifying the best targets. All three failed. The *CIA Program* first, on 20 May, detonated a charge that damaged an engine slightly. Shots from the train slew one rebel commando, whose companions returned fire killing a Guatemalan soldier. Two other attempts, on 23 and 25 May either failed to reach the target or inflict damage.[25] The arms reached the capital safely on the 26th.

Arbenz had momentarily outwitted the Agency, but by so doing he removed the constraints on the Agency's ability to retaliate. Before the *Alfhem* incident, David Phillips observed, there was still a chance that Holland or another official in the State Department would pull the plug on PBSUCCESS. The arms shipment "clearly defined the issue:

[22]Wisner to Robert B. Anderson, Under Secretary of Defense, "Guatemalan Procurement of Arms from the Soviet Orbit," 21 June 1954, Job 79-01025A, Box 24.

[23][   ] to LINCOLN, "Information re Alfhem Arms Shipment," HGG-A-1162, 28 May 1954, Job 79-01228A, Box 24; King to Dulles, "Quality and Future Disposition of Arms Received by Guatemala from the Ship Alfhem," 16 December 1954, Job 79-01228A, Box 23; Wisner to Holland, "Guatemalan Arms Acquisition," 21 June 1954, Job 79-01228A, Box 24. CIA had only a sketchy idea of the numbers of actual arms but a firm idea of their weight (4,122,145 pounds) and a value (approximately $5 million).

[24]Wisner, "Thoughts and Possible Courses of Action Concerning Latest Developments in PBSUCCESS—Arrival of the Alfhelm [sic]," 18 May 1954, Job 79-01228A, Box 24.

[25]See LINCOLN cables 2900–3099, Job 79-01025A, Boxes 4 and 5.

Guatemala had received arms from Russia, thus Guatemala and Russia were playing footsie. From that point, there was no question of the nature of the target, only the question of how soon and in what manner it would be destroyed."[26]

Operation HARDROCK

not CIA

The *Alfhem* incident touched off a massive escalation of the US effort to intimidate the Guatemalan Government. The State Department concluded a military assistance agreement with Honduras and began shipping planes and tanks to Tegucigalpa. On 24 May, the Navy provided a more daunting indicator of US resolve in operation HARDROCK BAKER, the sea blockade of Guatemala. Submarines and warships patrolled the sea approaches to Guatemala, stopping all ships and searching for arms. The task force was instructed to damage vessels if necessary to make them stop. Ships transiting the Panama Canal en route to Guatemala were detained and searched. The blockade's blatant illegality made it a powerful weapon of intimidation. The United States stopped and boarded French and British freighters in defiance of international law. France and Britain muted their protests in hopes that the United States would show similar restraint with regard to their colonial troubles in the Middle East. The message to Guatemala was clear: If the United States would violate freedom of the seas, it would not be stopped by so feeble an instrument as the nonintervention clause of the Rio Pact.[27]

PBSUCCESS, too, stepped up the pressure on the Army. On 26 May, one of Castillo Armas's warplanes flew low over the capital, buzzed the presidential palace and dropped leaflets in front of the headquarters of the presidential guard. The leaflets encouraged members of the Guardia to "Struggle against Communist atheism, Communist intervention, Communist oppression.... Struggle with your

[26]Debriefing Report, David Atlee Phillips, [undated], Job 79-01025A, Box 167.
[27]Gleijeses, *Shattered Hope*, pp. 312–313; [   ] to Graham L. Page, "K-Program," HUL-A-989, 6 June 1954, Job 79-01025A, Box 103.

patriotic brothers! Struggle with Castillo Armas!"[28] "I suppose it does-
n't really matter what the leaflets say," Barnes acknowledged. The real
massage was conveyed by the plane itself, an intimidating weapon in a
region that had never witnessed aerial warfare.[29] "If they had been napalm bombs and not leaflets, we wouldn't be here to talk about it,"
one editorialist observed. Leaflet drops on successive days were widely
interpreted as practice bombing runs.[30]

By the first week of June the population of Guatemala City expected
an invasion any day. Ambassadors left town "on urgent orders" from
their governments. The labor union federation placed its members on
alert against "reactionary elements." Somoza severed diplomatic relations. On 5 June, the retired Chief of Staff of the Air Force, Rodolfo
Mendoza Azurdia, fled in a small plane [

] In agony, the govern-
ment and the PGT sought a way out. Arbenz offered Gálvez a nonag-
gression pact and asked to meet with Eisenhower to relieve tensions,
but neither request elicited a response. The PGT, meanwhile, had begun to disintegrate. After the Caracas conference, Fortuny had voiced
concerns that the party had gone "beyond what was realistically possible," advancing its programs to an extent that endangered the state.
He called for "self-restraint," a pause in the agrarian reform, and
urged Communists in high government positions to resign. Even as he
did so, he was plagued by self-doubt and the near certainty that he was
asking too little, too late. Other leaders refused to listen. [   ]
propaganda attacks had whittled the party's membership down to an
unmovable core, unafraid and prepared to follow the revolution to the
end.[31] News of Fortuny's resignation reached Agency officials in the
first week of June, leaving them perplexed. Accustomed to dealing

[28][   ] to Chief of Station Guatemala, "Intended Leaflet Drop," HUL-
A-893, 23 May 1954, Job 79-01025A, Box 103.
[29][   ] interviewed by Nick Cullather, tape recording, Washington, DC, 19 June 1993 (hereafter cited as [   ] interview). Recording
on file in the DCI History Staff Office, CIA.
[30]Gleijeses, *Shattered Hope*, pp. 309–310.
[31]*Ibid.*, pp. 283–286.

with iron-willed totalitarians, they were unused to seeing an adversary flounder in the face of insurmountable problems and self-doubt.

Desperate, the regime lashed out at its internal opposition. On 8 June, Arbenz suspended civil liberties and began a roundup of suspected subversives. Police arrested 480 persons in the first two weeks of June, holding them at military bases. Many were tortured. On 14 June, one of the few survivors of the CEUA group found the mutilated and charred body of [   ] in the city morgue.[32] Barnes admitted that the net had "suffered losses" and suggested that it be reorganized for the operation's final phase, but there was nothing left to organize.[33] Some 75 detainees were killed and buried in mass graves in the regime's final days.

The Invasion

It was already muggy at 7:00 A.M. on 15 June when [   ] pulled into a driveway alongside a [   ] house belonging to [   ] wasn't used to the heat. He had replaced Tranger as Chief of Guatemala Station in early May, right at the beginning of the rainy season, when the mornings broke hot and the predictable afternoon showers brought no relief. [   ] was breathing down his neck for results on the military defection project, the "K-Program," and [   ] had opted for the coldest of cold approaches. He would go to [   ] house, ring the doorbell, and ask the man to stage a coup. Minutes later, in [   ] *sala*, he bluntly explained what [   ] always called the "facts of life." The time had come for [   ] to "get moving and take over the Army." This was "the last opportunity for the Army to salvage its honor and even its existence." [   ] listened, nodding in agreement. He was ready to help, he told [   ] but he would need some assistance in return. Arbenz still exercised a great deal of control over the officer corps [

---

[32] [Unsigned], "Informal Memorandum," 23 June 1954, Leddy file, Job 79-01025A, Box 81.

[33] Barnes to PBSUCCESS Headquarters, HUL-A-986, 16 June 1954, Job 79-01025A, Box 103.

] If Castillo
Armas would have [   ] would start the
coup. That would not be possible, [   ] replied. The times
called for courage, for taking risks. [   ] would have to do
things for himself. The two men agreed to meet again the following
day.[34]

The K-Program presented a paradox for PBSUCCESS. [   ]
believed the operation could not succeed without an Army revolt, but
his efforts to bully and frighten the officer corps into action left the
military's leaders divided and cowed. No *caudillo* emerged to lead soldiers against the government, and as the operation wore on it appeared less likely that one would emerge. Early on, [   ] had
picked [   ] as the most likely candidate. He had threatened to
revolt; he was ambitious and opportunistic. Peurifoy vouched for his
anti-Communism. When the time came, however, [   ] demanded more than he offered. At the second meeting, he told [
] that he had consulted [
] and the two had agreed that "a spectacle of
force" would be needed to swing the Army to the side of the opposition. Labor unions had organized progovernment demonstrations for
the following day. If Castillo Armas could drop a bomb in the infield
of the hippodrome, tear gas the crowd, and buzz Arbenz's house, the
Army would act. [   ] considered this a reasonable request
and promised to provide a suitable display.[35]

[   ] Barnes, and Wisner were less willing to accommodate a
weak-kneed *caudillo*. An aerial display would prove US involvement,
since few Central American governments, let alone rebel movements,
could mount a bombing mission. [   ] told [   ] the
air show was off and instructed him to go over the facts of life one
more time with [   ]. [   ] had other ways to put pressure on the Army. In his calculations, Castillo Armas [   ]
would soon be in competition, each trying to topple Arbenz first.

[34]Guatemala Station to Director, [   ], Job 79-
01025A, Box 11.
[35]Guatemala Station to Director, GUAT 874, 17 June 1954, Job 79-01025A,
Box 11.

Invasion plan, 18 June 1954. Copyright ©1998 by Indiana University.

PBSUCCESS now had "two strings in its bow," he told Allen Dulles, Castillo Armas and his forces on the Honduran border, and [   ] uprising in the capital. Both options would be pursued "since they do not become mutually exclusive until after the disposition of the present regime." Even if Castillo Armas suffered setbacks, his invasion would create the turmoil necessary for [   ] to seize control. Likewise, if [   ] failed, his rebellion would still immobilize the Army long enough to allow Castillo Armas to make gains in the countryside. Even "assuming Castillo Armas's defeat or assuming [   ] failure, there is no problem."[36]

The invasion plan went into effect on 15 June, the day [   ] made his cold approach. Divided into four teams, Castillo Armas's 480 "shock troops" arrived at staging areas on the Guatemalan border near the Honduran towns of Florida, Nueva Ocotepeque, Copán, and Macuelizo. From these areas they were to proceed to the border, arriving near midnight on the 17th. The plan called for four rebel bands to make five separate incursions into Guatemala in order to project the impression of an attack across a broad front and to minimize the chance that the entire force could be routed in a single encounter. The largest force, 198 soldiers, would cross the border near Macuelizo and attack the heavily guarded port city of Puerto Barrios. A group of 122 rebels would proceed from a base near Florida, Honduras, and march on Zacapa, the Guatemalan Army's largest frontier garrison. Castillo Armas would command a group of 100 soldiers split between the base areas in Copán and Nueva Ocotepeque. These forces would seize the lightly defended border towns of Esquipulas, Quezaltepeque, and Chiquimula before uniting and marching on the capital. Meanwhile, a smaller force of 60 soldiers would cross into El Salvador and invade Guatemala from the *finca* of [

                                    ] From there they would attack the provincial capital of Jutiapa (El Salvador had refused to allow Castillo Armas to invade from its territory, [

---

[36] LINCOLN to Director, LINC 3824, 15 June 1954, Job 79-01025A, Box 5.

] In addition to these regular troops, 10 trained saboteurs would fan out into the countryside ahead of the invading troops, blowing up railroads and cutting telegraph lines.[37] The rebels were to avoid direct confrontation with the Guatemalan Army, which would unify the officer corps and lead to a quick defeat of the rebellion. Harassing raids in remote areas would enable the rebels to keep a force intact while sowing panic in the capital and prodding the military to act. Rebel aircraft were instructed to avoid hitting military targets.

Even before H-hour, the invasion degenerated from an ambitious plan to tragicomedy. Salvadoran policemen spotted the Jutiapa force on a road outside Santa Ana on the afternoon of 17 June and decided to take a look. They discovered 21 machine guns, rifles, and grenades hidden in a wagon the men were riding. The police arrested the entire group and threw them in the Santa Ana jail.[38] Castillo Armas eventually got them deported to Honduras but without their weapons. Jutiapa was spared. Later that evening the Chiquimula force engaged in the first action of the campaign. Approaching the border near Esquipulas, they were surprised to discover a border guard and a customs official stationed on the previously unguarded road. They captured the soldier and shot the customs official. He was the first Guatemalan casualty.[39]

Dressed in a leather jacket and checked shirt and driving a battered station wagon, Castillo Armas led his troops across the border at 8:20 P.M. on 18 June. At about the same time, his planes, in partial fulfillment of [   ] request, buzzed the progovernment demonstrations at the railroad station in Guatemala City. SHERWOOD told its listeners that "there are reports of a battle at Esquipulas, but we do not yet have a tally of the dead."[40] Castillo Armas led the Chiquimula detachment, the one thought least likely to encounter serious resistance. On foot, and encumbered by weapons and supplies, the rebels made slow progress, and it would be some days before they actually captured Esquipulas, a few miles from the border.

[37]LINCOLN to Director, LINC 3937, 16 June 1954, Job 79-01025A, Box 6.
[38]LINCOLN to Director, LINC 4065, 19 June 1954, Job 79-01025A, Box 6.
[39]LINCOLN to Director, LINC 3997, 18 June 1954, Job 79-01025A, Box 6.
[40]Phillips, *Night Watch*, p. 58.

Meanwhile, [   ] continued to demand the bombing of the race track. With the invasion under way, [   ] was even less inclined to satisfy what he considered a frivolous demand. He told Bissell he was ready to give up on [   ] believing he could accomplish the Army's "intimidation or actual defeat through air to ground action supported by shock forces." Wisner and Bissell quickly brought him back to reality. The "entire issue in our opinion will turn on the position taken by the Guatemalan forces," they warned. If the rebels attacked Army garrisons, they would succeed only in uniting the military behind Arbenz. And even if the Army could be intimidated into inaction, police units and labor organizations could round up the small rebel force with little trouble.[41] With only one string in its bow, PBSUCCESS would fail. "Our next move," Dulles told [   ] "should be to exert all possible influence to persuade the Army that their next target must be Arbenz himself if they are themselves to survive. . . . If the Army acts it, not Castillo Armas will rule the country."[42]

[   ] continued to negotiate with [   ] while [   ] stepped up the air war. On 19 June, rebel planes blew up a railroad bridge at Gualán. Cargo planes dropped pallets of arms over the Guatemalan countryside to persuade the Army that a fifth column was ready to rise against the government. Guatemala Station reported that the city was "clearing rapidly. Cars, carts, tearing to outskirts. Fear, expectation spreading."[43] But [   ] remained stubbornly inert.

The initial panic generated by the invasion and air attacks wore off as Guatemalans realized nothing would happen immediately. On the 20th, Guatemala Station cabled that the government was "recovering its nerve." "Capital very still, stores shuttered. People waiting apathetically, consider uprising a farce, some even speculating it a government provocation."[44] Castillo Armas's invaders were not making

[41]Richard Bissell to [   ], DIR 05705, 19 June 1954, Job 79-01025A, Box 9; Wisner to [   ], DIR 05535, 18 June 1954, Job 79-01025A, Box 9.
[42]Dulles to [   ], DIR 05857, 21 June 1954, Job 79-01025A, Box 9.
[43]LINCOLN to SHERWOOD, LINC 4036, 19 June 1954, Job 79-01025A, Box 6.
[44]Guatemala Station to Director, GUAT 921, 20 June 1954, Job 79-01025A, Box 11.

the sort of bold strikes needed to inspire terror in the capital. On the 20th his forces captured Esquipulas, barely three miles from the border and defended only by a small police force.[45] Meanwhile a column of 122 rebels approaching Zacapa from the northeast encountered a small garrison of 30 soldiers led by Lt. César Augusto Silva Girón at the small town of Gualán. Without instructions or reinforcements from the larger garrison at Zacapa, Girón engaged the rebels in a 36-hour firefight, forcing them to flee toward La Union, between Gualán and Zacapa. Only 30 rebels escaped death or capture. The casualties included their commanding officer. The survivors reported that they had been "decisively defeated" by a superior force.[46]

The following day, the rebels' largest force suffered a colossal defeat at Puerto Barrios. Twenty insurgents landed a boat on the waterfront as 150 of their compatriots attacked the town from the east. Policemen and hastily armed dock workers rounded up the amphibious force and ran off the remainder, who fled across the border to San Miguel Correderos, Honduras, and refused to rejoin the fray. After repeated requests for a report, the defeated rebels turned off their radios and dispersed.[47] Their loss cost Castillo Armas almost half his regular army. After three days in action, two of the invasion's four prongs had been turned back (one by the Salvadoran police), and one had been halted by minor resistance.

In an effort to recover momentum, [   ] authorized air attacks on the capital the following day, but the results were unimpressive. A single plane, flying above 1,000 feet, managed to hit a small oil tank on the city outskirts igniting a fire that was doused in 20 minutes. [   ] described the attack as a "pathetic" gesture that left the public with an impression of "incredible weakness, lack of decision, fainthearted effort."[48] Attempts to use aircraft for propaganda advan-

---

[45] LINCOLN to Director, LINC 4153, 21 June 1954, Job 79-01025A, Box 6.

[46] Gleijeses, *Shattered Hope*, pp. 326–327; LINCOLN to Director, "Daily Sitrep No. 13," LINC 4440, 27 June 1954, Job 79-01025A, Box 6.

[47] *Ibid.*; LINCOLN to Director, LINC 4477, 28 June 1954, Job 79-01025, Box 6; LINCOLN to Director, "Daily Sitrep No. 9," LINC 4229, 23 June 1954, Job 79-01025A, Box 6.

[48] LINCOLN to SHERWOOD, LINC 4194, 22 June 1954, Job 79-01025A, Box 6.

Actual invasion, late June 1954. Copyright ©1998 by Indiana University.

tage were hampered by Castillo Armas's persistent demands for air support. Ensconced at Esquipulas, he reported his situations as "very grave as result two pronged enemy attacks from Zacapa and from Jutiapa via Ipala." If he did not receive "heavy bombardment" on these fronts, he would be "forced to abandon everything."[49]

Challenge at the UN

As Monzón dallied and Castillo Armas faltered, PBSUCCESS faced another, potentially fatal challenge on the diplomatic front. On 18 June, the day of the invasion, Guatemalan foreign minister Guillermo Toriello petitioned the UN Security Council to intervene to stop the outside aggression he blamed on Nicaragua, Honduras, and the United Fruit Company. On 20 June, the council approved a French motion enjoining all member nations to refrain from aiding the insurgency. John Foster Dulles was furious, but to save appearances he had to support the measure. On the 21st, Toriello asked the Security Council to take "whatever steps are necessary" to enforce the resolution.[50] The prospect that the council could dispatch a factfinding mission to Guatemala touched off a flurry of meetings and phone calls between Wisner, the Dulles brothers, Assistant Secretary Henry Holland, the President, and Henry Cabot Lodge, the US delegate to the UN. Eisenhower was ready to use the veto. The United States had never before vetoed a Security Council resolution and the first use would mean a grave propaganda defeat. Wisner argued that the United States should allow some kind of an inspection mission and then try to control it. The US should get the OAS Peace Council designated as the body of first recourse. "Friendly" delegates from the United States, Brazil, and Cuba dominated the council. If the UN insisted on sending its own mission, the United States should direct it to investigate the "causes" of the rebellion, including the *Alfhem* ship-

[49]LINCOLN to Director, LINC 4499, 28 June 1954, Job 79-01025A, Box 6.
[50][   ] Assistant Director for Current Intelligence, to Allen Dulles, "Significance of the 20 June UN Security Council Meeting," 21 June 1954, Job 79-01228A, Box 24.

ment, land reform, and the Communist influence in government.[51] Lodge adopted this position, but Holland and other State Department officials remained apprehensive about international press reaction.

For much of the world, the spring of 1954 seemed to carry a real chance for the two superpowers to ease world tensions after eight years of Cold War. Stalin had died in February 1953, and the new Soviet administration appeared less sinister and more ready to reach accommodations. In May 1954, the superpowers met to arrange a settlement of the difficult Indochina and Formosa disputes at the Geneva Conference. In the following weeks, however, tensions did not ease, and some in the international press blamed the Eisenhower administration for what was seen as a lost opportunity. Some generally pro-Western newspapers regarded Guatemala's plight as further proof that the United States had adopted a needlessly truculent posture. A former British Labor Government minister, Aneurin Bevan, not surprisingly wrote a column headlined "Guatemalan Invasion is Plot to Save American Property," which played prominently in *The Times of India* and other newspapers. On the morning of 18 June, CBS News aired a segment on the adverse reaction in Britain, quoting an official who observed that "despite the United Fruit Company, the United States does not yet own all of Central America and the Caribbean."[52] *Pravda* explained the invasion as an attempt by the United States to reignite the Cold War. USIA stations in Germany, Japan, and the Middle East reported the sympathy of the local press for Guatemala and the universal assumption of US complicity in the invasion. Even news organs unsympathetic to Arbenz—like the Iranian state press—

[51] Wisner, "Memorandum of Ideas Developed in Meeting in Mr. Murphy's Office Concerning Guatemalan Situation," 21 June 1954, Job 79-01228A, Box 24; Wisner to Holland, "Recommendations for Use in Connection with Further Proceedings in the United Nations and/or the OAS Peace Commission, Guatemala," 22 June 1954, *ibid.*; [   ] "Intelligence Provided Department of State Concerning Guatemala," 20 July 1954, *ibid.*; [   ] Assistant Director for Current Intelligence, to Allen Dulles, "Significance of the 20 June UN Security Council Meeting," 21 June 1954, *ibid.*

[52] Wisner to Holland, "British Attitude Toward the Guatemalan Situation," 18 June 1954, Job 79-01228A, Box 23.

acknowledged with certainty that the rebellion had US support. These reports made State Department officials nervous, and their jitters spread to the Agency. [   ] staff was "terrified" that the Guatemalans would make such a ruckus in international forums that Henry Holland or other State Department officials would pull the plug.[53]

The Agency, meanwhile, took steps to ensure that coverage in the American press had a favorable slant. Peurifoy met with American reporters in Guatemala City to discuss "the type of stories they were writing." At his suggestion, "all agreed to drop words such as 'invasion.'" The French and British consuls agreed to have a word with their correspondents.[54] Agency officials had earlier managed to have Sydney Gruson, the *New York Times* correspondent, reexpelled from Guatemala. In the wake of the *Alfhem* incident, Arbenz allowed Gruson back into the country. [   ] staff complained that after his return Gruson's reports parroted "Foreign Minister Toriello's statements regarding the Guatemalan position on arms purchases and denial of complicity in the Honduran strikes." [   ] speculated that either Arbenz had extracted a quid pro quo in exchange for lifting the expulsion, or that Gruson was unwilling to risk offending Guatemalan officials a second time. He plumbed Agency files and found that two years earlier Gruson had attended parties in Mexico City at which Czechoslovak diplomats had been present. He took this evidence to Dulles, and the Director passed it on to Arthur Hays Sulzberger, publisher of the *Times*, who reassigned Gruson.[55] During the battle for Guatemala, stories in the *Times* originated in Mexico City.

[53]For international press reaction see Bonn to USIA, 22 June 1954; the Hague to Secretary of State, 22 June 1954; New Delhi to Secretary of State, 25 June 1954, all three in Job 79-01025A, Box 82; Huntington D. Sheldon to Allen Dulles, "Significance of 20 June UN Security Council Meeting," 21 June 1954, Job 79-01228A, Box 24. [   ] interview.

[54]Peurifoy to Willauer and Holland, GUAT 940, 23 June 1954, Job 79-01025A, Box 11.

[55][   ] "Reporting on Guatemala by *New York Times* Correspondent Sydney Gruson," 27 May 1954, Job 79-01228A, Box 23; [   ] to PBSUCCESS Headquarters, "Sydney Gruson," HUL-A-1118, 2 June 1954,

The Jaws of Defeat

Prospects for a rebel victory steadily dimmed after the defeats at Gualán and Puerto Barrios. [   ] and his staff, unable to influence the events on which the outcome of PBSUCCESS now seemed to depend, relayed daily reports to Headquarters detailing the dwindling fortunes of Castillo Armas's forces. On the 23rd, the bulk of the *liberacionistas* remained at Esquipulas with their commander, while an advance party entered Chiquimula and traded shots with the Army barracks there. Remnants of the force defeated at Gualán and detachments from Esquipulas broke into bands of 10 to 20 men and scattered among the small towns surrounding Zacapa, Teculután, Vado Hondo, and Jocotán. From these positions, the rebels could observe large numbers of government troops moving by rail to Zacapa.[56]

Historians have debated the question of whether substantial numbers of sympathizers joined Castillo Armas's forces in the field.[57] There

Job 79-01025A, Box 10; [   ] Jr., "Sydney Gruson," 2 June 1954, Job 79-01025A, Box 104. Harrison Salisbury has alleged that Dulles "deliberately deceived" Sulzberger in order to get rid of Gruson, and that "Gruson was too good a reporter. He might spill the beans." In fact, [   ] was not worried about Gruson's investigative talents. He wanted at all costs to keep Toriello's version of events out of the newspapers during the UN debate, and he feared Gruson was more susceptible to official pressure than other correspondents. Dulles claimed he did not suggest a course of action to Sulzberger, and that "our interest in this individual was only to pass on the information we had obtained about him and any action taken thereon is the responsibility of Mr. Sulzberger." Deputies' Meeting, 10 June 1954, Dulles papers, Job 80B-01676R, Box 23. *[The New York Times disclosed additional details from its own files on the Gruson incident when this study was released. See Tim Weiner, "Role of CIA in Guatemala Told in Files of Publisher," New York Times, July 7, 1997—N.C.]*

[56]LINCOLN to Director, "Daily Sitrep No. 9," LINC 4229, 23 June 1954, Job 79-01025A, Box 6.

[57]Frederick Marks, "The CIA and Castillo Armas in Guatemala, 1954: New Clues to an Old Puzzle," *Diplomatic History* 14 (Winter 1990): 70. Marks alleges that "it is clear that as Castillo Armas advanced, his ranks were swelled by a massive influx of ranchers, peasants, and other sympathizers who together posed a real threat to the regular army."

is no doubt that [   ] strategy relied on such reinforcements. The original invasion force numbered only 480 and was broken into smaller contingents that would be outnumbered in a fight with even a small Guatemalan Army garrison. These original soldiers were intended to be the core of a larger force that would spontaneously rise and join Castillo Armas as he marched on the capital. Preparations were made for weapons to be airdropped to the swelling ranks. Agency records reveal that recruits did join Castillo Armas, and in substantial numbers, but only in places where the *liberacionistas* met no resistance. Where the rebels were engaged in actual combat, no recruits materialized and the original force suffered high rates of desertion. On the 21st, Castillo Armas had asked for supplies for 500 additional men at Esquipulas.[58] His forces there and in Chiquimula eventually came to comprise 1,200 men, all receiving food and weapons from airdrops. In the vicinity of Zacapa, however, where regular Army units constantly threatened rebel bands, the number of insurrectionists dropped from 180 to 30 between 23 and 29 June.[59] The recruits taxed the operation's overburdened supply system without allowing Castillo Armas to strike effectively at the enemy.

The Arbenz regime, meanwhile, laid plans to destroy Castillo Armas. The victories at Puerto Barrios and Gualán gave Arbenz confidence that the Army would do its duty and crush the invasion. He asked Díaz to allow the rebels to penetrate into the interior of the country unopposed. Neither man feared Castillo Armas's ragtag army, but both considered the invasion part of a larger US plan to create a pretext for direct intervention. They chose a strategy designed to defeat the rebels without furnishing a justification for landing the Marines. On 19 June, most of the soldiers of the Base Militar and the Guardia de Honor left by rail for Zacapa, where they were ordered to wait and engage the rebel army when it arrived. When Castillo Armas's scouts reached the outskirts of Zacapa, they found trainloads of soldiers and supplies arriving hourly in the already heavily occupied

[58]LINCOLN to Director, LINC 4153, 21 June 1954, Job 79-01025A, Box 6.
[59]Compare LINCOLN to Director, "Daily Sitrep No. 9," LINC 4229, 23 June 1954, Job 79-01025A, Box 6, with LINCOLN to Director, "Daily Sitrep No. 14," LINC 4507, 29 June 1954, Job 79-01025A, Box 6.

town. These war preparations masked the profound demoralization afflicting the officers responsible for saving the country. Like Arbenz, they feared US intervention, but unlike the president, they placed little faith in the ability of the United Nations to restrain Eisenhower. Sitting in Zacapa, they ruminated on the likely consequences of defeating Castillo Armas, murmuring that Marines might already be landing in Honduras.[60]

The Communists were the first to warn Arbenz that the Army would not defend the government. On 23 June, a PGT official visited Zacapa and found the officers cowering in their barracks, terrified and unwilling to fight. Fortuny reported the situation to Arbenz two days later. In disbelief, Arbenz sent a trusted officer to speak to the field commanders. He returned with the same report and a message: the officers "think that the Americans are threatening Guatemala just because of you and your Communist friends. If you don't resign, the Army will march on the capital to depose you." He predicted that if Arbenz did not act quickly, the Army would strike a bargain with Castillo Armas. Confirmation arrived later that day with the news that the 150-man Chiquimula garrison had surrendered to the rebels without a fight.[61]

Agency stations in Guatemala City, [   ] and [   ] never learned what happened at Zacapa. [   ] and Peurifoy were convinced that only [   ] could induce the Army to betray Arbenz, and [   ] remained in the capital, ignorant of the treason of his brother officers. For [   ] and other Agency observers in Miami and Washington, what happened in the next few days seemed curious and magical. Just as the entire operation seemed beyond saving, the Guatemalan Government suddenly, inexplicably collapsed. The Agency never found out why. After the conclusion of PBSUCCESS, no one asked the captured Guatemalan officers what happened in the regime's final days. Instead, an Agency legend developed, promoted by Bissell and other officials close to the operation,

[60]LINCOLN to Director, LINC 4412, 27 June 1954, Job 79-01025A, Box 6; Gleijeses, *Shattered Hope*, pp. 334–340.
[61]*Ibid.*, pp. 332–333.

that Arbenz "lost his nerve" as a result of the psychological pressure of air attacks and radio propaganda.[62] In fact, Arbenz was deposed in a military coup, and neither the radio nor the air attacks had much to do with it. It was natural, however, for PBSUCCESS officers to feel these elements had been decisive. In the operation's last days, they were all that was left.

As Arbenz learned the horrible truth, [   ] struggled with setbacks of his own. By 23 June, he judged the K-Program a failure and decided that the only remaining chance for success lay in a military victory. "Army defection now considered a matter of a test of arms," he cabled Headquarters.[63] He ordered CAT pilots to attack military targets, countermanding previous orders to spare the Army while defection efforts were under way. Informing Dulles that "airpower could be decisive" in the ensuing days, he asked for additional fighter aircraft. That day, the Director met at the White House with Eisenhower and Holland. The latter strongly opposed sending planes to Castillo Armas, a move that would confirm US involvement and violate a Security Council resolution approved by the United States. Eisenhower listened to these objections and then asked Dulles what chance the rebels would have without the aircraft.

"About zero," the Director replied.

"Suppose we supply the aircraft," the President asked. "What would be the chances then?"

"About 20 percent," Dulles allowed. The President considered the answer realistic and gave the order to send two fighters. "If you had told me that the chances would be 90 percent," he later told Dulles, "I would have had a much more difficult decision."[64] Unknown to both men, the chances of success were substantially higher. The Guatemalan Army had given Arbenz its ultimatum before the all-out air offensive began.

[62] Oral history interview with Richard M. Bissell, Jr., 5 June 1967, Dwight D. Eisenhower Library, Job 85-0664R, Box 5.

[63] LINCOLN to Director, "Daily Sitrep No. 9," LINC 4229, 23 June 1954, Box 6.

...isenhower, *Mandate for Change, 1953–1956* (Garden City, ...nd Co., 1963), pp. 425–426.

The aircraft had little apparent effect on the situation in the field. Pilots found most of their World War II surplus bombs failed to explode. Strafing produced the best results, but still failed to prevent or delay the Army buildup in Zacapa. Rebel planes strafed troop trains, exploding the boilers of several. The troops, however, continued toward their destination on foot. Repeated strafing runs would scatter but not deter them. Bombing runs on Zacapa also had no visible effect on the concentration of forces there. In a final attempt to spur [   ] rebel planes successfully bombed the Matamoros fortress in downtown Guatemala City on 25 June, touching off secondary explosions, but [   ] continued to wait. With the gloves off, the mercenary aviators became overenthusiastic in their choice of targets. One dropped his load on a British freighter, the *Springfjord*, in port at San José. This time the bombs exploded, sending the vessel to the bottom, an unfortunate incident for which the Agency later had to pay $1 million in restitution.[65]

[   ] augmented the air strikes with intensified radio propaganda, breaking into military channels and broadcasting stories of reverses at the front, without discernible effect. The capture of Chiquimula provided a momentary bright spot, but [   ] recognized that Castillo Armas owed his successes to the Guatemalan Army's restraint. If the Army moved, the rebellion would be crushed.[66]

---

[65] [Unsigned] to Leddy, 14 July 1954, Leddy file, Job 79-01025A, Box 81. The blame for this incident can be distributed across a wide front. Somoza told PBSUCCESS pilots at Puerto Cabesas on the 27th that the *Springfjord* was unloading fuel and arms (in fact, it was loading cotton). A bombing run on San José's fuel tanks was scheduled for that day, and [   ] the Agency officer in charge, did not instruct the pilot "specifically to avoid hitting any shipping." [   ] requested authority to bomb the British vessel from [   ] initiating a discussion between [   ] in Florida, and Barnes, at Langley, over whether bombing of international shipping would further the economic warfare objectives of PBSUCCESS. They finally decided not to authorize the bombing "at present," but by then the pilot was airborne. LINCOLN to Director, LINC 4509, 29 June 1954, Job 79-01025A, Box 6.

[66] LINCOLN to Director, "Sitrep No. 10," LINC 4271, 24 June 1954, Job 79-01025A, Box 6; LINCOLN to Director, "Sitrep No. 11," LINC 4368, 26 June 1954, Job 79-01025A, Box 6; LINCOLN to Director, "Sitrep No. 12," LINC 4319, 25 June 1954, Job 79-01025A, Box 6.

[   ] worried, too, about Toriello's diplomatic offensive. On the 25th, he foresaw a "serious possibility that cease fire may be enforced soon and inspection teams sent" to Guatemala, Honduras, and Nicaragua. He instructed Castillo Armas to try to "obtain the most advantageous position prior to any cessation of hostilities."[67]

Although Guatemalan troops remained quartered at Zacapa garrison, Castillo Armas faced a growing threat from police and armed peasants. On 26 June, nearly all of the widely dispersed rebel units radioed pleas for air strikes against armed opponents.[68] The following day, Castillo Armas mounted an attack on Ipala and was turned back. He reported a "strong column" moving from Ipala to Quezaltepeque to sever his line of retreat from Chiquimula.[69] Although he was fighting a guerrilla campaign, Castillo Armas conceptualized his position in conventional terms, and sought with his tiny army to seize and occupy territory. His response to an attack on any of his "fronts" was to demand an air strike. Agency officials tired of these demands and of the rebel commander's preference for frontal assaults on populated areas, which usually ended in disaster. Bissell and Wisner wanted the rebels to remain in the countryside, broken into small contingents that would strike and melt away in true guerrilla fashion. In that way the rebels could keep the Army occupied while eliminating the chance of losing their entire force in a single disastrous encounter. On 28 June, Bissell ordered [   ] to try to get Castillo Armas to change tactics.[70]

There was no need. Castillo Armas's troops had done their job. On 25 June, Arbenz had summoned his Cabinet, party officials, and union leaders to inform them that the Army was in revolt and that the only hope was to arm the populace. Díaz and union leaders agreed to cooperate, but the following day no citizen army materialized. Union members had previously fought for the government alongside the Army, but the prospect of fighting *both* the Army and Castillo Armas

[67]LINCOLN to Director, "Sitrep No. 12," LINC 4319, 25 June 1954, Job 79-01025A, Box 6.
   [68]LINCOLN to Director, LINC 4931, 26 June 1954, Job 79-01025A, Box 6.
   [69]LINCOLN to Director, LINC 4477, 28 June 1954, Job 79-01025A, Box 6.
   [70]Bissell to LINCOLN, DIR 06786, 28 June 1954, Job 79-01025A, Box 9.

was too daunting. SHERWOOD was broadcasting that columns of rebel troops were converging on the capital. Only a handful showed up to ask for arms, but there were none available. Díaz reneged on his promise. He was closeted with Sánchez, Monzón, and other military leaders plotting to seize power for themselves.[71]

The Capitulation

Peurifoy met with the plotters on the afternoon of 27 June and learned that they planned to take power that night. They promised to "move immediately on seizing commie leaders and sending them out of the country," but they refused to deal with Castillo Armas, and asked Peurifoy to arrange a cease-fire. The Ambassador wanted Arbenz out but he did not intend to "become part of another Mihailovich-Tito deal." He did not "trust the Army leaders, either on anti-Communism or on keeping faith with the United States. They are collaborators with Communism and must pay penalty in form Castillo Armas assumption of presidency." He remained silent, allowing the colonels to think they would be allowed to take power with US consent.[72] [   ] ordered a "maximum air show" over Guatemala City for the following afternoon.[73]

That evening at 8:00 Arbenz announced his resignation. He was turning over executive power to Colonel Díaz, he explained, "because I am certain he will guarantee democracy in Guatemala and all the social conquests of our people will be maintained." "The enemy who commands the bands of foreign mercenaries recruited by Castillo Armas is not only weak but completely cowardly" as was proven at Puerto Barrios and Gualán. He expressed full confidence that, with the Army united behind Díaz, the rebels would be quickly routed.[74] He had not "cracked." Díaz had persuaded him that an arrangement—a

[71] Gleijeses, *Shattered Hope*, pp. 342–345.
[72] Peurifoy to Willauer, GUAT 986, 28 June 1954, Job 79-01025A, Box 11.
[73] LINCOLN to Director, "Daily Sitrep No. 14," LINC 4472, 28 June 1954, Job 79-01025A, Box 6.
[74] Schlesinger and Kinzer, *Bitter Fruit*, pp. 199–200.

"Mihailovich-Tito deal" in Peurifoy's words—could be reached that would allow the Army to coopt and then discard Castillo Armas. By turning over power to the military, Arbenz hoped to salvage most of the gains of the 1944 revolution while defeating the rebellion and defusing US opposition.

Moments later, Díaz took the microphone and proclaimed that he was seizing power in the name of the Revolution of 1944, and that the Army would continue the fight against Castillo Armas. "We have been double-crossed," Peurifoy cabled Headquarters. Díaz, Sánchez, and Monzón formed a junta that retained in power most of the Arbenz Cabinet. When Peurifoy asked if they would negotiate with the rebels, the junta leaders "evaded all issues, praised their own anti-Communism, slandered Castillo Armas." They warned Fortuny and other Communist leaders to seek asylum in foreign embassies. Peurifoy cabled Washington to "urgently recommend bombing Guatemala City. . . . Bombs would persuade them fast."[75]

That night [   ] and [   ] who had arrived in Guatemala City for the denouement, decided to do some persuading of their own. At 6:00 in the morning, they called on Díaz to give him an update on the facts of life. [   ] began to spell out the importance of acting quickly against the Communists. [   ] interrupted him. "Colonel," he explained, "you are not convenient for American foreign policy."[76] Díaz had to hear it from Peurifoy himself, and a few hours later the Ambassador confirmed [   ] interpretation of American foreign policy. The colonel grudgingly stepped aside.

With Díaz out of the way, Peurifoy decided the Agency ought to step aside and allow the State Department to negotiate with Guatemalan officials. He asked Wisner to "have a little talk" with [   ] who had done an "outstanding job" but needed now to "retire more to the background."[77] On 30 June, Wisner sent [   ] a

[75]Guatemala Station to Director, GUAT 992, 28 June 1954, Job 79-01025A, Box 6.
[76][   ] interview.
[77]Peurifoy to Leddy, 13 July 1954, Job 79-01228A, Box 23.

message known afterwards as the 'shift of gears cable." With hostilities concluded and a settlement in sight, he observed, the Station should concern itself with activities "for which this Agency is more strictly responsible and peculiarly qualified." The time had come "for the surgeons to step back and the nurses to take over the patient." All questions of policy and matters that could be handled overtly should be dealt with by the State Department. Agency officials would stay on to collect captured documents and continue propaganda activities in support of Castillo Armas.[78] PBSUCCESS was over.

In the 11 days after Arbenz's resignation five successive juntas occupied the presidential palace, each more amenable to American demands than the last. Peurifoy wanted a junta that included both Castillo Armas and Monzón. Substantive issues like land reform disappeared after the first two coups, and discussion centered on ways to satisfy the pride of the two military groups. Castillo Armas wanted to march into Guatemala City at the head of his men. Monzón refused to allow a triumphal march and insisted on being allowed to remain in office for a month before ceding power to Castillo Armas. Peurifoy and President Osorio presided over the talks in San Salvador. Anxious to arrest the few Communists remaining at large, Wisner dismissed Castillo Armas's demands as "dangerous nonsense." Peurifoy bullied and cajoled until on 2 July, the two men signed the "Pacto de San Salvador," forming a combined Army-*liberacionista* junta.[79]

Wisner cabled his congratulations for a performance that "surpassed even our greatest expectations." Peurifoy "can take great comfort and satisfaction from fact that his accomplishments are already well known and fully appreciated in all important quarters of government."[80] But it was not a complete victory. A week of chaos had allowed leading Communists to escape. Many took refuge in embassies. [   ] went to see Fortuny, the former head of the PGT, at

[78] Wisner to Chief of Station Guatemala, DIR 07144, 30 June 1954, Job 79-01025A, Box 9.

[79] Gleijeses, *Shattered Hope*, pp. 353–355; Wisner to Chief of St temala City, DIR 07304, 1 July 1954, Job 79-01025A, Box 9.

[80] Wisner to Chief of Station Guatemala City, DIR 08299, 30 Ju 79-01025A, Box 9.

the Mexican Embassy and found him a shattered man, unable to speak. As he left, a young attaché stopped him with a question, "does this mean the United States will not allow a Communist government anywhere in the hemisphere?" [   ] put on his hat. "Draw your own conclusions," he said, and walked out.[81]

[81] [   ] interview.

CHAPTER 4

The Sweet Smell of Success

What we'd give to have an Arbenz now. We are going to have to
invent one, but all the candidates are dead.

US State Department official, 1981[1]

PBSUCCESS officers concluded their business and began with-
drawing on 1 July 1954. The *Voz de la Liberación* went off the air the
following day, and David Atlee Phillips packed its mobile transmitter
for shipment to the States. In [   ] began collecting files and preparing to close [   ] He ordered Guatemala Station to destroy documents pertaining to PBSUCCESS.[2] As
Frank Wisner had said, it was time for the Agency to return to the
tasks for which it was "peculiarly qualified."[3] But the Agency would
never be the same after PBSUCCESS. The triumph showed what could
be accomplished through covert action, and its lessons, learned and
unlearned, would have ramifications for years to come.

The Agency's initial jubilation gave way to misgivings as it became
clear that victory in Guatemala had been neither as clear nor as unam-
biguous as originally thought. In Latin America, the Eisenhower administration came under heavy fire for its actions, and Guatemala be-

---

[1]Quoted in Marlise Simons, "Guatemala: The Coming Danger," *Foreign
Policy* 43 (Summer 1981): 103.
[2]Cyrus Burnette to J. C. King, "Plot by Arbenz Government Against United
Fruit Co.," HGG-A-1285, 29 July 1954, Job 79-01025A, Box 100.
[3]Wisner to [   ] DIR 07144, 30 June 1954, Job 79-01025A, Box 9.

came a symbol of the stubborn resistance of the United States to progressive, nationalist policies. Castillo Armas's new regime proved em-
barrassingly inept. Its repressive and corrupt policies soon polarized
Guatemala and provoked a renewed civil conflict. Operation PBSUC-
CESS aroused resentments that continue, almost 40 years after the
event, to prevent the Agency from revealing its role.

Mopping Up

After sending his "shift of gears" cable, Wisner turned his attention
to finding ways to exploit the victory of PBSUCCESS. The defeat of
Arbenz not only boosted the Agency's reputation in Congress and the
administration, it provided a chance to expose Soviet machinations
throughout the hemisphere. Wisner was anxious not to allow any opportunity to pass. Amid the ruins of Arbenz's government lay prizes
worth collecting: documents, defectable Communists, and openings
for propaganda. Wisner tried to seize what he could.

In early July, he sent two officers, [   ] and [
] of the Counterintelligence Staff, to Guatemala City to do a
"snatch job on documents while the melon was freshly burst open."[4]
He hoped to find papers that would enable the Agency to trace Soviet
connections throughout Latin America and identify "people who can
be controlled and exploited to further US policy."[5] In addition, he
thought the captured papers would conclusively prove the Communist
nature of the Arbenz regime. He named the project PBHISTORY. [
] arrived on 4 July along with a two-man State Department team. They discovered that the PGT headquarters and offices of labor unions and police organizations had already been plun-
dered systematically by the army and unsystematically by looters and
street urchins. [   ] who arrived a few days earlier, had
bought secret police documents from a small boy. Party and govern-

[4]Wisner, "Exploitation and Follow Ups," [undated], Job 79-01228A, Box
23.
[5][   ] Chief RQM, OIS, to Wisner, "Mechanics for Exploitation of Guatemalan Documents," 28 July 1954, Job 79-01228A, Box 23.

ment offices stood unguarded, their doors and windows broken, with official documents lying on the floor in heaps.[6]

With the help of the Army and Castillo Armas's junta, the team gathered 150,000 documents, but most of what it found had only "local significance." Few of the papers concerned "the aspects that we are most interested in, namely the elements of Soviet support and control of Communism in Guatemala."[7] Nor did the documents identify individuals vulnerable to exploitation. Ronald M. Schneider, an outside researcher who later examined the PBHISTORY documents, found no traces of Soviet control and substantial evidence that Guatemalan Communists acted alone, without support or guidance from outside the country.[8]   *unneeded intervention*

The operation produced enough material to fill a booklet distributed to the National Security Council, members of the Senate, and other interested officials. It contained photographs of Arbenz's library of Marxist literature, Chinese Communist materials on agrarian reform, pages from Mrs. Arbenz's copy of Stalin's biography, evidence that Arbenz had tried to purchase arms from Italy, and various letters and cables revealing a "strong pro-Communist bias." Wisner wanted more incriminating material, but the brochure was sufficient to impress the NSC staff.[9]

Apart from documents, the Agency also had interest in two other remnants of the Arbenz regime—the *Alfhem* arms and the assortment of political refugees encamped in embassy compounds around Guatemala City. After the United States provided Guatemala with military aid, Castillo Armas offered to sell the Czech arms to the Agency in order to raise money to purchase aircraft. Agency officials were initially

[6][   ] Counterintelligence Staff, "Report on Activity in Guatemala City, 4–16 July 1954," 28 July 1954, Job 79-01228A, Box 23.

[7]*Ibid.*

[8]Schneider's *Communism in Guatemala, 1944–1954,* was based on PBHISTORY materials.

[9]Counterintelligence Staff C, "Documents Obtained in a Brief, Preliminary Sampling of the Documentary Evidence of Communist Infiltration and Influence in Guatemala," 28 July 1954, Job 79-01228A, Box 23.

not even investing back

intrigued, but when military advisers surveyed the equipment they found it obsolete and in poor condition. Logistics warned that the arms could be easily traced, and the Western Hemisphere Division advised that it could think of no use for them. Allen Dulles declined the offer.[10]

Wisner and Barnes initially regarded the presence of several dozen high government and party officials in the embassies of Mexico, Argentina, El Salvador, and Chile as a propaganda opportunity. In early August, they proposed to have Castillo Armas's junta attempt to deport the asylum seekers to the Soviet Union. If the Soviets agreed, it would confirm the former regime's relationship with Moscow and remove Arbenz and his cronies from the hemisphere. If they did not, Wisner beamed, "then we have another excellent propaganda gambit, viz.: 'See what happens to Moscow's unsuccessful agents and operatives.'"[11] The scheme proved impossible to execute. Guatemala had no diplomatic relations with the Soviet Union, so a request required Moscow's cooperation, which was not forthcoming. Wisner remained fond of the idea, but by the beginning of September, Assistant Secretary of State Henry Holland was trying to get Mexico to turn former Guatemalan officials over to the junta for trial. Mexico's Embassy held the most distinguished cohort, including Fortuny and Arbenz. Holland tried to persuade the Mexicans to accept the "principle that the traditional benefits of asylum should be denied international Communists," but they would have none of it.[12]

State and Agency officials now began to regard the asylum seekers as a "troublesome and unsettled matter."[13] They worried that Guatemalan Communists would be allowed free passage to Mexico City, where they could plot their return. It was a useless worry. The PGT

[10]Wisner to Dulles, "Utilization of the Alfhem Arms Shipment to Guatemala," 14 December 1954, with attachments, Job 79-01228A, Box 23.

[11]Wisner to Holland, "Proposal of Combined Department of State and CIA for Action to Exploit Asylee Situation in Guatemala," 3 August 1954, Job 79-01228A, Box 23.

[12]Holland to J. Foster Dulles, "Asylee Problem in Guatemala," 10 August 1954, Job 79-01228A, Box 23.

[13]Wisner to King, "Guatemala; Conference with Messrs Leddy and Mann," 31 August 1954, Job 79-01228A, Box 23.

members who wished to stay active in politics remained at large, un-
molested by Castillo Armas's police, who concentrated on arresting
thousands of peasants who tried to remain on the land granted them
by Decree 900. The PGT remained active underground until the late
1960s, when a more proficient Guatemalan police force arrested, tortured, and killed Víctor Gutiérrez and 11 other leaders, sewed their
bodies into burlap sacks, and dropped them in the ocean from an army
transport plane.[14] Castillo Armas, embarrassed by the deposed president's continued presence in the capital, allowed Arbenz free passage
to Mexico on 12 September 1954. He insisted on a final humiliation
and ordered Arbenz to be strip searched at the airport. For the next 17
years Arbenz lived a peripatetic existence in France, Uruguay, Switzerland, and Cuba, returning finally to Mexico, where in 1971 he
drowned in his bathtub.[15] Fortuny also went to Mexico City, where he
still lives.

Communists moved to Mexico

In mid-August, Eisenhower summoned the operation's managers to
the White House for a formal briefing. There, before the Cabinet, Vice
President Nixon, and Eisenhower's family, [   ] Phillips, [
] Dulles, Barnes, Wisner, and King explained the operation with
maps and slides. The audience listened respectfully. At the end, the
President asked how many men Castillo Armas had lost. "Only one,"
a briefer lied.[16] Eisenhower shook his head; "Incredible," he mur-
mured.[17] Indeed, it had been incredible. Had the Guatemalan Army
crushed Castillo Armas at Chiquimula, as it easily could have done,
investigations would have uncovered the chronic lapses in security, the
failure to plan beyond the operation's first stages, the Agency's poor
understanding of the intentions of the Army, the PGT, and the government, the hopeless weakness of Castillo Armas's troops, and the
failure to make provisions for the possibility of defeat. All of these

---

[14] Gleijeses, *Shattered Hope*, p. 388.
[15] *Ibid.*, pp. 390–392.
[16] The number of opposition casualties (as well as the total number of casualties) is unknown, but Agency files indicate that at least 27 were killed at Puerto
Barrios, another 16 at Gualán. In addition, some 75 members of the civilian
opposition were killed in Guatemalan jails before the fall of Arbenz.
[17] Phillips, *The Night Watch*, pp. 62–64.

were swept away by Arbenz's resignation, and PBSUCCESS went into Agency lore as an unblemished triumph. Eisenhower's policymakers drew confidence from the belief that covert action could be used as a convenient, decisive final resort.

Over the following years, the Eisenhower administration employed covert actions to build a government in South Vietnam and support an abortive separatist movement in Sumatra. In early 1960, when the Agency needed to overthrow the regime of Fidel Castro in Cuba, it reassembled the PBSUCCESS team in [

] Bissell, Barnes, and Phillips all took leading positions in operation JMARC, an operation designed to create a "liberated area" in Cuba. As originally conceived, the area would contain a radio propaganda operation like SHERWOOD and become a focal point to which opposition elements could rally. Like PBSUCCESS, the operation relied on a rebel army of exiles and air support from World War II–era aircraft manned by Cuban and American pilots. It was not a copy of PBSUCCESS, but an improvement built around the elements of the Guatemala operation that had been considered effective: radio, airpower, and an insurrectionary army.[18] The operation underwent many changes before ending in fiasco at the Bay of Pigs, but these elements remained central to the plan. Afterwards, many of those involved in the two operations linked the success in Guatemala with the failure at the Bay of Pigs. "If the Agency had not had Guatemala," E. Howard Hunt, a case officer who served in both PBSUCCESS and JMARC later observed, "it probably would not have had Cuba."[19] Even after the Cuban disaster discredited its strategies, PBSUCCESS continued to cast a shadow on policy in Latin America. "The language, arguments, and techniques of the Arbenz episode," one analyst observed in the 1980s, "were used in Cuba in the early 1960s, [

] in the Dominican Republic in 1965, and in [

]"[20]

[18][

]
[19]Quoted in Immerman, *CIA in Guatemala*, p. 190.
[20]Simons, "Guatemala," p. 94. [*The full quote reads, "were used in Cuba in*

International Condemnation

Even before the afterglow of the White House briefing wore off, the Eisenhower administration had reason to question whether PBSUCCESS had delivered an undiluted victory. Agency and State Department officials were shocked at the ferocity of international protest after the fall of Arbenz. The London *Times* and *Le Monde* attacked the cynical hypocrisy behind America's "modern forms of economic colonialism," while in Rangoon protesters stoned the American Embassy.[21] UN Secretary General Dag Hammarskjold charged that "the United States' attitude was completely at variance with the [UN] Charter." The British Foreign Office found German newspapers "surprisingly critical," even ones "not usually hostile to America." British officials considered John Foster Dulles's gloating remarks after the coup as virtually "an admission that the rebellion was an outside job." *everyone knew*

Whitehall soon put aside its initial disgust and helped unruffle European feathers. Foreign Office officials were ready to lodge complaints over the naval blockade, the *Springfjord* incident, and the failure of the OAS investigation team to get closer than Mexico City. Prime Minister Winston Churchill, however, persuaded then that forbearance in this instance might be rewarded when Britain needed to quell the next disturbance in its empire. "I'd never heard of this bloody place Guatemala until I was in my seventy-ninth year," he growled. Britain helped cover up the *Springfjord* affair and issued a "white paper" that ratified the Agency's version of events. Eisenhower, how-

---

the early 1960s, in Brazil in 1964, in the Dominican Republic in 1965, and in Chile in 1973."—N.C.] Some have claimed an even longer shadow for PBSUCCESS. Philip C. Roettinger, a PBSUCCESS case officer, wrote in 1986 that "it is painful to look on as my Government repeats the mistakes in which it engaged me thirty-two years ago. I have grown up. I only wish my Government would do the same." Philip C. Roettinger, "The Company, Then and Now," *The Progressive*, July 1986, p. 50.

[21] Rangoon to Secretary of State, 27 June 1954, Job 79-01025A, Box 82.
[22] Meers, "The British Connection," pp. 422–423.

ever, felt no obligation to return the favor in kind, as Churchill's successor learned two years later at Suez.[23]

In Latin America, the Arbenz regime's demise left an enduring leg-
acy of anti-Americanism. In Havana, Santiago, Mexico City, Buenos
Aires, and Rio de Janeiro, large crowds gathered to burn the Stars and
Stripes and effigies of Eisenhower and Dulles. "Societies of the Friends
of Guatemala" sprang up to keep alive the memory of American imperialism and Guatemala's martyrdom.[24] The State Department was
"frightened by reactions all over," according to the Secretary.[25] An
Agency official reported that the demonstrations "revealed a surprising and embarrassing influence of Communists on public opinion."
Daniel James, the influential editor of *The New Leader*, predicted that
"in death the Guatemalan party may prove to be a bigger asset to the
Kremlin than in life."[26]

This was an overstatement, but victory over Arbenz proved to be a
lasting propaganda setback. Resentment even found artistic expression in the work of Mexican muralist Diego Rivera, who depicted in
fresco Peurifoy and the Dulles brothers passing money to Castillo Armas and Monzón over the bodies of Guatemalan children. Several
Mexican magazines reproduced the mural.[27] Among the crowds that
spat and threw vegetables at Vice President Richard Nixon in 1957
were signs condemning the suppression of Guatemala. For Latin
Americans determined to change their countries' feudal social structures, Guatemala was a formative experience. "The Guatemala intervention," according to one historian, "shaped the attitudes and stratagems of an older generation of radicals, for whom this experience
signaled the necessity of armed struggle and an end to illusions about

---

[23] *Ibid.*, pp. 422–428.
[24] Wisner, "The Friends of Guatemala," 19 June 1954, Job 79-01228A, Box 23.
[25] Gleijeses, *Shattered Hope*, p. 371.
[26] [   ] "Comment on 'Lessons of Guatemala' by Daniel James," 19 August 1954, Job 79-01228A.
[27] "Yo No Miento! Grita Diego," *Impacto*, 29 January 1955, pp. 20–25; *Lux: La Revista de los Trabajadores* (magazine of the Mexican Electricians Union), 15 February 1955, cover.

[Handwritten margin note: blank Communists always]

peaceful, legal, and reformist methods."[2] This generation included Che Guevara and Fidel Castro, who learned from Guatemala's experience the importance of striking decisively against opponents before they could seek assistance from outside.

↳ actually led to

The Liberator Cuban communism

While PBSUCCESS succeeded in removing a government, it failed to install an adequate substitute. Agency officials might have felt more sanguine in their victory if Castillo Armas had been an able leader. The invasion's disastrous setbacks dispelled all illusions about his capabilities, and US officials had low expectations at the outset of his presidency. Even these proved optimistic. Hopes that he would align himself with centrist and moderate elements were dashed within weeks, as the new junta sought out the only elements not tainted by ties to the Arbenz regime, the aged and embittered retainers of Ubico. Castillo Armas named José Bernabé Linares, Ubico's hated secret police chief, to head the new regime's security forces. Linares soon banned all "subversive" literature, including works by Victor Hugo and Fyodor Dostoevsky. Castillo Armas completed his lunge to the right by disfranchising illiterates (two-thirds of the electorate), canceling land reform, and outlawing all political parties, labor confederations, and peasant organizations. Finally, he decreed a "political statute" that voided the 1945 constitution and gave him complete executive and legislative authority.[29]

These depredations worried John Foster Dulles less than the new regime's chronic insolvency. Castillo Armas came to power just as international coffee buyers, convinced that prices had risen too high, mounted a "buyers' strike" against Central and South American growers. A few months later, Guatemala felt the first effects of a year-long drought that devastated the corn crop. The new regime opened its arms to American investors, but the only takers were Mafia figures

---

[28] James Dunkerly, *Power in the Isthmus: A Political History of Modern Central America* (London: Verso, 1988) p. 429.
[29] Schlesinger and Kinzer, *Bitter Fruit*, p. 221.

who joined with Guatemalan Army officers in opening gambling halls.[30] Meanwhile, American "promoters, carpetbaggers and others" raised expectations in Guatemala City that a large US aid package would be easy to get. Castillo Armas surprised the State Department's Thomas Mann in September with a request for $260 million in aid, including plans for a $60 million national highway network.[31] The Department had planned to give $4 million in grant aid and to ask the International Monetary Fund for a $20 million loan for road development, fearing that higher levels would provoke other Latin countries to submit requests.[32] By the end of the year, it was apparent that each country had entirely unrealistic expectations of the other. The United States wanted Castillo Armas to maintain a fiscally responsible government, while Castillo Armas recognized that his claim to authority rested on his ability to deliver goods from the United States.

Guatemala quickly came to depend on handouts from the United States. The government's foreign reserves dropped from $42 million at the end of 1953 (when it was easy for Arbenz to spare $5 million for Czech arms), to a rockbottom $3.4 million in April 1955.[33] At this point, the regime could no longer borrow internally. Capital flight, black markets, and other signs of approaching bankruptcy discredited the regime. Wisner complained of "the inability on the part of the Government to realize sufficient revenues to operate."[34] When aid and multilateral loans ran out, the State Department offered to help Castillo Armas obtain private loans, but the Agency worried about the propaganda ramifications of making its client beholden to New York banks and recommended against it.[35] In April, Holland increased his

[30]*Ibid.*, p. 234.

[31]Memorandum of Conversation, Ambassador Norman Armour, Holland, Mann, 25 January 1955, *Foreign Relations of the United States, 1955–1957,* 7: 59.

[32]Memorandum of Conversation, "Current Situation in Guatemala and Projected Aid Program," 28–29 April 1955, *Foreign Relations of the United States, 1955–1957,* 7: 71–75.

[33]*Ibid.*, p. 73.

[34]Wisner to Allen Dulles, "Guatemala—Continuing economic difficulties," 30 November 1954, Job 79-01228A, Box 23.

[35][   ] to Allen Dulles, "Current US position with

request for grant aid from $4 million to $14 million. The following month, the National Security Council, determining that the "collapse of the present Guatemalan government would be a disastrous political setback for the United States," decided on an aid package totaling $53 million.[36]

The Eisenhower administration had to underwrite an increasing Guatemalan deficit aggravated by corruption and mismanagement. As [   ] had observed, the United States was prepared to subsidize some wastage, but the scale of corruption surprised US officials. In 1955, at the height of the corn famine, Castillo Armas granted several former *Liberacionistas* a license to import corn in return for a personal kickback of $25,000. United Nations officials inspected the corn and found it contaminated and unfit for consumption. Shortly afterward, a Guatemalan student newspaper exposed the scandal, reprinting a copy of the canceled check used to bribe the president. Castillo Armas responded by ordering a police crackdown on his critics.[37]

Opposition to the regime grew more vocal as the second anniversary of the liberation approached. On 1 May 1956, workers booed government speakers off the platform at a labor rally and cheered former *Arbencista* officials. In early June, Embassy officials reported that the Guatemalan Communist Party was "well on its way toward recovery," with underground cells assuming effective leadership of the opposition. On 25 June, government agents fired into a crowd of student protesters marching on the presidential palace, killing six and wounding scores more. Castillo Armas declared a "state of siege" and suspended all civil liberties. The US Ambassador stressed to the president "the importance of publicizing, with supporting evidence, the events as part of a Communist plot."[38] The United States Information Agency (USIA) agreed to help. Holland met with Guatemalan officials

---

regard to Government loan requested by Guatemala," 22 October 1954, Job 79-01228A, Box 23.

[36]Holland to Under Secretary of State Herbert Hoover, Jr., 20 May 1955, *Foreign Relations of the United States, 1955–1957*, 7: 80–81.

[37]Schlesinger and Kinzer, *Bitter Fruit*, pp. 234–235.

[38]Holland to J. F. Dulles, 29 June 1956, *Foreign Relations of the United States, 1955–1957*, 7: 124.

and "suggested that in dealing with demonstrators tear gas was effective and infinitely preferable to bullets."[39]

Quelling unrest, however, proved more difficult than finding the right propaganda slant. After another year of escalating violence between the opposition and the authorities, Castillo Armas was assassinated by a member of the presidential guard. USIA dutifully portrayed the killing as another Communist plot. The Liberator's death opened the way for elections, which produced a plurality for Ortiz Passarelli, a centrist candidate. Followers of the defeated nominee of the right, Ydígoras Fuentes, rioted, and the Army seized power and invalidated the election. In January 1958, Guatemalans voted again, and this time they knew what was expected of them. Ydígoras won by a plurality, and shortly after taking office declared another "state of siege" and assumed full powers.[40]

Amid the convulsions of the 1950s, Guatemala's political center, which had created the Revolution of 1944 and dominated politics until 1953, vanished from politics into a terrorized silence. Political activity simply became too dangerous as groups of the extreme right and left, both led by military officers, plotted against one another. In the early 1960s, guerilla groups began operating in the eastern part of the country, and in 1966 the United States responded by sending military advisers and weapons, escalating a cycle of violence and reprisals that by the end of the decade claimed the lives of a US Ambassador, two US military attachés, and as many as 10,000 peasants. In 1974, the Army stole another election, persuading another generation of young Guatemalans to seek change through intrigues and violence. Increasingly, Indians and the Catholic Church—which had formerly remained aloof from politics—sided with the left, isolating the Army on the far right.[41]

Ironically, by attaining its short-term goal—removing Jacobo Ar-

---

[39] Memorandum of Conversation, Holland and José Cruz Salazar, Ambassador of Guatemala, 29 June 1956, *Foreign Relations of the United States, 1955–1957*, 7: 126.
[40] Schlesinger and Kinzer, *Bitter Fruit*, pp. 236–239.
[41] Simons, "Guatemala," pp. 95–99.

benz—PBSUCCESS thwarted the long-term objective of producing a stable, non-Communist Guatemala. [   ] hopes that Castillo Armas would establish a moderate, reformist regime and follow the instructions of US financial experts were destroyed by the same process that had placed the Liberator in power. Because Arbenz and the PGT had advocated and implemented progressive reforms, [   ]—for tactical reasons—had needed to direct his appeals at the groups most hurt by land reform and other progressive policies. Moderate elements disliked parts of Arbenz's agenda, but were repelled by the bitter disaffection of the opposition. Resentful landowners and partisans of the pre-1944 regime were the rebels' natural allies, and Castillo Armas, as their leader, acted as a broker between these "men of action" and the United States.

During PBSUCCESS, US officials had reason to believe Castillo Armas's rightist tendencies would be offset by his openness to advice from the United States. Case officers found him malleable and receptive to suggestions. But, as the State Department soon learned, Castillo Armas's relationship to CIA had been dictated by his circumstances. As president of Guatemala, he was in a better position to press the demands of his primary constituency, conservative land barons and political opportunists. When the United States failed to provide enough aid to satisfy these groups, Castillo Armas was forced to appease them in other ways, though graft and preferment. The United States' heavy stake in Castillo Armas's success reduced its leverage in dealing with him. State Department officials were unable to bargain with the junta on a quid pro quo basis because they knew—and the Guatemalans knew—the United States would never allow Castillo Armas to fail. In Guatemala, US officials learned a lesson they would relearn in Vietnam, Iran, [   ] and other countries: intervention usually produces "allies" that are stubborn, aid-hungry, and corrupt.[42]

[42] The increased-stake, decreased-leverage paradox is explored by Leslie Gelb and Richard Betts in *The Irony of Vietnam: The System Worked* (Washington: Brookings Institution, 1979), pp. 11–13

El Pulpo

The United Fruit Company did not profit from victory. Castillo Armas restored many of the company's privileges, but they were worth less than before. The more affluent American consumers of the 1950s consumed less fruit per capita, and independent companies cut into United Fruit's share. The company's profit margin dropped from 33.4 percent in 1950 to 15.4 percent in 1957, and share prices, which peaked at $73 in 1951, fell to $43 in 1959. The company courted environmental disaster by experimenting with pesticides and selective breeding. Taller, more productive trees turned out to be more vulnerable to hurricanes, and winds felled 20 million trees a year in 1958 and 1959. A chemical agent used to control a banana blight killed predators that kept insect pests in check. By the end of the 1950s, the company faced higher costs and declining yields.[43]

Political setbacks compounded these disasters. To improve relations with Latin America, the State Department demanded that the company grant higher wages, not just in Guatemala but throughout the hemisphere. Once United Fruit's usefulness to PBSUCCESS was at an end, the Eisenhower administration proceeded with its suspended antitrust action, and in 1958 the company signed a consent decree divesting it of its holdings in railroads and marketing operations. Thomas Corcoran's heroic lobbying and the addition of Walter Bedell Smith to the board of directors in 1955 failed to turn the company around. Smith joined a Boston-bred, Harvard-educated corporate leadership described by *Fortune* as "complacent, unimaginative, and bureaucratic," too rigid and conservative to contend with the company's multiplying difficulties.[44]

United Fruit continued to decline during the 1960s, and in 1972 sold the last of its Guatemalan land to the Del Monte corporation. A few years later, the company merged with Morrell Meats to form United Brands, but the merger failed to stop the slide. In 1975, after a

[43]Herbert Solow, "The Ripe Problems of United Fruit," *Fortune*, March 1959, pp. 97–233.
[44]*Ibid.*, p. 98.

year in which the company lost $43.6 million and came under Federal investigation for paying a $2.5 million bribe to the Government of Honduras, United Brands' president, Eli Black, smashed out the window of his corner office in the Pan Am Building and jumped to his death. Two years later, two New York real estate developers bought the company and managed to turn a profit. In 1984, United Brands was purchased by a Cincinnati-based insurance holding company, American Financial Corporation, which owns it today. Thanks to Americans' changing diets, banana importing has once again become profitable, and United's Chiquita brand has recaptured a majority share of the market. The company's Tropical Radio division (which once employed the Salamá conspirators) ventured into the cellular telephone business in the early 1980s and now dominates the mobile phone business in 20 Latin American cities.[45]

The Story Unfolds

Today, most of the story of PBSUCCESS is available in published accounts. In Latin America, scholars and journalists assumed US complicity in the Guatemalan affair from the outset, but in the United States the details of official involvement came slowly to light in the 1960s and 1970s. During the Eisenhower administration, the Agency took pains to cover its tracks, [

][46] But after Eisenhower and Dulles left office, references to the

[45] Jefferson Grigsby, "The Wonder Is That It Works at All," *Forbes*, 18 February 1980, pp. 104–105; "United Brands' Hidden Charms for Carl Lindner," *Fortune*, 19 March 1984, p. 41; Kerry Hannon, "Ripe Banana," *Forbes*, 13 June 1988, p. 86.
[46] [

]

Only hidden by Dulles + Eisenhower

operation began appearing in open sources. In 1961, Whiting Willauer, in public testimony before Congress, revealed that he had been part of a special team of ambassadors sent to Central America to aid an Agency-sponsored plan to overthrow Arbenz. He further testified that the Agency had trained and equipped Castillo Armas's forces. Thruston B. Morton, Eisenhower's Assistant Secretary of State for Congressional Affairs, boasted of his role in PBSUCCESS on television while campaigning for the Senate in 1962. The following year, Eisenhower, sharing a podium with Allen Dulles, conceded that "there was one time" when "we had to get rid of a Communist government" in Central America.[47] He told the story of how Dulles had come to him with a request for aircraft for the rebel forces. That same year he repeated the story in his memoirs, *Mandate for Change*, and Dulles provided additional details in his 1963 study, *The Craft of Intelligence*.[48] At about the same time, Ydígoras Fuentes published a memoir in the United States in which he described the Agency's involvement while concealing his own role in the operation.

David Wise and Thomas B. Ross put these pieces together in the 1964 exposé on the CIA, *The Invisible Government*, which devoted a chapter to Guatemala. [   ] who flew with the rebel force, described his own experiences with considerable embellishment.[49] The Agency was disturbed by the book's revelations, and DCI John McCone tried unsuccessfully to get Wise and Ross to make changes. McCone raised no objections to the Guatemala chapter, which, he said, described events "before my time."[50] Like Eisenhower,

[47]David Wise and Thomas B. Ross, *The Invisible Government* (New York: Random House, 1964), pp. 166–168.

[48]Dwight D. Eisenhower, *Mandate for Change, 1953–1956* (Garden City, NY: Doubleday and Co., 1963), pp. 425–426; Allen Dulles, *The Craft of Intelligence* (London: Weidenfield and Nicolson, 1963), pp. 219, 229. Dulles revealed no sources or methods but made it clear that the United States had been involved.

[49][   ] *[Wise and Ross tell the story of Jerry DeLarm, a former skywriter and barnstormer, who "was flying for Castillo Armas and the CIA."—N.C.]*

[50]Transcript of conversation between DCI McCone, Lyman Kirkpatrick, David Wise, and Thomas Ross, 15 May 1964, Job 80B-01285A, Box 13, Folder 10.

Dulles, and Willauer, he regarded the operation, after 10 years, as a subject that could now be discussed, so long as names and places remained unmentioned.

Amid the push for increased government accountability in the 1970s, leaks by former Agency employees continued to outnumber official disclosures. The Pike and Church committees, which investigated CIA activities in the 1970s, refrained—at least in public—from commenting on the Guatemala operation, but ex-CIA officers continued to fill in the details. In early 1972, Richard Bissell told John Chancellor on national television that "the whole policy-making machinery of the executive branch of the government was involved," with CIA taking a leading role.[51] Soon afterward, an Associated Press reporter, Lewis Gulick, decided to test a new executive order on declassification (Executive Order 11652) by requesting documents on PBSUCCESS. His request, on 6 July 1972, was the first declassification inquiry received under the new order, and since it came from a prominent media figure, Agency officials knew it could not be dismissed lightly. Nonetheless, after reviewing the documents, DCI Richard Helms denied the request in full.[52] David Atlee Phillips, who was then the chief of the Western Hemisphere Division in the Directorate of Operations, argued that exposing the Guatemala materials would "only stir more Hemispheric controversy about CIA when our plate overflows already in the wake of [

]**[53]** Gulick appealed, but the Interagency Classification Review Committee, chaired by John Eisenhower, son of the former president, backed up the Agency.[54]

Former Agency officials, meanwhile, continued to tell their stories. Publishers found a popular genre in CIA memoirs. In *Undercover*, published in 1974, E. Howard Hunt disclosed his role in the psycho-

[51] Untitled transcript, 2 August 1972, Job 79-01025A, Box 153.

[52] Angus MacLean Thuermer, Assistant to the Director, to Lewis Gulick, 16 August 1972, Job 79-01025A, Box 153.

[53] Phillips to Executive Assistant, Directorate of Operations, "Proposed Topics for Unclassified History," 17 October 1973, Job 79-01025A, Box 153.

[54] Thuermer to Marvin L. Arrowsmith, Associated Press Bureau Chief, 28 August 1973, Job 79-01025A, Box 153.

logical and paramilitary aspects of the operation.[55] Four years later, Phillips described the SHERWOOD operation, a part of PBSUCCESS that had not previously received press attention, in an account copied almost verbatim from a debriefing report that is still classified.[56] Many more officials told their stories to Richard Harris Smith, a former Agency official who was working on a biography of Allen Dulles. Smith missed his publisher's deadline, and in 1980 he showed his uncompleted manuscript to two *Newsweek* reporters, Stephen Schlesinger and Stephen Kinzer, who were working on a book on Guatemala.

In their pursuit of documents, Schlesinger and Kinzer tested the limits of the newly amended Freedom of Information Act. In 1974, Congress substantially strengthened the 1966 Act, giving scholars a powerful instrument for extracting documents from government agencies. When CIA denied their request, the two journalists took the Agency to court with help from the American Civil Liberties Union's National Security Project. The lawsuit caused the Agency to collect all of the available documents on the operation and place them in Job 79-01025A, the collection on which this history is based. The suit also revealed the operation's name, PBSUCCESS, to the public for the first time. CIA won the court action, and no Agency documents were revealed. Schlesinger and Kinzer, however, used the Act to obtain documents from the Departments of State and Defense and the Federal Bureau of Investigation. These documents, and the revelations of former American and Guatemalan officials, substantiated the story told in their book *Bitter Fruit* and the more scholarly studies on PBSUCCESS that have appeared since.

In announcing CIA's new "openness" policy, made possible by the end of the Cold War, former Director of Central Intelligence Robert M. Gates in February 1992 included PBSUCCESS along with the 1953 coup in Iran and the Bay of Pigs, as covert action operations whose records will be reviewed for declassification by CIA's new Historical

[55]E. Howard Hunt, *Undercover: Memoirs of an American Secret Agent* (New York: Berkeley Publishing, 1974), pp. 96–101.
[56]Phillips, *The Night Watch*, pp. 37–68.

Review Group. Although this new Group's work on its own priorities was delayed by legislation later in 1992 that required CIA (and all other agencies and departments) to review all their records relevant to the assassination of President John F. Kennedy, the review of PBSUC-CESS records is now scheduled to begin in 1994.

Although the opening of CIA's records on this 1954 operation may well revive old controversies and criticisms, it will nevertheless at last allow the Agency to place this episode firmly behind it. Releasing the Guatemala records should symbolically separate CIA from the kind of actions it once considered crucial in the struggle against world Communism. Moreover, these documents will reveal not only the Cold War pressures, but also the restraining power of multilateral accords like the OAS treaty, which nearly prevented covert action despite the consensus of high officials supporting the operation. Finally, and perhaps most importantly, disclosing information about this formative and still controversial incident in intelligence history will show that the United States can honestly confront the painful incidents in its past and learn from its experience.

Appendixes

APPENDIX A

PBSUCCESS Timeline

18 July 1949	Col. Francisco Arana, Guatemalan armed forces chief, assassinated.
15 May 1950	Thomas Corcoran, United Fruit Company lobbyist, meets with Deputy Assistant Secretary for Inter-American Affairs, Thomas Mann, to suggest action to oust Guatemalan President Juan José Arévalo.
3 September 1950	Case officer [ ] assigned to project [ ] arrives in Guatemala City [ ] establishes contact with [ ]), a student group.
11 November 1950	Jacobo Arbenz elected president.
15 March 1951	Arbenz inaugurated.
22 August 1951	United Fruit Company warns employees that any increase in labor costs would make its operations in Guatemala uneconomic and force it to withdraw from the country.
15 September 1951	Windstorm flattens United Fruit's principal Guatemalan banana farms at Tiquisate; United Fruit later announces it will not rehabilitate plantation until it

	has completed study of economics of Guatemalan operation.
26 September 1951	United Fruit suspends 3,742 Tiquisate employees, refuses to comply with order of Inspector General of Labor to reinstate the suspended employees.
30 October 1951	Walter Turnbull, Vice President of United Fruit, gives Arbenz ultimatum. United Fruit will not rehabilitate plantation without assurance of stable labor costs for three years and exemption from unfavorable labor laws or exchange controls.
19 December 1951	United Fruit announces reduction in passenger ship service to Guatemala.
2 January 1952	Labor Court of Appeals rules United Fruit must resume operations at Tiquisate and pay 3,742 employees back wages.

[   ]   [

                                                        ]

[   ]   [

                                                        ]

25 March 1952	Mexico City [ ] begins receiving weekly reports from Castillo Armas.
16 June 1952	Case officer [ ] arrives in Guatemala [ ]
17 June 1952	Arbenz enacts Agrarian Reform Law.
10 July 1952	DDP Allen Dulles meets with Mann to solicit State Department approval for plan to overthrow Arbenz.
7 August 1952	Distribution of land under the Agrarian Reform Law begins.

18 August 1952	DCI gives approval for PBFORTUNE.
2 October 1952	Pan American Airways settles three-month-old strike in Guatemala by raising wages 23 percent.
11 December 1952	Guatemalan Communist party opens second party congress with senior Arbenz administration officials in attendance.
12 December 1952	Workers at United Fruit's Tiquisate plantation file for expropriation of 55,000 acres of United Fruit land.
19 December 1952	Guatemalan Communist party, PGT, legalized.
5 February 1953	Congress impeaches the Supreme Court for "ignorance of the law which shows unfitness and manifest incapacity to administer justice" after the Court issued an injunction against further seizures of land.
25 February 1953	Guatemala confiscates 234,000 acres of United Fruit land.
18 March 1953	NSC 144/1, "United States Objectives and Courses with Respect to Latin America," warns of a "drift in the area toward radical and nationalistic regimes."
29 March 1953	Salamá uprising. Abortive rebellion touches off suppression campaign against anti-Communists in Guatemala.
12 August 1953	National Security Council authorizes covert action against Guatemala.
11 September 1953	[ ] adviser to King, submits "General Plan of Action" for PBSUCCESS.
October 1953	John Peurifoy, new US Ambassador, arrives in Guatemala City.
9 November 1953	José Manuel Fortuny flies to Prague to negotiate purchase of arms.
16 November 1953	DDP Frank Wisner approves [ ] plan and recommends acceptance by DCI.
9 December 1953	DCI Allen Dulles approves general plan for PBSUCCESS, allocates $3 million for the program.
23 December 1953	CIA's LINCOLN Station opens [ ]

18 January 1954	Alfonso Martínez, head of the Agrarian Department, "flees" to Switzerland. Proceeds to Prague to negotiate arms deal.

[   ] [

]

25 January 1954	Guatemalan Government begins mass arrests of suspected subversives.
29 January 1954	Guatemalan white paper accuses US of planning invasion. Reveals substantial details of PBSUCCESS.
2 February 1954	Sydney Gruson, *New York Times* correspondent, expelled from Guatemala by Guatemalan Foreign Minister Guillermo Toriello. [ ] Wisner, King meet to decide whether to abort PBSUCCESS due to white paper revelations.
19 February 1954	Operation WASHTUB, a plan to plant a phony Soviet arms cache in Nicaragua, begins.
24 February 1954	Guatemala confiscates 173,000 acres of United Fruit land.
1 March 1954	Caracas meeting of the OAS opens.
4 March 1954	Dulles speaks to Caracas meeting.
5 March 1954	Toriello rebuts US charges.
13 March 1954	OAS votes 17 to 1 to condemn Communism in Guatemala. Secretary of State John Foster Dulles briefed on PBSUCCESS.
21 March 1954	Paramilitary training program graduates 37 Guatemalan sabotage trainees.
9 April 1954	Guatemalan Archbishop Mariano Rossell y Arrellana issues a pastoral letter calling for a national crusade against Communism.
10 April 1954	Wisner briefs Assistant Secretary of State Henry Holland on PBSUCCESS. Holland, shocked by security lapses, demands top-level review of project.
15–16 April 1954	Black flights suspended pending top-level review of PBSUCCESS.

17 April 1954	John Foster Dulles and Allen Dulles give [ ] the "full green light."
20 April 1954	Paramilitary training program graduates 30 leadership trainees.
[ ]	[ ]
1 May 1954	*La Voz de la Liberación*, Operation SHERWOOD, begins broadcasts.
14 May 1954	Paramilitary training program graduates communications trainees.
15 May 1954	SS *Alfhem* docks in Puerto Barrios with cargo of Czech weapons.
20 May 1954	Commando raid on trainload of *Alfhem* weapons. One soldier and one saboteur killed. Further sabotage attempts on 21 and 25 May. All fail. Official Guatemalan radio goes off the air to replace transmitter. Does not restart broadcasts until mid-June. Nicaragua breaks diplomatic relations with Guatemala.
24 May 1954	US Navy begins Operation HARDROCK BAKER, sea blockade of Guatemala.
29 May 1954	Arbenz rounds up subversives, netting nearly all of Castillo Armas's clandestine apparatus.
31 May 1954	Arbenz offers to meet with Eisenhower to reduce tensions.
4 June 1954	Col. Rodolfo Mendoza of Guatemalan air force defects to El Salvador with private plane.
8 June 1954	Víctor Manuel Gutiérrez, secretary general of the Guatemalan trade union federation, holds a special meeting of farm and labor unions to urge them to mobilize for self-defense.
15 June 1954	Sabotage teams launched. Invasion forces moved to staging areas. Chief of Station [ ] makes cold approach to [ ] prime defection candidate.
17 June 1954	[ ] meets again with [ ]

	requests bombing of Guatemala City race track as demonstration of strength.
18 June 1954	At 1700 hours, Arbenz holds mass rally at railroad station. Buzzed by CIA planes. At 2020 hours, Castillo Armas crosses the border.
19 June 1954	At 0150 hours, bridge at Gualán blown up.
20 June 1954	Esquipulas captured. Rebels defeated at Gualán.
21 June 1954	Largest rebel force suffers disastrous defeat at Puerto Barrios.
25 June 1954	Matamoros Fortress bombed. Chiquimula captured. CIA planes strafe troop trains.
27 June 1954	Arbenz capitulates. Castillo Armas attacks Zacapa, is defeated, and falls back to Chiquimula. Agency plane bombs British freighter at San José.
28 June 1954	Díaz, Sánchez, and Monzón form junta at 1145 hours. Refused to negotiate with Castillo. F-47 dropped two bombs at 1530 hours.
29 June 1954	Monzón seizes junta, requests negotiations with Castillo Armas. Zacapa garrison arranges cease-fire with Castillo Armas.
30 June 1954	Wisner sends "Shift of Gears" cable, urging officers to withdraw from matters of policy.
1 July 1954	Monzón and Castillo Armas meet in Honduras to mediate differences.
2 July 1954	SHERWOOD ceases broadcasts, begins withdrawal.
4–17 July 1954	CIA documents recovery team, PBHISTORY, collects 150,000 Communist-related documents in Guatemala City.
12 July 1954	LINCOLN office closed.
1 September 1954	Castillo Armas assumes presidency.
26 July 1957	Castillo Armas assassinated.

APPENDIX B

Bibliography

Agency Records

Director of Central Intelligence. Executive Registry Records. Job 80R-01731R, CIA Archives and Records Center.
———. Job 83-00739R. CIA Archives and Records Center.
———. Job 85-00664R. CIA Archives and Records Center.
Directorate of Operations Records. Job 79-01025A. CIA Archives and Records Center.
———. Job 79-01228A. CIA Archives and Records Center.

National Archives

General Records of the Department of State. Record Group 59. US National Archives and Records Administration.
Records of the Office of Inter-American Affairs. Lot 57D95. Record Group 59. US National Archives and Records Administration.

Interviews

[   ] Interview by Nick Cullather, 19 April 1993, Washington, DC, Tape Recording. DCI History Staff, CIA.

Articles and Books

Braden, Spruille. *Diplomats and Demagogues*. New Rochelle, NY: Arlington House, 1971.

Castillo Armas, Carlos. "How Guatemala Got Rid of the Communists." *American Mercury*, January 1955, pp. 137–142.

Clark, Paul Coe. *The United States and Somoza, 1933–1956: A Revisionist Look*. Westport: Praeger, 1992.

Dulles, Allen. *The Craft of Intelligence*. London: Weidenfield and Nicolson, 1963.

Dunkerly, James. *Power in the Isthmus: A Political History of Modern Central America*. London: Verso, 1988.

Eisenhower, Dwight David. *Mandate for Change, 1953–1956*. Garden City, NY: Doubleday and Company, 1963.

Fauriol, Georges A., and Eva Loser. *Guatemala's Political Puzzle*. New Brunswick: Transaction Books, 1988.

Ferrell, Robert H. *American Diplomacy: A History*. 3rd ed. New York: W. W. Norton and Co., 1975.

Fried, Jonathan L., et al. *Guatemala in Rebellion: Unfinished History*. New York: Grove Press, 1983.

Gelb, Leslie H., and Richard K. Betts. *The Irony of Vietnam: The System Worked*. Washington, DC: Brookings Institution, 1979.

Gleijeses, Piero. "The Death of Francisco Arana: A Turning Point in the Guatemalan Revolution." *Journal of Latin American Studies* 22 (October 1990): 527–552.

———. *Shattered Hope: The Guatemalan Revolution and the United States, 1944–1954*. Princeton: Princeton University Press, 1991.

Gordon, Max. "A Case History of US Subversion: Guatemala, 1954." *Science and Society* 35 (Summer 1971) 2: 129–155.

Handy, Jim. " 'The Most Precious Fruit of the Revolution': The Guatemalan Agrarian Reform, 1952–54." *Hispanic American Historical Review* 68 (1988): 675–705.

———. " 'A Sea of Indians': Ethnic Conflict and the Guatemalan Revolution, 1944–1952." *The Americas* 46 (Oct. 1989): 189–204.

Hitchens, Christopher. "Minority Report." *The Nation*, July 6, 1985, p. 8.

Hunt, E. Howard. *Undercover: Memoirs of an American Secret Agent*. New York: Putnam, 1974.

Immerman, Richard H. *The CIA in Guatemala: The Foreign Policy of Intervention*. Austin: University of Texas Press, 1982.

———. "Guatemala as Cold War History." *Political Science Quarterly* 95 (Winter 1980–81) 4: 629–653.

Jensen, Amy Elizabeth. *Guatemala: A Historical Survey*. New York: Exposition Press, 1955.

[

]

LaBarge, Richard Allen. "Impact of the United Fruit Company on the Economic Development of Guatemala." In *Studies in Middle American Economics*, ed. Richard LaBarge, Wayne Clegern, and Oriol Pi-Sunyer. New Orleans: Tulane University, 1968. pp. 1–72.

Linebarger, Paul. *Psychological Warfare.* Washington: Infantry Journal Press, 1948.

Manz, Beatriz. *Refugees of a Hidden War: The Aftermath of Counterinsurgency in Guatemala.* Albany: State University of New York Press, 1988.

Marks, Frederick W., III. "The CIA and Castillo Armas in Guatemala, 1954: New Clues to an Old Puzzle." *Diplomatic History* 14 (Winter 1990): 67–86.

Martínez, Pedro. "Lessons of the Guatemalan Tragedy." *World Marxist Review* 27 (July 1984): 101–106.

McCamant, John F. "Intervention in Guatemala: Implications for the Study of Third World Politics." *Comparative Political Studies* 17 (October 1984): 373–407.

McCann, Thomas P. *An American Company: The Tragedy of United Fruit.* New York: Crown Publishers, 1976.

[

]

Meers, Sharon I. "The British Connection: How the United States Covered its Tracks in the 1954 Coup in Guatemala." *Diplomatic History* 16 (Summer 1992) 3: 409–428.

Montague, Ludwell Lee. *General Walter Bedell Smith as Director of Central Intelligence.* University Park: Pennsylvania State University Press, 1992.

[

]

Payne, Walter A. "The Guatemalan Revolution, 1944–1954: An Interpretation." *The Pacific Historian* 17 (Spring 1973): 1–32.

Petersen, John Holger. "The Political Role of University Students in Guatemala, 1944–1968." Ph.D. dissertation, University of Pittsburgh, 1969.

Phillips, David Atlee. *The Night Watch.* New York: Ballantine Books, 1977.

Rabe, Stephen G. "The Clues Didn't Check Out: Commentary on 'The CIA and Castillo Armas.'" *Diplomatic History* 14 (Winter 1990): 87–95.

Roettinger, Philip C. "The Company, Then and Now." *The Progressive*, July 1986, p. 50.

Schneider, Ronald M. *Communism in Guatemala, 1944–1954.* New York: Frederick A. Praeger Publishers, 1958.

Schlesinger, Stephen, and Stephen Kinzer, *Bitter Fruit: The Untold Story of the American Coup in Guatemala*. Garden City: Doubleday and Company, 1982.

Simons, Marlise. "Guatemala: The Coming Danger." *Foreign Policy* 43 (Summer 1981): 93–103.

Smith, Joseph Burkholder. *Portrait of a Cold Warrior*. New York: G. P. Putnam's Sons, 1976.

Wise, David, and Thomas B. Ross. *The Invisible Government*. New York: Random House, 1964.

US Congress. House Select Committee on Communist Aggression. *Communist Aggression in Latin America*. 83rd Cong., 2d sess., 1954.

Zunes, John Stephen. "Decisions on Intervention: United States Response to Third World Nationalist Governments, 1950–1957." Ph.D. dissertation, Cornell University, 1990.

APPENDIX C

A Study of Assassination

Along with the foregoing study, the CIA released a report by agency historian Gerald K. Haines entitled "CIA and Guatemala Assassination Proposals, 1952–1954," written in June 1995. It concludes that while the agency never authorized or conducted assassinations in Guatemala, "proposals for assassination pervaded both PBFORTUNE and PBSUCCESS." High agency officials discussed the option, and agents in the field undertook planning and preparation. "Some assassins were selected, training began, and tentative 'hit lists' were drawn up." The two documents below are taken from the collection released along with the Haines study. Both are from a folder marked "Training File of PBSUCCESS" in Box 73 of Job 79-01025A.

According to Haines, "A Study of Assassination" was prepared in January 1954 to brief the training chief of PBSUCCESS who was preparing to leave for Castillo-Armas's camp in Honduras. It is in rough form, with passages crossed out and rewritten in pencil.

Definition

Assassination is a term thought to be derived from "hashish," a drug similar to marijuana, said to have been used by Hassen-Ben-Sabah to induce motivation in his followers, who were assigned to carry out political and other murders, usually at the cost of their lives.

It is here used to describe the planned killing of a person who is not under the legal jurisdiction of the killer, who is not physically in the hands of the killer, who has been selected by a resistance organization for death, and whose death provides positive advantages to that organization.

Employment

Assassination is an extreme measure not normally used in clandestine operations. It should be assumed that it will never be ordered or authorized by any U.S. Headquarters, though the latter may in rare instances agree to its execution by members of an associated foreign service. This reticence is partly due to the necessity for committing communications to paper. No assassination instructions should ever be written or recorded. Consequently, the decision to employ this technique must nearly always be reached in the field, at the area where the act will take place. Decision and instructions should be confined to an absolute minimum of persons. Ideally, only one person will be involved. No report may be made, but usually the act will be properly covered by normal news services, whose output is available to all concerned.

Justification

Murder is not morally justifiable. Self-defense may be argued if the victim has knowledge which may destroy the resistance organization if divulged. Assassination of persons responsible for atrocities or reprisals may be regarded as just punishment. Killing a political leader whose burgeoning career is a clear and present danger to the cause of freedom may be held necessary.

But assassination can seldom be employed with a clear conscience. Persons who are morally squeamish should not attempt it.

Classifications

The techniques employed will vary according to whether the subject is unaware of his danger, aware but unguarded, or guarded. They will also be affected by whether or not the assassin is to be killed with the subject; hereafter, assassinations in which the subject is unaware will be termed "simple"; those where the subject is aware but unguarded will be termed "chase"; those where the victim is guarded will be termed "guarded."

If the assassin is to die with the subject, the act will be called "lost." If the assassin is to escape, the adjective will be "safe." It should be noted that no compromise should exist here. The assassin must not fall alive into enemy hands.

A further type of division is caused by the need to conceal the fact that the subject was actually the victim of assassination, rather than an accident or natural causes. If such concealment is desirable the operation will be called "secret," if concealment is immaterial, the act will be called "open," while if the assassination requires publicity to be effective it will be termed "terroristic."

Following these definitions, the assassination of Julius Caesar was safe, simple, and terroristic, while that of Huey Long was lost, guarded and open.[1] Obviously, successful secret assassinations are not recorded as assassinations at all. Ananda of Thailand and Augustus Caesar may have been the victims of safe, guarded and secret assassination.[2] Chase assassinations usually involve clandestine agents or members of criminal organizations.

The Assassin

In safe assassinations, the assassin needs the usual qualities of a clandestine agent. He should be determined, courageous, intelligent, resourceful, and physically active. If special equipment is to be used, such as firearms or drugs, it is clear that he must have outstanding skill with such equipment.

Except in terroristic assassination, it is desirable that the assassin be a transient in the area. He should have an absolute minimum of contact with the rest of the organization, and his instructions should be given orally by one person only. His safe evacuation after the act is absolutely essential, but here again contact should be as limited as possible. It is preferable that the person issuing instructions also conduct any withdrawal or covering action which may be necessary.

In lost assassination, the assassin must be a fanatic of some sort. Politics, religion, and revenge are about the only feasible motives. Since a fanatic is unstable psychologically, he must be handled with extreme care. He must not know the identities of the other members of the organization, for although it is intended that he die in the act, something may go wrong. While the assassin of Trotsky has never revealed any significant information, it was unsound to depend on this when the act was planned.[3]

Planning

When the decision to assassinate has been reached, the tactics of the operation must be planned, based upon an estimate of the situation similar to that used in military operations. The preliminary estimate will reveal gaps in in-

---

[1]Julius Caesar, a Roman general, was assassinated on March 14, 44 B.C., by Gaius Cassius and Marcus Brutus before a meeting of the Senate. Sen. Huey P. Long of Louisiana was shot by Dr. Carl Weiss in the state house in Baton Rouge on September 8, 1935.

[2]Ananda Mahidol, King Rama VIII of Thailand, was shot to death on June 9, 1946 in the royal palace. Mystery surrounding the shooting led to the collapse of the civilian government. Caesar Augustus, the first Roman emperor, died in 14 A.D. at the age of 76. Historians attribute his death to natural causes, but the author of this study appears to have other information.

[3]Ramón Mercador, a Spanish Communist, was convicted of the murder of Leon Trotsky and sentenced to 20 years in prison.

formation and possibly indicate a need for special equipment which must be procured or constructed. When all necessary data has been collected, an effective tactical plan can be prepared. All planning must be mental; no papers should ever contain evidence of the operation.

In resistance situations, assassination may be used as a counter-reprisal. Since this requires advertising to be effective, the resistance organization must be in a position to warn high officials publicly that their lives will be the price of reprisal action against innocent people. Such a threat is of no value unless it can be carried out, so it may be necessary to plan the assassination of various responsible officers of the oppressive regime and hold such plans in readiness to be used only if provoked by excessive brutality. Such plans must be modified frequently to meet changes in the tactical situation.

Techniques

The essential point of assassination is the death of the subject. A human being may be killed in many ways but sureness is often overlooked by those who may be emotionally unstrung by the seriousness of this act they intend to commit. The specific techniques employed will depend upon a large number of variables, but should be constant in one point: Death must be absolutely certain. The attempt on Hitler's life failed because the conspiracy did not give this matter proper attention.[4]

Techniques may be considered as follows:

[In the fifteen pages that follow, the author describes the advantages and drawbacks of a variety of killing methods, including firearms, explosives, edge and blunt weapons, and manual techniques.—N.C.]

---

[4]In July 1944, conspirators in the German Army placed a bomb in a briefcase in Hitler's headquarters in East Prussia. The explosion killed four people, but Hitler escaped.

As early as January 1952, Directorate of Plans officers began drawing up lists of persons to "eliminate" after a successful anti-Communist coup. The last such list, appended to the memorandum below, was discussed in April 1954 with Castillo Armas. He and CIA officers agreed that assassinations would take place during the invasion or after its success. Confident that Castillo Armas's tiny force would actually reach the capital, agency officials spent nearly as much time laying plans for victory as they did preparing for the actual operation.

(HAND CARRY)

31 March 1954

MEMORANDUM
TO   :   All Staff Officers
FROM   :   C/[   ]
SUBJECT: Selection of individuals for disposal by Junta Group.

C/[   ] has requested a list of names to be compiled for study by Staff Officers to determine if they meet the latest criteria for inclusion on the Junta's disposal list.

Consideration for inclusion on the final list should positively establish that the individual falls into one or more of the following groups:

1) High government and organizational leaders whose outward position has not disclosed the fact they are motivated and directed by the Cominform and who are irrevocably implicated in Communist doctrine and policy.

2) Out-and-out proven Communist leaders whose removal from the political scene is required for the immediate and future success of the new government.

3) Those few individuals in key government and military positions of tactical importance whose removal for psychological, organizational or other reasons is mandatory for the success of military action.

This document is routed to Staff Officers for deletions, additions, and/or comments. It is requested that a final list of disposees be approved promptly to permit P.M. planning to proceed on schedule.

The following list of individuals for consideration has been assembled from old lists supplied by the Junta and from recent intelligence available[5] at [
] Your careful consideration is requested in making additions or deletions. Each officer is to indicate his concurrence by placing his initials after each

---

[5]The words "recent intelligence available" are underlined and a handwritten notation reads, "*no* not done."

name on the attached list which he believes should remain in this list. Exceptions, additions or deletions are to be noted on the blank pages following the attachment.

Attachments:
1. Disposal list
2. Blank pages
3. Biographic data[6]

[6]Five pages follow, redacted in full.

New Documents

Since the first edition of *Secret History*, more documentation has come to light on the CIA's activities in Guatemala. The Clinton administration released agency files to assist a truth and reconciliation process that was part of the accord that ended Guatemala's civil conflict in 1996. Others were released through the efforts of scholars using the Freedom of Information Act, and still others were published in a volume of the State Department's *Foreign Relations of the United States* series in 2003. This appendix includes a selection of these along with excerpts from speeches, writings, and official reports on the covert action and its aftermath.

The Assessment

Agency analysts recognized that Guatemala's Communists were few in number and had only indirect influence over the Arbenz government (Document 1). But in assessing Guatemala, intelligence officials were thinking of China, which had fallen to Communism with unexpected suddenness three years earlier. In China, the Communists' association with a progressive social policy and with land reform, along with the disorganization of the opposition had been crucial. Both symptoms were evident in Guatemala. Arbenz (Document 3) attracted less concern than the people around him, particularly Alfonso Martinez, head of the land reform program. Characteristically, analysts were concerned about contingencies, as well as objective conditions, and so evaluation lent as much weight to imagined scenarios, such as a left-wing assassination plot, as it did to observable trends.

Agrarian reform presented a dilemma for U.S. officials (Document 4). They saw it as a necessary step for creating a capitalist economy in Guatemala, but believed it would enhance the prestige of Guatemala's communists. The United Fruit Company's holdings would be affected, but this was not the Department's primary concern.

The Agency attempted to gain approval for a covert operation while assessment proceeded (Document 2). They remained frustrated at the State Department's reluctance to give an unequivocal "green light" for the operation. Until April 1954, Department officials would give only verbal or implied approval, and Director Allen Dulles expected a reversal at any time.

Document 1. Central Intelligence Agency, "Present Political Situation in Guatemala and Possible Development During 1952," NIE-62, March 11, 1952[1]

The Problem

To analyze the present political situation in Guatemala and possible developments during 1952.

Conclusions

1. The Communists already exercise in Guatemala a political influence far out of proportion to their small numerical strength. This influence will probably continue to grow during 1952. The political situation in Guatemala adversely affects US interests and constitutes a potential threat to US security.

2. Communist political success derives in general from the ability of individual Communists and fellow travelers to identify themselves with the nationalist and social aspirations of the Revolution of 1944. In this manner, they have been successful in infiltrating the Administration and the pro-Administration political parties and have gained control of organized labor upon which the Administration has become increasingly dependent.

3. The political alliance between the Administration and the Communists is likely to continue. The opposition to Communism in Guatemala is potentially powerful, but at present it lacks leadership and organization. So far Communist-inspired Administration propaganda has succeeded in stigmatizing all criticism of Communism as opposition to the Administration and to the principles of the still popular Revolution of 1944.

4. Future political developments will depend in large measure on the outcome of the conflict between Guatemala and the United Fruit Com-

[1]Source: U.S. Department of State, *Foreign Relations of the United States, 1952–1954, Guatemala* (Washington: U.S. Government Printing Office, 2003), pp. 6–9.

pany. This conflict is a natural consequence of the Revolution of 1944, but has been exacerbated by the Communists for their own purposes.

5. If the Company should submit to Guatemalan demands the political position of the Arbenz Administration would be greatly strengthened. It is probable that in this case the Government and the unions, under Communist influence and supported by national sentiment, would exert increasing pressure on other US interests, notably the Railway.

6. If the Company should withdraw from Guatemala a worsening economic situation would probably result. It is unlikely, however, that the economic consequences during 1952 would be such as to threaten political stability unless there were a coincident and unrelated decline in coffee production, prices, or markets.

7. Any deterioration in the economic and political situations would tend to increase the Administration's dependence on and favor toward organized labor, with a consequent increase in Communist influence. However, it is unlikely that the Communists could come directly to power during 1952, even though, in case of the incapacitation of President Arbenz, his present legal successor would be a pro-Communist.

8. In present circumstances the Army is loyal to President Arbenz, although increasingly disturbed by the growth of Communist influence. If it appeared that the Communists were about to come to power in Guatemala, the Army would probably prevent that development.

9. In the longer view, continued Communist influence and action in Guatemala will gradually reduce the capabilities of the potentially powerful anti-Communist forces to produce a change. The Communists will also attempt to subvert or neutralize the Army in order to reduce its capability to prevent them from eventually taking full control of the Government.

Discussion

The Arbenz Administration

10. The present political situation in Guatemala is the outgrowth of the Revolution of 1944. That Revolution was something more than a routine military coup. From it there has developed a strong national movement to free Guatemala from the military dictatorship, social backwardness, and "economic colonialism" which had been the pattern of the past. These aspirations command the emotional loyalty of most politically conscious Guatemalans and the administration of President Arbenz derives corresponding strength from its claim to leadership of the continuing national Revolution.

11. President Arbenz himself is essentially an opportunist whose politics are largely a matter of historical accident. Francisco Arana, the principal military leader of the Revolution of 1944, became Chief of the

Armed Forces under President Arévalo and Arbenz, a lesser member of the military junta, became Minister of Defense. As the Arévalo Administration turned increasingly leftward in its policies Arana opposed that trend. His possible election to the Presidency in 1951 became the one hope of moderate and conservative elements in Guatemala. In view of Arana's political position, Arbenz, his personal rival for military leadership, became the more closely associated with Arévalo and the leftist position in Guatemalan politics. The assassination of Arana in 1949 cleared the way for Arbenz' succession to the Presidency in 1951.

12. By 1951 the toleration of Communist activity which had characterized the early years of the Arévalo Administration had developed into an effective working alliance between Arévalo and the Communists. Arbenz, to attain the Presidency, made with the Communists commitments of mutual support which importantly affect the present situation. He did not, however, surrender himself completely to Communist control.

Communist Strength and Influence

13. The Communist Party of Guatemala has no more than 500 members, of whom perhaps one-third are militants. The Party, however, has recently reorganized and is actively recruiting, especially in Guatemala City, on the government-owned coffee plantations, and among United Fruit Company workers. It is in open communication with international Communism, chiefly through the Communist-controlled international labor organizations, the Latin American CTAL and the worldwide WFTU.

14. The Communists have achieved their present influence in Guatemala, not as a political party, but through the coordinated activity of individual Communists in the leftist political parties and labor unions which emerged from the Revolution of 1944. The extension of their influence has been facilitated by the applicability of Marxist clichés to the "anti-colonial" and social aims of the Guatemalan Revolution.

Document 2. [Name not declassified] of the Central Intelligence Agency to J. C. King, Chief of the Western Hemisphere Division, Central Intelligence Agency, "Guatemala," October 8, 1952.[2]

1. Early in July Mr. Dulles, Mr. Hedden, [name not declassified] and myself visited the State Department where we had a conference at which were present Assistant Secretary of State Miller, his Deputy, Mr. Mann, and Mr. Robert P. Joyce. The CIA delegation posed the following three questions: (as well as I can remember)

[2]Source: U.S. Department of State, *Foreign Relations of the United States, 1952–1954, Guatemala* (Washington: U.S. Government Printing Office, 2003), p. 31.

1. Would the State Department like to see a different government in Guatemala?
2. Would the State Department oppose a government established by the use of force?
3. Does the State Department wish CIA to take steps to bring about a change of government?

2. The first question was answered positively. The second question was answered negatively. The third question was not answered clearly but by implication, positively.

3. Mr. Dulles asked me to make a Memorandum of Conversation in long-hand and deliver the one copy to him. I did this and waited in his office while he showed it to the Director. In a few minutes I was called into the Director's office, and it was soon clear that the Director was dissatisfied with the lack of a direct answer to the third question. He then telephoned to Mr. Bruce to make arrangements for a meeting.

4. I later gathered from Mr. Dulles that the Director had received a satisfactory answer from Mr. Bruce.

[name not declassified]

Document 3. **"Personal Political Orientation of President Arbenz / Possibility of a Left-Wing Coup," Central Intelligence Agency Information Report No. 00-B-57327, October 10, 1952**[3]

Guatemala City, October 10, 1952.

COUNTRY
Guatemala

SUBJECT
Personal Political Orientation of President Arbenz/Possibility of a Left-Wing Coup

PLACE ACQUIRED (BY SOURCE)
Guatemala

DATE ACQUIRED (BY SOURCE)
Sep 52 and earlier

DATE (OF INFO.)
Sep 52

SOURCE
[1 paragraph (11-1/2 lines of source text) not declassified]

[3]Source: U.S. Department of State, *Foreign Relations of the United States, 1952–1954, Guatemala* (Washington: U.S. Government Printing Office, 2003), pp. 38–40.

Summary

1. Although President Arbenz appears to collaborate with the Communists and extremists to the detriment of Guatemala's relations with the US, I am quite certain that he personally does not agree with the economic and political ideas of the Guatemalan or Soviet Communists, and I am equally certain that he is not now in a position where they can force him to make decisions in their favor. The reasons for my opinion are as follows:

(a) The President's social reform ideas stem from the US New Deal rather than from Soviet Communism.

(b) President Arbenz is still convinced that he is "using" Communists and Communism to further his own ends.

(c) He is fully aware of Guatemala's economic dependence on the US.

(d) Arbenz has no fear of a conservative coup and has taken no active steps to guard against one.

(e) The "opposition" of business groups and conservatives (with the exception of a few landowners) has been greatly exaggerated. This is evidenced by the "surprising" lack of serious concern in most business circles about the effects of the new land reform bill.

It is my personal fear that the chief threat to the Arbenz regime is a coup by rank opportunists within the "palace clique" who have sold out to Communist penetration. Such a coup would first assassinate the popular Arbenz, blame the reactionaries for his death, and then proceed to violently wipe out all conservative opposition.

2. Rather than setting up a Communist state, Arbenz desires to establish a "modern democracy" which would improve the lot of its people through paternalistic social reforms. Arbenz' personal idol is FDR and his reforms are patterned after New Deal reforms and adjusted to the backward economy and social structure of Guatemala. None of the reforms is substantially extreme as compared to many of those in the US, Europe, and even in other Latin American countries. The extremities are relative and seem radical in Guatemala only because of the backward feudal situation they are meant to remedy. Also they seem extreme compared to the ineffective piecemeal measures of his predecessor, Arevalo. During Arevalo's term, Arbenz often became angry at his weakness as a chief-of-state and realized that no effective social measures could be implemented while Arevalo was president. Satisfying his ambition to become president himself, and also with a sincere desire to fulfill his promises to his people, Arbenz went to work immediately and impatiently to implement his reforms and, as he put it, "to jar Guatemala out of the Middle Ages." . . .

Document 4. State Department, Office of Intelligence Research, "Agrarian Reform in Guatemala," Report No. 6001, March 5, 1953.[4]

ABSTRACT

On June 17, 1952, a comprehensive agrarian reform program became law in Guatemala. Its professed objective is the development of a capitalistic agricultural economy through the abolition of semi-feudal owner-worker relationships, the redistribution of land, and the improvement with state assistance of cultivation methods. The implications of the legislation, however, go beyond agrarian reform inasmuch as its provisions furnish a basis for the strengthening of political and Communist control over the rural population.

Full implementation of the law would free thousands of agrarian workers from a centuries-old dependence upon the privileged landholding class, but would subject the majority, in all probability, to close control by the state. This would be exercised through a virtually autonomous National Agrarian Department. Certain limitations, also, would be incumbent upon those using redistributed land. Since the great bulk of the land expropriated would be incorporated into the imprescriptible public domain, holdings could be acquired only on the basis of a life grant or by rental. Private title, however, would be possible by the direct transfer to the peasant of land expropriated from private estates. Another feature of the law facilitating state control is provision for the concentration of agrarian workers on each private plantation into a single village.

Administration forces undoubtedly envisage political benefits from the legislation. They are presumably anxious to break the control of the conservative anti-administration large landholders over the farm labor force in order to organize it behind the government. Advantages to the Communists are likely to be enhanced by the opportunity to extend the influence in farm areas through infiltration of the National Agrarian Department, through their expanded control over Guatemalan labor organization, and through greater opportunities to attack the United Fruit Company. The deepening cleavage between moderates and left caused by government sponsorship of the agrarian program will benefit the Communists.

Full and rapid implementation of the land distribution program would be likely to produce serious economic repercussions. Already ner-

---

[4]Source: U.S. Department of State, *Foreign Relations of the United States, 1952–1954, Guatemala* (Washington: U.S. Government Printing Office, 2003), pp. 70–72.

vousness has depressed business activity. Thus far, however, agricultural production, which provides the basis of Guatemala's economy, apparently has not been affected.

Implementation of the law will be difficult and politically dangerous. Although an abundance of land is made available for redistribution, only a small part of it is desirably located. The extent to which land controlled by foreign agricultural corporations—the greater part of United Fruit Company holdings are possibly subject to expropriation—may be made available for redistribution is largely a matter of speculation. As far as can be ascertained, these enterprises have no special protection under their operating concessions. While they may appeal decisions affecting their interests to the National Agrarian Department, this agency and the civil courts, which probably could not be utilized, are closely subjected to the will of an administration determined to accelerate the agrarian program. Also difficult for the administration to overcome will be the long-standing living habits and prejudices of the largely Indian agrarian population. Most significant of all will be the perfecting of a competent administrative organization. The strong probability exists that too rapid acceleration of the agrarian program coupled with increasing Communist strength and influence may lead to violence difficult for the Arbenz administration to contain. . . .

The Plan

The Agency saw Guatemala as a "prototype area" where psychological tactics could be devised and tested (Document 5). In a draft plan, prepared in November 1953, Castillo Armas is designated at the "constitutional leader." The plan anticipates an almost entirely psychological operation proceeding through a series of abstract steps creating "maximum pressure" and "serious difficulties" for the Arbenz regime (Document 6). The plan's uncertainties fall into a yawning gap between items 5D and 5E, at which point the government leadership and its popular support was to vanish in an unspecified manner.

The Agency had growing misgivings about its chosen instrument "Calligeris," Castillo Armas, whose passive-aggressive habits irritated his handlers. A month before the operation culminated, PBSUCCESS officials expressed doubts about his qualifications to lead Guatemala after the operation (Document 7).

Document 5. Richard Hirsch, "Debriefing of Ambassador
Rudolf E. Schoenfeld, October 28, 1953," October 28, 1953.[5]

Of the various comments made by Ambassador Schoenfeld on the
communist situation in Guatemala, the following are most relevant to
OCB interests:

1. The communist power-drive in Guatemala has reached an advanced state of infiltration, they hold key positions in (a) the agrarian
movement, (b) the labor movement, (c) government administration
short of cabinet level.

2. President Arbenz, who is half Swiss, has a granite streak of stub-
bornness in addition to his volatility and is firmly convinced that he can
deal with the communists whenever he has to. This optimism is not
shared by Ambassador Schoenfeld, who feels that Arbenz has not even
begun to appreciate the real purposes and techniques of communism as
a power-seeking movement, not a social reform.

3. On the anti-communist side, there are very few positions of
strength. The church is extremely weak, all of its property having been
confiscated, and a strong anti-clerical attitude exists. The intellectuals
are either bemused by the appeals of communism, or are hypersensitive
to the U.S. The land-owners are strictly apolitical and will not permit
themselves, or their sons, to engage in political activity. They feel that
Guatemalan politics has three unattractive destinations: the palace, the
jail, or the cemetery. The independent press, however, is very alert to
the communist danger.

4. Guatemala represents in miniature all of the social cleavages, tensions, and dilemmas of modern Western society under attack by the
communist virus. Conditions will worsen considerably before we can
improve them, and we should regard Guatemala as a prototype area for
testing means and methods of combatting communism.

5. It will be of primary importance for U.S. labor organizations to
encourage the growth of free trade unions in Guatemala, for U.S. corporations to adopt enlightened labor policy in the area, and for the U.S.
Government to develop information activities along non-attributable
lines.

Richard Hirsch

[5]Source: U.S. Department of State, *Foreign Relations of the United States, 1952–1954, Guatemala* (Washington: U.S. Government Printing Office, 2003), p. 121.

Document 6. "Program for PBSUCCESS," November 12, 1953.[6]

SUBJECT

Program for PBSUCCESS

REFERENCES

A. "Guatemala—General Plan of Action", TS# dated 11 September 1953
B. Project PBSUCCESS Status Report, dated 29 October 1953

A. Objectives

1. To remove covertly, and without bloodshed if possible, the menace of the present Communist-controlled government of Guatemala.

2. To install and sustain, covertly, a pro-US government in Guatemala.

B. Statement of the Problem

1. The Communists have become strongly entrenched in Guatemala and in the Guatemalan government, thus constituting a threat to United States welfare in the Western Hemisphere.

2. The Guatemalan non-Communist opposition has become disillusioned and disunited. However, a latent anti-Communist resistance potential is believed to exist.

3. The resistance potential must be built up to the point where it can contribute materially to the accomplishment of the objectives of PBSUCCESS.

4. In view of growing Communist strength and declining non-Communist cohesion in Guatemala, the implementation and successful completion of the objectives of PBSUCCESS must proceed without delay.

5. It must be recognized that any major effort to dislodge the Communist-controlled government of Guatemala will probably be credited to the United States, and possibly on CIA. Covert accomplishment of the objectives of PBSUCCESS is therefore defined as meaning accomplishment with plausible denial of United States or CIA participation.

C. Plan of Operations

1. Stage One—Staffing and Assessment—
   a. Assignment of Project Personnel.
   b. Field Survey by Communications Adviser.
   c. Briefing and despatch of Project field personnel.

[6]Source: U.S. Department of State, *Foreign Relations of the United States, 1952–1954, Guatemala* (Washington: U.S. Government Printing Office, 2003), pp. 136–139.

    d. Assessment and analysis of friendly assets.

    e. Assessment and analysis of enemy assets.

    f. Preparation of detailed operational plans for Headquarters approval.

2. Stage Two—Preliminary Conditioning (D-?)

    a. Project Headquarters moves to the field.

    b. Create dissension and defection within the target.

    c. Discredit target at home and abroad.

    d. Demonstrate inability of target regime to represent best interests of the people.

    e. Create hope and encourage patience among non-Communists.

    f. Complete military agreements with Nicaragua, Honduras and El Salvador.

    g. Withdraw US military personnel from target at appropriate time.

    h. Begin economic pressure.

    i. Begin formation and training of a para-military force in exile.

    j. Assess accomplishments.

    k. Obtain Headquarters approval before proceeding to next stage.

3. Stage Three—Build-Up (D-75)

    a. Create maximum antagonism to target regime.

    b. Fan passive will to resist.

    c. Apply internal and external economic pressure to create serious difficulties.

    d. In concert with majority of OAS members, apply diplomatic pressures.

    e. Demonstrate urgency by speeding military build-up of neighboring countries (not including Mexico).

    f. Accentuate para-military preparation.

    g. Initiate passive sabotage program.

    h. Assess accomplishments.

    i. Obtain Headquarters approval before proceeding to next stage.

4. Stage Four—Critical Period (D-25)

    a. Apply maximum economic pressure.

    b. Accentuate divisionist activity within target.

    c. Intensive rumor campaign stimulating fear of war for the purpose of drawing enemy forces away from capital.

    d. Constitutional revolutionary forces claim support of people.

    e. Para-military force in readiness.

    f. Passive sabotage evident.

    g. Assess accomplishments.

    h. Obtain Headquarters approval before proceeding to next stage.

5. Stage Five—Showdown (D-5)
   a. Implement aggressive sabotage plan against key targets.
   b. Constitutional leader claims capability to seize power by force and issues ultimatum to target regime to capitulate in order to avoid needless bloodshed.
   c. Populace is told to await target regime's reply and further instructions from constitutional leader.
   d. If ultimatum fails, popular uprising begins; para-military force enters target country, proclaims authority, declares target regime null and void.
   e. Secure position and restore order.
6. Stage Six—Consolidation (D-?)
   a. Roll-up of Communists and collaborators.
   b. Dramatic initial proclamations and edicts.
   c. Formation of government.
   d. Announcement of long-range domestic and foreign policy.
   e. OAS countries announce immediate recognition and support of new regime.
   f. United States offers aid.
   g. PBSUCCESS terminated.

D. Organization and Authority
   1. Priority
      a. "Top Operational Priority" given PBSUCCESS.
   2. Authority and Responsibility
      a. Primary field authority and responsibility is vested in the Officer in Charge, PBSUCCESS.
      b. This officer is designated "Special Deputy for PBSUCCESS, WHD."
      c. The command channel will be direct from Special Deputy to CWH.
   3. Staff Requirements
      a. The following staff requirements for PBSUCCESS are believed to be the minimum for adequate implementation and control of the Plan of Operations envisaged herein. Additional personnel may be required for varying periods of TDY.
      b. The T/O outlined below is exclusive of WHD's current T/O.

[Omitted here is a proposed Table of Organization with position titles and grades.]

   7. Finance
      a. Upon arrival of this program, financial accountability will be vested in CWH, under whose direction CWH/Ad will be the

accountable disbursing officer for Headquarters expenditures. Under the general direction of the CWH, the Special Deputy for PBSUCCESS will be the accountable disbursing officer for Field expenditures.

b. Procedures for allocation, disbursement, and accounting of funds will be in a manner acceptable to the DD/A, and as shall be arranged between him and the CWH/Ad.

[name not declassified]

Document 7. [Name not declassified), "Calligeris," Memorandum for the Record, May 14, 1954.[7]

SUBJECT
Calligeris

1. The following comments and opinions regarding Calligeris are being submitted for the record to assist in any possible future evaluation of his personality. The basis for these remarks is the following: a ten day personal association in January 1954, a six day personal association in April 1954, a review of Subject's correspondence with [name not declassified] during the period January-May 1954, and a résumé of [name not declassified]'s remarks during the above noted period. . . .

a. This brings to light a Calligeris personality trait which is now clearly recognizable. He is a firmly stubborn man who in the face of indisputable evidence is prone to maintain his own point of view. The manner in which he defends his own decisions is interesting. Personal experience has shown that Calligeris will yield readily on general points and appear to be most willing to conciliate, promising that changes as suggested will be carried out. However, his execution of the details of any agreement will be as he sees fit. This completely modifies his original agreement with general plans. His geographical position plus the lack of a group contact with him who can effectively assure his completion of activities, has given him reason to believe that he can modify to suit his own desires any orders or instructions from [name not declassified] or the Group. It should be pointed out that Calligeris has not developed this line of thinking with an altogether malicious intent. Delays, lack of decisions, reversal of decisions by the Group have tended to increase his necessity to take the initiative when he, from his Honduran outpost, saw the necessity for some course of action.

b. The undersigned now realizes that Calligeris, when shorn of intel-

[7]Source: U.S. Department of State, *Foreign Relations of the United States, 1952–1954, Guatemala* (Washington: U.S. Government Printing Office, 2003), pp. 282–284.

ligence and propaganda responsibilities in January 1954, keenly resented this decision to which he agreed without any undue enthusiasm.
His subsequent actions soon abrogated the agreement in such a direct
manner that his excuses of a lack of adequate communication [less than
1 line of source text not declassified] only made the case more obvious.
In the end the Group yielded to Calligeris' wishes, thus giving him a
clear idea that if he persisted his ideas would be accepted. . . .

7. Calligeris, in the undersigned's opinion, could not last too long in
the rough and tumble of Guatemalan politics without the support of the
men [less than 1 line of source text not declassified]. From the visible
support which he has received to date, he counts on not too many military men. He could expect no support from the elements of the present
regime. Any alienation of the [less than 1 line of source text not declas-
sified] would estrange him immediately with individuals more conservative than the [less than 1 line of source text not declassified]. Calligeris
would therefore be dependent on a very small base of people who have
resided with him in exile. It is not logical that such a small element of
people, few of whom have had political experience, could long survive
the ordeal of righting the "mess" made by the communists. A representative from Group, properly installed, could easily in the course of a few
weeks, make the above points painfully clear to Calligeris.

[name not declassified]

The Operation Unfolds

*The arrival of the Alfhem with a cargo of Czech arms at Puerto Bar-
rios on May 15 led the agency to activate its plans early. Saboteurs
made an unsuccessful attempt to sabotage rail shipments of the arms en
route to the capital (Document 8).*

*Meanwhile agency official confidently laid plans for the collapse of
the Arbenz government, dividing responsibilities between ODACID, the
U.S. embassy in Guatemala, and ODYOKE, the U.S. government in
Washington. JMBLUG, Ambassador John Peurifoy, recommended post-
poning actions advantageous to the United Fruit Company in order to
avoid damage to the prestige of the new regime (Document 9).*

*Peurifoy had earlier urged a military coup as the surest means of de-
posing Arbenz, but the K-Program (Document 10), aimed at recruiting
military defectors, had made little headway. Officials at PBSUCCESS
headquarters recommended bombing military garrisons in the capital
(Document 12) as an inducement. By the first week of June (Document
11) the rebel planes buzzing the capital, the U.S. Navy blockade of
Guatemala, and SHERWOOD broadcasts had produced a climate of
fear that led the government to crack down on its political opponents.*

On June 27, Arbenz resigned, turning the powers of the presidency over to Col. Enrique Diaz who refused to negotiate with Castillo Armas. PBSUCCESS headquarters (Document 13) urged continued pressure from aircraft and SHERWOOD to force Diaz to include SYN-CARP, Castillo Armas's organization, in the junta.

Reports in the U.S. press, such as this sample from the Washington Post (Document 14), applauded the outcome and acknowledged the decisive role played by the United States (but not the CIA), which had the power to "stop the fighting in 15 minutes" if it wanted to.

Document 8. John Peurifoy, U.S. Ambassador to Guatemala, to the Department of State, May 22, 1954, 5 p.m.[8]

759. Up to this morning, 69 carloads of material unloaded from Alfhem had arrived in Guatemala City and unloading and shipments were continuing regularly. Ship may finish unloading Monday.

Charnaud MacDonald, Minister of Interior, revealed last night that attempt to blow up train morning of May 19 had cost lives of one Guatemalan soldier and one saboteur. Three other soldiers were wounded in battle described as lasting half hour between soldiers armed with rifles and saboteurs armed with submachine guns. Latter then retired toward Honduras frontier and escaped.

Press this morning carried photographs nitroglycerine cartridges which failed to explode and were used to connect charge with detonator. Minister reportedly emphasized this type explosives not used by any branch of Guatemalan Government and "possibly not in any Central American country."

Peurifoy

Document 9. [Name not declassified] of the Central Intelligence Agency to Frank Wisner, Deputy Chief of Plans and the Chief of Plans, Central Intelligence Agency, "Consolidation of New Guatemalan Regime," May 24, 1954.[9]

SUBJECT
Consolidation of New Guatemalan Regime

1. The task of consolidating the new Guatemalan regime falls into two parts:

[8]Source: U.S. Department of State, *Foreign Relations of the United States, 1952–1954, Guatemala* (Washington: U.S. Government Printing Office, 2003), p. 297.
[9]Source: U.S. Department of State, *Foreign Relations of the United States, 1952–1954, Guatemala* (Washington: U.S. Government Printing Office, 2003), pp. 298–299.

a. Duties devolving on the Guatemalans. This is currently being discussed with [name not declassified] and will be covered in a later memorandum.

b. Duties devolving upon ODYOKE. These form the subject of the present memorandum.

2. The duties devolving upon ODYOKE are:

a. Diplomatic recognition of the new government. ODACID must clearly take the lead in recognizing the new government, not only because other Hemisphere nations expect it, but also because such early recognition will capitalize most effectively on the overt moves that ODYOKE has made against the Guatemalan Communists. Early recognition by ODACID could do much to re-affirm ODYOKE leadership in the Hemisphere. (The cover and deception requirements of covert action should be satisfied by other means and should not be allowed to hamper early overt recognition.) Action: ODACID.

b. Economic and technical assistance. There should not be extension of American economic aid and technical assistance to Guatemala alone; this could be interpreted by other Central American and Hemisphere countries as "rewarding" a recently Communist and aggressive nation, without corresponding help to nations that never were Communist. There should be an overall economic aid and technical assistance program for all Central America, as recommended in LINC 2885. Action: ODACID and FOA.

c. Coordination of UFCO Action. Immediate conversations should be initiated with the UFCO, with a view toward coordinating ODACID and UFCO action in the consolidation period. Specifically, UFCO should be advised that ODACID will not support UFCO requests with diplomatic notes during the early months of the new government; while it was necessary and proper for ODACID to support UFCO against a Communist government, it will be improper for ODACID to make the same demands of an anti-Communist government. Likewise, UFCO should be asked not to mortgage the political viability of the new regime by pressing its claims too soon. Rather, as JMBLUG has recommended, UFCO should await the call of the new government to a joint parley in view of the influence that pro-UFCO elements and individuals will have in the new government ([name not declassified], SUPERIOR, etc.) the UFCO should be able to await and join in such a parley with equanimity. It may be advisable for the parley to agree to turn over the Guatemalan-UFCO dispute to an impartial commission, chosen by the parties to the dispute. It may also be advisable for the new government to levy promptly the increased taxes that the UFCO has declared itself willing to pay; then the issue of compensation for expropriated land can be masked by the tax "victory" of the new government; compensation might actually be made in the form of taxes lower than they would be otherwise. Action: ODACID.

d. Labor leadership. The AFL, either acting through the ORIT or independently, should be urged to send immediately a highly qualified team of labor instructors to assist anti-Communist Guatemalan labor leaders in the purging and re-organization of both urban and rural unions. These instructors should be men willing and able to cooperate with the Catholic Church in Guatemala. Action: ODACID-KUBARK.

e. Special Security Commission. A special team of qualified personnel should be dispatched to Guatemala, on request from the new government, to assist the new government in the detection and elimination of all Communists and pro-Communists from positions of influence in Guatemala. This mission should have its costs shared between the two governments. Action: ODACID to secure the request from the new Guatemalan government, KUBARK to prepare and dispatch the team.

[name not declassified]

Document 10. Graham L. Page, "K-Program," Guatemala City, June 1, 1954.[10]

SUBJECT
K-Program
Notes

1. Your letter, dated 30 May 1954, prompts me to line up once more my premises and conclusions. If you should detect any inconsistencies put that down to a situation in flux.

2. The recruitment of [name not declassified] was effected under PBSUCCESS auspices. He has become reconciled to Calligeris' role, but there are no indications of subservience. Nor has he waived his stipulation that Calligeris be kept uninformed. [name not declassified] realizes that the underlying concept of PBSUCCESS is a workable one and that—at least at the time of his recruitment—there existed no workable alternative.

3. [name not declassified]'s sole asset is a personal following among ranking Army officers. He is our channel to Colonel [initials not declassified], an officer who—according to [name not declassified]—is fully committed to our cause. He is working on SMILAX. He is turning over in his mind ways and means of defecting Colonel [initials not declassi-

[10]Source: U.S. Department of State, *Foreign Relations of the United States, 1952–1954, Guatemala* (Washington: U.S. Government Printing Office, 2003), pp. 300–301.

fied]. Regarding the latter he has provided us with a frame of reference that makes sense to me.

4. I have increasing doubts whether additional recruitments can be effected under PBSUCCESS auspices. I know for certain that in the cases of SMILAX, Colonel [initials not declassified], and Colonel [initials not declassified], the involvement of Calligeris is likely to stiffen their resolve to protect the regime at all cost. They detest Calligeris and his enterprise to them holds connotations of a "foreign invasion", calling forth a strictly emotional reaction (see SMILAX broadcast).

5. Now this is where the inconsistency comes in: I maintain—so far a priori—that the manifest threat of United States intervention is the sole lever that might conceivably unhinge the allegiance of the "Anti Calligeris faction" to the Arbenz regime. Of course, they wouldn't cotton to the prospect of landing marines any more than to that of invading revolutionaries. But—I maintain—the certain prospect of a unilateral United States move would give them ample food for thought. In an atmosphere of reflection, my message conveying to them an "Easy way out" formula, would be bound to make an impact. In effect they would be offered an opportunity to stave off intervention by the simple expedient of overthrowing the regime and usurping power for themselves. Of course, there would be some weighty political strings attached to our countenancing this shift, but nothing that could possibly be construed as an abridgment of Guatemala's sovereignty.

6. You of course realize that I am not advocating that we scrap PBSUCCESS or modify its objectives. I am discussing defection techniques and approaches. By a process of elimination I believe to have isolated the one motivating factor that may lead to significant defections in the Army High Command. If those defections come off, it may conceivably provide the spark setting off Calligeris' effort, because there will undoubtedly ensue a period of turmoil during which [lots] of things can happen. But the "crucial spark" has to be generated by heat—United States heat. . . .

Document 11. Telegram From the CIA Station in Guatemala to Operation PBSUCCESS Headquarters in Florida, June 8, 1954, 2328Z.[11]

780. 1. Govt declared suspension constitutional guarantees at 4 a.m. 8 June.

2. This most drastic step taken in recent times by WSBURNT govt.

3. Morning edition Impacto seized.

4. Declaration curfew possible.

[11]Source: U.S. Department of State, *Foreign Relations of the United States, 1952–1954, Guatemala* (Washington: U.S. Government Printing Office, 2003), p. 316.

5. Plane reported dropped leaflets over Quetzaltenango night 7 June.
6. Fear panic spreading in government circles and offices. Constant meetings govt high command with Fortuny ranking Commies attending. Fortuny allegedly successfully recommending policy appeasement toward ODYOKE. Bannister comment: Believe govt becoming desperate attempting shore up position. Suspension guarantees and subsequent activities repression may rebound govt detriment rather than benefit. Consider army key situation and believe army situation again becoming fluid. Flight ESODICS caused sensation showed army not whole heartedly supporting govt. Individual army officers griping at constant state alert and believed dissatisfaction could mount to point action if govt makes foolish moves in attempting keep afloat. Sources: ESPARTO, ESCHEL, ESPERANCE, ESCONSON-2.

Document 12. Telegram From the CIA Chief of Station in Guatemala to the Central Intelligence Agency, June 19, 1954, 2042Z.[12]

906. From JMBLUG to Ascham.

1. There is no further use moralizing about or with [name not declassified]. We have gone as far as we can with talk. [name not declassified] is what he is. He has said what he needs. We may regret or dislike or disagree with his request but if we refuse it, we are abandoning what ever potential [name not declassified] may have and we can not afford that since Calligeris assets are too small.

2. [name not declassified] knows what effect bombs will have on the Latin temperament including his own. Aerial acrobatics are not the same thing.

3. Meanwhile the govt and Commies are arresting and killing. Martinez del Rosal got a bullet in the center of his forehead. They shot Perfecto Villegas and then ran a truck over him. Kaufman had his feet carbonized before he died.

4. While this goes on, we fail to bomb. This is what William James called "atrocious harmlessness."[13]

---

[12]Source: U.S. Department of State, *Foreign Relations of the United States, 1952–1954, Guatemala* (Washington: U.S. Government Printing Office, 2003), p. 352.

[13]The philosopher William James was referring to a lecture retreat at Chatauqua, New York when he wrote, "Ouf, what a relief! Now for something primordial and savage, even though it were an Armenian massacre, to set the balance straight again. This order is too tame, this culture too second-rate, this goodness too uninspiring. This human drama without a villain or a pang; this community so refined that ice-cream soda is the utmost offering it can make to the brute animal in man; this city shimmering in the tepid lakeside sun; this atrocious harmlessness in all things." William James, *The Letters of William James* (Boston: Atlantic Monthly Press, 1920), 2: 43.

5. If we bomb, that does not guarantee [name not declassified] will act but then we will have done our utmost. And there is no danger of a boomerang. At this stage, both friend and foe respect force alone.

6. We have already missed the moment to bomb, mainly last night. We still have a chance today and tomorrow.

7. Many people have been to see me saying one bomb on palace would do the job.

8. Bomb repeat Bomb.

Document 13. Telegram From Operation PBSUCCESS Headquarters in Florida to the Mission Broadcasting Station, June 28, 1954, 0558Z.[14]

4459. For Langevin and Cadick.

1. Arbenz is out but Diaz refuses to accept Calligeris's terms. Only 500 regular army and 2500 untrained reserves in Adam.

2. Immediately inform public what has happened and that if cease and terms LINC 4362 (IN 22435) not complied with immediately SYNCARP will launch all out bombing attack and assault and destroy all those not joining anti-Communist forces. Communism must go and Diaz must agree to terms or army of liberation will continue its victorious march to Adam and fight Communists to last one.

3. Appeal to people that Communist Arbenz has resigned, first victory won and everyone should now join side of liberation movement for a greater WSBURNT. The government is obviously crumbling and further bloodshed futile. Prepare leaflets for troops in field.

4. Tell Diaz bombings to start noon 28 June and will not stop until liberation army occupies palace or Diaz agrees to terms announced.

5. Target but don't announce for noon 28 June is Matamoros again and knock out brief pilots from Langevin's staff or [name not declassified]. Put on maximum air show. Strafe all AA batteries.

6. SHERWOOD to keep steady strong appeal that anti-Communists are victorious and Diaz must agree cease fire before hundreds of innocent army men die in lost cause. Only way to stop bloodshed is to drive communism out. No other solution acceptable.

Document 14. Edwin A. Lahey, "Arbenz 'Resigns,' Behind the Scenes in Guatemala," *The Washington Post and Times Herald,* **June 29, 1954, p. 13.**

Guatemala City—The Guatemalan government of President Jacobo Arbenz fell Monday.

[14]Source: U.S. Department of State, *Foreign Relations of the United States, 1952–1954, Guatemala* (Washington: U.S. Government Printing Office, 2003), p. 393.

With it went the Soviet Union's last remaining hospitality center in the Western Hemisphere.

Arbenz didn't go quietly. In bitterness and tears he turned over the government to the military because the alternative was a hole in the head.

The military chiefs told the President that the buzzards were feasting on the bodies of innocent Guatemalans in the dusty streets of villages 100 miles north of the capital, and that the 10-day battle for Guatemala must be ended.

Invading planes under the command of Col. Carlos Castillo Armas have been raking villages in the Department of Zacapa without mercy since the weather turned in their favor a few days ago.

The Guatemalan army, loyal to the left-wing government of Arbenz at the beginning of the anti-Communist invasion led by Castillo Armas, forced Arbenz to step down in favor of Col. Carlos Enrique Diaz, chief of the armed forces.

There was some initial doubt whether Castillo Armas, who gets the credit for knocking off the Arbenz government, will achieve any place on the public payroll.

The group headed by Colonel Diaz was reported as dead set against permitting Castillo Armas to have power in the new government.

But Castillo Armas, who had been on the lam from Guatemala until the invasion began, still had some bargaining power in the P-47s that have been hammering the open villages to the north of Guatemala City. For the last two weeks the planes have spread terror in the capital city itself.

Officially, the United States had no part of this little war, but the real hero in this business was Jack Peurifoy, our Ambassador to Guatemala.

He knows the Communist pitch from his service as Ambassador in Greece, the first spot on the globe where we really built a dike against the spread of communism.

When the Arbenz government started to crack, it was to Peurifoy that the leaders turned.

Guillermo Toriello, the Foreign Minister, broke first, and asked Peurifoy to come and see him Sunday morning. Toriello, horribly aware of the mounting carnage on the northern front, told Peurifoy that he, the U.S. Ambassador, could stop the fighting in 15 minutes if he would.

The Foreign Minister asked Peurifoy if a new government under a military junta would be agreeable to him. Toriello turned violently anti-Communist during the interview, and promised Peurifoy that all the Communists in Guatemala would be sent back to Moscow.

Peurifoy, dressed in sports clothes for the golf course, dragged calmly on his cigarette holder and told Toriello that he really had no control over the situation.

He did suggest modestly, however, that a clean sweep of the officers of the Arbenz government, including Foreign Minister Toriello himself, would seem to be in order if peace were to be restored to this anguished little republic.

Colonel Diaz next summoned Peurifoy to a meeting, which lasted most of Sunday afternoon.

Defense Minister Jose Angel Sanchez and other military leaders were present at this meeting.

Diaz told Peurifoy that the streets of the villages to the north were littered with dead bodies, abandoned by the fleeing populace, and that "the buzzards are feasting on these bodies at this minute."

Then he asked Peurifoy if the United States would recognize him if he, Diaz, took over the government. Peurifoy replied that he could not make such a guarantee.

•

The Ambassador said that the only concern of the United States was the rising tide of Communist influence that had been revealed in Guatemala.

He went on to say that the differences between the United Fruit Co. and the Guatemalan government, which have figured largely as propaganda weapons of the Guatemalan Communists, were things that could be worked out easily by reasonable men.

Diaz immediately promised that he would "eliminate" the Communists and abolish the "Labor Party" in which they operate, if he took over the government.

Peurifoy said that this didn't sound sufficient to him. He thought the Communists literally must go. "The Communists will go," Diaz promised. Diaz insisted, however, that he did not want to bargain with Castillo Armas.

Peurifoy did not press this point, but repeated to Diaz that there ought to be a clean sweep over at the National Palace. Diaz agreed, and that was the beginning of the end of the so-called "Revolution of 1949" so aggressively represented by Jacobo Arbenz, and so avidly infiltrated by home-grown and imported Communists.

The Cycle of Instability and Repression

U.S. officials discovered that controlling events in Guatemala became even more difficult after the removal of Arbenz. As predicted, Castillo Armas proved a poor leader (Document 15), but his successors fared little better. The U.S. wanted a progressive modernizing dictator-

ship, but the counterrevolution drew support from Guatemala's most reactionary elements. Agency reports (Document 17) acknowledged the paradox: the government could gain stability and widen its appeal only through economic or social reforms, but the government's conservative backers would resist reform, by overthrowing the government if necessary. The only solution was increased dependence on U.S. funds and advice.

As the U.S. government went on to overthrow other Latin American governments by election-rigging, invasion, or other means in British Guiana (1964), the Dominican Republic (1965), and Chile (1973), PBSUCCESS came to be remembered as part of a pattern of American intervention (Document 16). In the 1980s, as conflict spread throughout Central America and the Reagan Administration sought public support for a covert war against Nicaragua's Sandinista government, a former CIA officer, Philip Roettinger, told of his participation in PBSUCCESS and expressed regret (Document 18).

An international Commission on Historical Clarification, part of the agreement that ended the Guatemalan civil war, concluded in 1998 that the U.S. and the Guatemalan state had created "a system of multiple exclusions" designed to protect elite privilege and U.S. security at the expense of justice for the majority of Guatemala's citizens (Document 19). In 1999, President Bill Clinton acknowledged (Document 20) that U.S. actions had been "wrong," but he declined to offer an apology.

Document 15. [Name not declassified] to Director Central Intelligence, "The Political Situation in Guatemala," June 19, 1956.[15]

1. The Communist Party of Guatemala, which was decisively defeated two years ago, seems to be well on its way toward recovery, while the present government under Castillo Armas is displaying increasingly serious weaknesses. Although there is no reason to believe that the government is likely to be overthrown by external or internal forces within the next few months, there is good ground for concern over its longer range prospects.

2. The CP of Guatemala, outlawed since the overthrow of the Arbenz regime and harassed by the security forces of the present government, has managed to reconstitute its underground organization, to set up new cells and to recruit new members "according to plan." [   ] Its exiled groups appear to be well entrenched in neighboring countries, es-

[15]Source: Declassified Documents Reference System (Farmington Hills, Mich.: Gale Group, 2004), Document # CK3100081410.

pecially in Mexico. They have been able to smuggle clandestine literature into the country. [   ] Some exiled officials of the Guatemalan CP
hold positions in international Communist organizations. For example,
the Communist labor union leaders Victor Gutierres and Manuel Pellecer are employed by the CTAL in Mexico and by the WFTU in Prague,
respectively. [   ]

3. Both in the underground inside the country and among the exiles
abroad, the Communists, though a minority appear to play a key role.
As a result of better organization, stricter discipline and foreign support,
they are able to continue the function of "leading minority" which they
exercised so effectively during the Arbenz regime. There have been reports that "The Communists are now in control. They occupy more and
more public posts." [   ] Or "The Communist exiles are in day-to-day
contact with covert associates within the present government." [   ]
These reports are probably biased and exaggerated, but they indicate
that at least the "negative prestige" of the Communist Party is again
rising among its enemies.

4. Whatever the actual strength of the Guatemalan CP may be, it
would not cause us serious concern if we could rely on the basic stability of the Castillo Armas regime. Its security forces seem to be alert
against the Communist underground, as the latter is forced to admit.
[   ] The government is reported to have undertaken considerable
anti-Communist propaganda (of. Joint Weeka 120, U.S. Embassy Despatch 683). Nevertheless the overall political, and social position of the
Government is such as to cast doubts on its ability to maintain a firm
check on the forces of subversion.

5. When Castillo Armas overthrew the Arbenz regime, he was welcomed and supported by most of the non-communist elements in the
country. Today, however, many of Castillo's supporters appear either to
have turned against him or to have withdrawn into apathetic indifference. His support among the professional officers of the Army appears
to have been weakened, and some of the officers in key positions are reported to have joined the opposition. His political party won the elections to the Constituent Assembly only through the use of concentrated
government pressure and in the face of popular lack of interest. Several
anti-Communist sources have accused his government of widespread
corruption in high places and of general inefficiency. [   ]

6. The mass of the population of Guatemala consists of poor peasants, including laborers, farm and industrial workers or artisans. These
were the two sources of Communist strength under the Arbenz regime.
Castillo Armas removed the Communists from the leading positions in
farmers' and labor unions and corrected certain excesses of the Com-

munist-sponsored agrarian reforms, but he has failed thus far to offer peasants and workers a constructive alternative. Peasant labor unions have been restricted to farms employing more than 500 hands leaving the great majority without any representation. [   ] Labor dissatisfaction with the Castillo Armas regime came into the open on May day. "The workers, in an apparently well-planned maneuver, booed the scheduled speakers, some of them government officials, off the platform and cheered five substitutes, some of them leaders under the regime of Arbenz. These speakers took over the meeting and vigorously attacked the Government's labor policies." (NEW YORK TIMES, 6 May 1956, "Unrest of Labor Stirs Guatemala").

7. In the opinion of SRS, steps should be taken immediately to cope with the adverse trends which are beginning to appear in Guatemala. It goes without saying that the downfall of the Castillo Armas regime would be a major blow to US prestige and a powerful propaganda theme for International Communist. We suggest that measures to strengthen the present government should not be limited to economic aid, but should provide guidance toward greater political stability, broader popular support, increased administrative efficiency and progressive solutions of the social and economic problems of the country.

[name not declassified]
Chief, MRS/DDI

Document 16. Juan José Arévalo, *The Shark and the Sardines*. New York: Lyle Stuart, 1961.[16]

The United States became great while progress in Latin America was brought to a halt. And when anything or anyone tried to interfere with the bankers or the companies, use was made of the Marines. Panama, 1903. Nicaragua, 1909. Mexico and Haiti, 1914. Santo Domingo, 1916. Along with the military apparatus, a new system of local "revolutions" was manipulated—financed by the White House or by Wall Street—which were now the same. This procedure continued right up to the international scandal of the assault on Guatemala in 1954, an assault directed by Mr. Foster Dulles, with the O.K. of Mr. Eisenhower who was your president at that time.

North American friends, this is history, true history, the briefest possible sketch of history. . . . Because of my own nationality, I have chosen to illustrate my fable with a presentation of this particular historical example. But the past and the present of our unfortunate Latin America are full of examples like Nicaragua, other assaults leading either to a

---

[16]Translated by June Cobb and Dr. Raul Osegueda, pp. 11, 73–74.

loan or a brotherly treaty, other fraternal treaties or loans leading to assaults. And when this is not the case, simple and awkward invasions or disembarkations or aerial landings. . . .

The Shark plays with the sardine before swallowing her down. The Shark makes use of Law and "believes" in Law before making a joke of Law. He stimulates universal tragedies, human dramas, ideologic comedies to end in a vulgar farce of bankers, loan-makers, and marines who want to glut themselves in somebody else's house. And the Shark does this with the sardines and with the law, just "because." Just because he is a Shark.

Document 17. Central Intelligence Agency, "Prospects for Stability in Guatemala," National Intelligence Estimate no. 82-66, June 24, 1966.[17]

THE PROBLEM

To estimate the situation in Guatemala and the prospects for stability over the next year or two.

CONCLUSIONS

A. The staying power of the new, moderate-left government of Mendez will depend primarily on its relationship with the Guatemalan military. The military leaders, recalling the Communist surge to power in the early 1950s, may tend to overreact to any administration appointments or policy moves which they regard as favorable to the far left. Mendez, a proud and somewhat sensitive man, is likely to become restive over such circumscription of his powers.

B. In our view, his chances of maintaining himself in power through 1966 are good. During this period he will have the opportunity to improve his ties with military leaders and the economic elite, but probably this would require the sacrifice of some of the reform measures he favors. The Communist guerrilla bands, although out capable of taking power, are strong enough to carry out terrorist campaigns that could keep the government under heavy pressure from the military. These campaigns might be used to justify military intervention if the right and the military leadership became dissatisfied with Mendez' conduct of his administration.

C. In view of the economic, social and political problems which will confront Mendez beyond 1966, we are not confident that he will survive in office through the next two years. His administration's chances for accomplishing much, either in reform or in significant economic growth and development, will depend heavily upon whether it accepts

[17]Source: Declassified Documents Reference System, Farmington Hills, Mich.: Gale Group, 2004, Document # CK3100153247.

substantial outside assistance with its attendant obligations and uses it effectively

DISCUSSION

I. BACKGROUND

1. Guatemala has had little experience with representative government, and the military establishment continues to be the most important political factor. Until World War II, the country was little affected by the political and social currents of the twentieth century. The reform-minded government which came to power in 1944, after a long period of dictatorial rule, undertook a far-reaching program of change aimed at eradicating the remnants of the feudal past. But the Guatemalan Communists gained strong influence in the Arevalo administration (1945–1951) and, under President Arbenz (1951–1954), they became the controlling force in the government.

2. During these years the political predominance of large landowners and merchants, in alliance with the military, was undercut, but their economic power was not much reduced. Though the Communists had control of organized labor, their efforts to build strength throughout the countryside were not successful. In 1954 when anti-Communist Guatemalans launched an invasion from neighboring Honduras, neither peasants nor workers showed much inclination to flight for the Arbenz regime. The military chiefs refused to commit troops against the invaders and Arbenz was quickly deposed. The leader of the victors, Col. Carlos Castillo Armas, proceeded to conduct a purge of the Communists and their associates in which the country's labor and small-landowner organizations were almost completely destroyed. Thus the way was opened for the right to regain its former political predominance; it has not done so largely because of personal rivalries among rightist leaders, and the failure of any rightist leader to develop a popular and effective program.

3. The military establishment, however, has clearly indicated that it will not permit a recurrence of the 1944–1954 pattern of Communist infiltration. In March 1963, the Minister of National Defense, Col. Enrique Peralta, led a coup which removed President Ydigoras for his equivocal handing of former President Arevalo's candidacy in the scheduled 1963 elections. The military leaders made clear their intention of retaining direct control of the caretaker government by decreeing that the Minister of National Defense would also serve as Chief of Government.

4. Guatemala remains underdeveloped. Although new exports have been developed, including some manufactured products for the Central American Common Market, the economy remains vulnerable to down-

swings in world commodity price for coffee and cotton, its principal exports. The reaction to the Arevalo-Arbenz period has been characterized by a resistance to change that has impeded movement toward a more modern society. About half the population, which at present totals some 4,500,000, continues to follow traditional Indian ways in largely self-contained communities that participate only marginally, if at all, in national economic and political life. . . .

27. Mendez' survival in office over the longer run will depend on his ability to hold to a narrow and delicate course. On the one hand, he is keenly aware of Guatemala's need for modernization of its institutions and for numerous reforms, political, social, and economic. To retain the support of those who elected him will require initiatives and some progress on his part on these fundamental matters. But unless the measures he puts forward are carefully tailored, cautiously presented, and tactfully implemented, any one of them may weaken his administration's political position by dangerously offending the military, or its economic position by shaking the confidence of the private sector. Allaying the apprehensions of the sharply differing interest groups will not be easy on any one proposal or measure of major importance; doing the same successfully over time on a whole series of measures will be difficult in the extreme.

28. Economic problems will present a similar dilemma. World market conditions for coffee and cotton will almost certainly inhibit any significant improvement in Guatemala's export earnings. At the same time, domestic credit probably will continue to be restricted, and direct import controls may be imposed, in order to limit foreign trade imbalances and to conserve foreign exchange reserves. The Mendez government would probably like to expand public investment in infrastructure and in various socially oriented programs. But the present regressive tax system is not suited to provide the necessary funds, and it would be necessary to seek higher taxes on personal incomes, property, and exports, which at present yield only about one-sixth of total tax revenues. Such measures would strike directly at the economic position of powerful agricultural and commercial interests in a fashion to jeopardize Mendez' continuance in office. The outlook for the economy, then, is for moderate growth with GNP increasing, at best, four or five percent annually in 1967 and 1968.

29. Maintaining a positive relationship with the Guatemalan military has always been difficult for civilian political figures. Moreover, certain of Mendez' characteristics can be expected to add to the difficulty. He is a proud and sensitive man who may become restive about sharing his presidential powers de facto with the military leaders. His

own political tendencies are liberal and rather legalistic, and there are figures in the military, and the economic elite as well, so conditioned by the Communist surge to power in the early 1950's that they may over-react to an appointment or a policy move by the administration which they interpret as favorable to the far left. However, Mendez has shown good judgment and flexibility in dealing with the problems which he has thus far confronted.

30. Considering all these difficulties we are not confident that Mendez will survive in office through the next two years. His chances of holding on to power would be maximized by a realignment of political forces from which the PR emerged as a centrist movement with a moderate reform program which the military and enlightened right would tolerate. Even under these circumstances his administration's chances for accomplishing much on either reform or significant economic growth and the development will depend heavily upon whether it accepts substantial outside assistance with its attendant obligations and uses it effectively. . . .

Document 18. Philip C. Roettinger, "The Company, Then and Now," 1986.[18]

It is night and we are encamped in a remote area. A ragtag group rests around a fire. They are rebels, trading war stories and laughingly planning what they will do when they take over the capital. Uninterested in social reforms and untouched by ideological conviction, they haven't heard the President of the United States describe their mission as "preventing the establishment of a communist beachhead in the Western Hemisphere." They just want to overthrow the government. . . .

As a CIA case officer, I trained Guatemalan exiles in Honduras to invade their country and oust their democratically elected president, Jacobo Arbenz. Our plotting enjoyed great secrecy until its final stages, when rumors prompted the Organization of American States to dispatch a delegation to Honduras to investigate our activities. Forewarned by a cable from Miami, we quickly broke camp and retreated to Nicaragua to avoid exposure. It was there, in a bar in a Managua hotel, that I received the news: Arbenz was out. Anastazio Somoza, then the chief of the Nicaraguan armed forces, joined us to drink and celebrate.

I now think my involvement in the overthrow of Arbenz was a terrible mistake. The reasons the Eisenhower administration gave were false; the consequences were disastrous.

In March 1954, three months before we toppled Arbenz and installed

---

[18]*The Progressive*, July 1986, p. 50.

Colonel Carlos Castillo Armas, our handpicked "liberator," CIA director Allen Dulles convened his Guatemalan operatives at Opa Locka Ma-
rine Air Base in Miami for a pep talk. Seated in front of us, resplendent
in a tweed sport coat and puffing his pipe, Dulles exhorted us to do our
jobs well and told us the same lie Ronald Reagan is telling the American
people today: The purpose of U.S. support for the rebels is to stop the
spread of communism.

But communism was not the threat we were fighting. The threat was
land reform. Fulfilling a pledge to transform Guatemala into a "modern
capitalist state," Arbenz had taken over some unused land belonging to
the United Fruit Company. The Boston-based company, which considered its rights superior to those of Guatemalans, retaliated with a publicity campaign to paint Guatemala red. . . .

"Operation Success" was a failure. The new regime burned books. It
disfranchised three-fourths of Guatemala's people. It dismantled social
and economic reforms such as land redistribution, social security, and
trade-union rights. Our overthrow began thirty-one years of repressive
military rule and the deaths of more than 100,000 Guatemalans. . . .

The coup I helped to engineer in 1954 inaugurated an unprecedented
era of intransigent military rule in Central America. Generals and colonels acted with impunity to wipe out dissent and amass wealth for
themselves and their cronies. The 1979 overthrow of Nicaraguan dictator Somoza shook the status quo, and now that nation thwarts the will
of the U.S. government by governing with the support of most of its
people.

I am seventy years old now. I have lived and worked in Latin America for more than thirty years. Done with skullduggery, I devote my
time to painting the region's beautiful scenery. It is painful to look on as
my Government repeats the mistake in which it engaged me thirty-two
years ago. I have grown up. I only wish my government would do the
same.

Document 19. Comisión para el Esclarecimiento Histórico, *Guatemala: Memory of Silence: Report of the Commission for Historical Clarification* (Guatemala City: CEH, 1998).

Conclusions

    I. The tragedy of the armed confrontation

    1. With the outbreak of the internal armed confrontation in 1962,
Guatemala entered a tragic and devastating stage of its history, with
enormous human, material and moral cost. In the documentation of
human rights violations and acts of violence connected with the armed
confrontation, the Commission for Historical Clarification (CEH) regis-

tered a total of 42,275 victims, including men, women, and children. Of these, 23,671 were victims of arbitrary execution and 6,159 were victims of forced disappearance. Eighty-three percent of fully-identified victims were Mayan and seventeen percent were Ladino.

2. Combining this data with the results of other studies of political violence in Guatemala, the CEH estimates that the number of persons killed or disappeared as a result of the fratricidal confrontation reached a total of over 200,000.

Historical roots of the armed confrontation

3. The Commission for Historical Clarification (CEH) concludes that the structure and nature of economic, cultural, and social relations in Guatemala are marked by profound exclusion, antagonism, and conflict—a reflection of its colonial history. The proclamation of independence in 1821, an event prompted by the country's elite, saw the creation of an authoritarian State which excluded the majority of the population, was racist in its precepts and practices, and served to protect the economic interests of the privileged minority. The evidence for this, throughout Guatemala's history, but particularly so during the armed confrontation, lies in the fact that the violence was fundamentally directed by the State against the excluded, the poor and above all, the Mayan people, as well as against those who fought for justice and greater social equality.

4. The anti-democratic nature of the Guatemalan political tradition has its roots in an economic structure, which is marked by the concentration of productive wealth in the hands of a minority. This established the foundations of a system of multiple exclusions, including elements of racism, which is, in turn, the most profound manifestation of a violent and dehumanising social system. The state gradually evolved as an instrument for the protection of this structure, guaranteeing the continuation of exclusion and injustice.

5. The absence of an effective state policy, with the exception of the period from 1944 to 1954, accentuated this historical dynamic of exclusion. In many cases, more recent state policy has produced inequality, or, at the very least, endemic institutional weaknesses have accentuated it. Proof of this can be seen in the fact that during the last twenty years of Guatemala's most rapid economic growth (1960–1980), state social spending and taxation were the lowest in Central America.

6. Due to its exclusionary nature, the State was incapable of achieving social consensus around a national project able to unite the whole population. Concomitantly, it abandoned its role as mediator between divergent social and economic interests, thus creating a gulf which made direct confrontation between them more likely. . . .

8. Thus a vicious circle was created in which social injustice led to protest and subsequently political instability, to which there were always only two responses: repression or military coups. Faced with movements proposing economic, political, social, or cultural change, the State increasingly resorted to violence and terror in order to maintain social control. Political violence was thus a direct expression of structural violence. . . .

The closing of political spaces

11. After the overthrow of the government of Colonel Jacobo Arbenz in 1954, there was a rapid reduction of the opportunity for political expression. Inspired by fundamentalist anti-communism, new legislation outlawed the extensive and diverse social movement and consolidated the restrictive and exclusionary nature of the political system. These restrictions on political participation were agreed to by the country's real powers and activated by the period's civil and political forces. In itself, this process constitutes one of the most overwhelming pieces of evidence for the close relationship between the military, the economic powers, and the political parties that emerged in 1954. From 1963 onwards, in addition to the legal restrictions, growing state repression against its real or suspected opponents was another decisive factor in the closing of political options in Guatemala. . . .

The cold war, the National Security doctrine and the role of the United States

13. The CEH recognises that the movement of Guatemala toward polarization, militarization and civil war was not just the result of national history. The cold war also played an important role. Whilst anti-communism, promoted by the United States within the framework of its foreign policy, received firm support from right-wing political parties and from various other powerful actors in Guatemala, the United States demonstrated that it was willing to provide support for strong military regimes in its strategic backyard. In the case of Guatemala, military assistance was directed toward reinforcing the national intelligence apparatus and for training the officer corps in counterinsurgency techniques, key factors which had significant bearing on human rights violations during the armed confrontation.

14. Anti-communism and the National Security Doctrine (DSN) formed part of the anti-Soviet strategy of the United States in Latin America. In Guatemala, these were first expressed as anti-reformist, then anti-democratic policies, culminating in criminal counterinsurgency. The National Security Doctrine fell on fertile ground in Guatemala, where anti-communist thinking had already taken root and from the 1930s, had merged with the defense of religion, tradition and con-

servative values, all of which were allegedly threatened by the world-wide expansion of atheistic communism. Until the 1950s, these views were strongly supported by the Catholic Church, which qualified as communist any position that contradicted its philosophy, thus contributing even further to division and confusion in Guatemalan society. . . .

Document 20. William J. Clinton, "Remarks in a Roundtable Discussion on Peace Efforts," March 10, 1999, Guatemala City.[19]

Thank you very much, Mr. President. First let me say how much I appreciate this opportunity that has been provided for me to meet with citizens of your country to hear about the progress of the peace process and the challenges ahead. Because of the involvement of the United States, I think it is imperative, as we begin, for me just to say a few words about the report of the Historical Clarification Commission.

The commission's work and the support it has received from the government shows how far Guatemala has traveled in overcoming that painful period. I have profound respect for the victims and the families who had courage to testify and for the courage of a nation fo coming to terms with the past and moving forward.

For the United States, it is important that I state clearly that support for military forces or intelligence units which engage in violent and widespread repression of the kind described in the report was wrong, and the United States must not repeat that mistake. We must and we will, instead, continue to support the peace and reconciliation process in Guatemala. As many of you know, we provided $1½ million in support of the commission. We declassified over 4,000 documents at the commission's request. Now we will encourage the translation of the report into indigenous languages and its wide dissemination. Consistent with the commission's recommendations, we also will continue our support of development programs in those communities which suffered most from violence and repression. This year, we plan to provide an additional $25 million to support the peace accords through aid to the justice sector, to education, to literary training, to the generation of income, and to citizen participation in government.

You have come a long way, as President Arzu just said, in forging a consensus in support of democracy and human rights and in finding a way to discuss your differences openly and peaceably. I applaud the difficult but essential effort you have undertaken.

Beyond the commission issues, I would also hope to discuss other

[19]Source: United States, *Public Papers of the Presidents of the United States, William J. Clinton, 1999* (Washington: U.S. Government Printing Office, 2000), 1: 340.

matters critical to peace and to development and reconciliation, including economic liberalization, market-opening measures, increased trade and investment, all of which are crucial to the overall well-being of the people of Guatemala. Now that you have chosen democracy and peace, it is imperative that the United States be a good partner in making sure that it works for all your people.

Document 21. Jim Lobe, "Guatemala: U.S. Resumes Military Aid After Hiatus Over Rights," March 28, 2005, Inter Press Service, (c) 2005 Global Information Network

WASHINGTON, Mar. 25, 2005 (IPS/GIN)—The restoration of U.S. military aid to Guatemala 15 years after it was suspended for human rights abuses was assailed late Thursday by several rights groups, who said the move was premature.

On a visit to the Guatemalan capital earlier in the day, U.S. Defense Secretary Donald Rumsfeld announced that the George W. Bush administration was releasing 3.2 million dollars in aid to reward the government of President Oscar Berger for overhauling the armed forces whose human rights record in the 1980s was considered the worst in the Americas.

"I've been impressed by the reforms that have been undertaken in the armed forces," Rumsfeld told reporters. "I know it is a difficult thing to do, but it's been done with professionalism and transparency."

But rights groups did not agree with his assessment, although they did give Berger credit for making efforts in the right direction.

"Despite its commitment to ending impunity and combating clandestine groups, the Berger administration has demonstrated a lack of political will and ability to make progress in establishing an effective mechanism to investigate and dismantle clandestine groups," according to a joint statement by the Washington Office on Latin America (WOLA), the Robert F. Kennedy Memorial Centre for Human Rights, and other groups.

It noted that these clandestine groups or illegal armed groups, which were supposed to have been dismantled after the signing of the 1996 peace accords, are believed to have ties to Guatemala's military intelligence, which is also widely believed to have become increasingly active in drug trafficking and organized crime.

The rights groups, which also included the Network in Solidarity with the People of Guatemala (NISGUA) and the Guatemala Human Rights Commission, added that at least 26 human rights defenders have been threatened or attacked, presumably by or at the instigation of the clandestine groups, so far this year after a reported 122 attacks in 2004.

Afterword

Afterword

The Culture of Fear

Guatemala has many faces. There is the smiling face of the Indian in costume serving guests in the gentle atmosphere of hotels and restaurants; there is the cultivated upper class, at home in the United States, speaking excellent English, many as white as Anglo-Saxons; there is the middle class, with its dreams of consumer goods and its admiration for all things American. And there is the sick, undernourished lower class.

Fear and hatred, not a sense of common purpose, unite the ten million Guatemalans. Through the cacophony of the many Guatemalan cultures—the Indian and the Ladino, the elite few and the miserable many, the town dweller and the peasant, the civilian and the military—cuts one keynote: the culture of fear. Violence, torture, and death are the final arbiters of Guatemalan society, the gods that determine behavior. The culture of fear is the taproot of Guatemalan history. It is not attributable to one particular dictatorship, one man, or one family. It hails from the long night that began with the Spanish conquest, a conquest that is, for the Indians, a trauma from which they have not yet recovered. The lament of the Cakchiquels is as true today as it was four centuries ago, when they first bowed under the Spaniard's lash:

> Little by little, heavy shadows
> And black night enveloped
> Our fathers and grandfathers
> And us also, oh, my sons . . .
> All of us were thus.
> We were born to die.[1]

The Guatemalan revolution—Jacobo Arbenz above all, with his Communist friends—challenged this culture of fear. In eighteen months, from January 1953 to June 1954, 500,000 people (one-sixth of Guatemala's population) received the land they desperately needed. For the first time in the history of Guatemala, the Indians were offered land rather than being robbed of it. The culture of fear loosened its grip over the great masses of the Guatemalan people. In a not unreachable future, it might have faded away, a distant nightmare.

The United States, however, did not approve of Arbenz. Through intense psychological warfare, it convinced Guatemala's military officers that if they did not get rid of Arbenz, the United States would—and then make them pay for their loyalty to the Communist. In fear, the officers betrayed their president.

Arbenz was overthrown, the Communists were persecuted, the army was purged, and the peasants were thrown off the land they had just received. As the culture of fear reestablished its grip over the great many, the elite few strengthened their resolve: never had they felt as threatened as under Arbenz; never had they lost land to the Indians; never would it happen again.

The upper class has ruled Guatemala since the overthrow of Arbenz in partnership with the military. After Castillo Armas's assassination in 1957, Ydígoras Fuentes, whom the CIA had rejected as leader of the exile band against Arbenz, became president. In 1963, the army and the upper class worried (mistakenly) that he would allow free elections to choose his successor, and free elections, they

[1]From the sixteenth-century chronicle *The Annals of the Cakchiquels*, quoted in
ll, "Surviving Conquest: The Maya of Guatemala in Historical Perspec-
America Research Review 23 (1988): 25. On the culture of fear see
es, *Politics and Culture in Guatemala* (Ann Arbor: Center for Political
ersity of Michigan, 1988).

knew, would be won by Juan José Arévalo, the man who had paved the way for Arbenz's reforms. A coup was launched and a military government was installed; then, in 1966, relatively free elections were won by Julio César Méndez Montenegro of the centrist Partido Revolucionario, the furthest left of the parties allowed to participate. He was to be the last civilian president for sixteen years. Between 1970, when his term ended, and 1982, three generals succeeded one another every four years, each duly elected amidst massive fraud and widespread intimidation. In 1982 another military coup ushered in direct military rule for three years, when an election, this one without fraud, reestablished a line of civilian presidents that continues to this day.

The Guatemalan upper class has changed. It has branched out of landholding into industry, commerce, and banking. Its children now go to the United States, not Europe, to study, and they major in business and economics, not in the social sciences, art, or literature. Many of the elite are competent businessmen, as familiar with the latest technology as they are with the latest fads in New York and Paris. Many upper-class families receive the *New York Times* daily; those who have not quite arrived read only the Sunday edition.

There is one way, however, in which this elite has not changed: it still fiercely opposes social reform. The upper class in other Latin American countries has defused social tensions by making some concessions, by forgoing some privileges. Not in Guatemala. There, violence alone has maintained the status quo. Journalists, professors, priests, men and women of the political center have lost their lives to the culture of fear. They have died alongside members of rural cooperatives, grassroots organizers, labor leaders, left-wing students, and armed guerrillas. "Tortures and murders are part of a deliberate and long-standing program of the Guatemalan Government," Amnesty International stated in 1981.[2] Tortures and murder are the cement of Guatemalan society. Waves of wholesale violence are followed by periods of moderate, selective repression. The intensity of the violence has been a function of the intensity of the fear

---

[2]Amnesty International, *Guatemala: A Government Program of Political Murder* (London, 1981), p. 3.

felt by the upper class and the military, not the whims of the man in the presidential palace. Thus President Méndez Montenegro, a well-respected moderate, oversaw an unprecedented wave of violence. After winning election in 1966, this "proud and sensitive man," as U.S. intelligence described him, was allowed to assume the presidency only after signing a statement that gave the army "carte blanche in the field of internal security."[3] Thus he stood by as the military descended into what the CIA gently called "its extralegal terror campaign"—that is, a wave of "kidnappings, torture, and summary executions"[4] of thousands of peasants in order to eliminate the handful of guerrillas. "The assumption of power by Mendez will represent an impressive victory for democracy in this hemisphere," Lyndon Johnson's National Security Adviser wrote shortly after the Guatemalan election. "The formula of civilian, reform-minded presidents with the political knack for reaching practical working relationships with the military and other conservative elements is one which I hope will continue to prosper in this hemisphere."[5] In Guatemala, the formula meant slaughter.

It was only under Méndez Montenegro's successor, General Carlos Arana, that Guatemala returned to normal, i.e. selective murder. The guerrillas had been crushed, and extreme measures were no longer necessary. The generals felt so confident, in fact, that when the incoming Carter administration mildly criticized their human rights record, they proudly renounced U.S. military aid.

---

[3]National Intelligence Estimate, "Prospects for Stability in Guatemala," June 24, 1966, p. 9, National Security File, Box 9, Lyndon B. Johnson Library (hereafter LBJL); Thomas Hughes (Director of the Office of Intelligence and Research of the U.S. Department of State [hereafter INR]) to SecState, "Guatemala: A Counter-Insurgency Running Wild?" Oct. 23, 1967, p. 1, National Security File, Country File [hereafter NSFCF]: Guatemala, Box 54, LBJL. For the text of the secret agreement signed by Méndez Montenegro on May 4, 1966, see *La Hora* of Nov. 26 and 27, 1973.

[4]CIA, Directorate of Intelligence, "The Communist Insurgency Movement in Guatemala," Sept. 20, 1968, p. 4, NSFCF: Guatemala, Box 54, LBJL; Hughes (INR Director) to SecState, "Guatemala: A Counter-Insurgency Running Wild?" Oct. 23, 1967, p. 1, *ibid.*

[5]W. W. Rostow, Memorandum for the President, Apr. 5, 1966, NSFCF: Guatemala, Box 54, LBJL.

The tranquillity that seduced the Guatemalan generals was deceptive. New guerrilla groups were organizing, and unlike their fallen comrades they were developing a peasant base. By the late 1970's the war had resumed in earnest, and this time the Indians joined the guerrillas.

While the army had fought a few hundred guerrillas in the 1960's, it faced several thousand in the early 1980's; while the guerrillas had been largely isolated in the 1960's, they had widespread support in the early 1980's, particularly among the Indians in the highlands. And so the army resorted again to heroic methods. A whirlwind of death swirled through the Indian highlands of Guatemala. The mountains and the valleys were littered with corpses of men, women, infants. Rape was a banal event, charred villages a fact of life.

These atrocities were the work of the demented, but the demented had their logic: the army was responding to Mao Tse-tung's dictum, "The guerrillas must swim among the population as the fish in the water." How could the army differentiate the tame and the rebellious among the Indians in the highlands? "The guerrillas," an army officer wrote, "have penetrated entire populations which now support them unconditionally."[6] All that the army knew was that there were guerrillas in the highlands, that the Indians were rising in revolt, and that selective repression no longer cowed them. Only the massacre of whole communities could drain the river in which the fish swam.

Terror was effective. As the guerrillas retreated, tens of thousands of Indians died.[7] Others, possibly 200,000, escaped to Mexico. Still more fled deeper into the mountains. As the country was swept up in unspeakable horrors, the Reagan administration comforted the murderers. Thus in 1981, the State Department attributed most of the violence to "self-appointed vigilantes" beyond the government's control,

[6]César Augusto Ruiz Morales, "Por qué solos?" *Revista Militar* (Guatemala City), Sept.–Dec. 1981, p. 89.

[7]Excesses were committed by the guerrillas, but the voluminous evidence from Amnesty International, Americas Watch, and other human rights organizations, as well as from observers, is conclusive: the immense majority of the killings were committed by the Guatemalan army.

and Deputy Assistant Secretary of State Stephen Bosworth blamed leftists for the violence and discerned "positive developments" in security forces "taking care to protect innocent bystanders."[8] In March 1982, as the slaughter reached unprecedented levels under General Efraín Ríos Montt, Reagan told the world that the general had gotten a "bum rap" on human rights.[9] Fourteen years later, the U.S. government set the record straight, belatedly and without fanfare. "In the late 1970's and early 1980's," the Intelligence Oversight Board stated, "the Guatemalan army . . . waged a ruthless scorched-earth campaign against the Communist guerrillas as well as noncombatants. In the course of this campaign . . . more than 100,000 Guatemalans died."[10]

The war against the guerrillas helped the army forget its shame. In June 1954, it had betrayed President Arbenz, and, fearing America's wrath, it had surrendered to the parody of an invasion staged by Castillo Armas. The Guatemalan officers returned from the "front" after their capitulation "despondent, and with a terrible sense of defeat."[11] They, who had proudly supported the nationalism of the revolutionary years, had behaved at the decisive moment like officers of a banana republic. Now they were subjected to the contempt of those whom they had betrayed, of those who had benefited from their betrayal, and of U.S. officials. On August 1, 1954, military troops on parade were jeered by the masses and by the upper class, by the defeated and by the victors alike, seen as traitors by the former and as cowards by the latter. It was a moment the Guatemalan officers never forgot. Henceforth, they vowed, they might be the object of hatred, they might be cursed, but never again would

---

[8]Quotations from United States Department of State, *Country Reports on Human Rights Practices for 1981* (Washington DC: GPO, 1982), p. 442, and from prepared statement of Stephen Bosworth before the Subcommittees on Human Rights and International Organizations and on Inter-American Affairs, House Committee on Foreign Affairs, July 30, 1981 (Washington DC: GPO, 1981), p. 6.

[9]*New York Times* (hereafter *NYT*), Dec. 5, 1982, p. 1.

[10]Intelligence Oversight Board, "Report on the Guatemala Review," June 28, 1996, p. 18.

[11]Interview with Colonel Oscar Mendoza, Guatemala City, Sept. 6, 1982. Mendoza was appointed army chief of staff in early July 1954. "Therefore," as he said, "I saw all this very closely."

they be the object of ridicule, never again would they be jeered. And they would never forgive the United States for forcing this humiliation on them.[12]

The guerrillas helped them recover their pride. In the late 1960's, as the army crushed the fledgling guerrilla movement, the officers boasted, "We won in Guatemala while the United States was losing in Vietnam." And in the early 1980's they defeated a far stronger guerrilla movement.[13]

As the pride of the Guatemalan officers grew, so too did their power. Until 1944, they had been the instrument of the dictators. After the overthrow of Arbenz, they ruled the country as the junior partner of the upper class, but the marriage underwent a subtle transformation in the late 1960's as the army battled the guerrillas. "The army, which had entered the partnership as the bride, gradually grew whiskers and developed strong muscles."[14] In 1966, as Méndez Montenegro assumed the presidency, civilian death squads operated independently of the military, but by 1970, when he stepped down, the machinery of murder was concentrated in the hands of the military, and civilian terrorist groups acted only under its orders.[15] Henceforth the army encroached upon the political and economic preserves of the upper class and even dared to kill its members if they challenged its primacy. The military had become, the CIA declared, "the final arbiters of political power in Guatemala."[16]

The army developed an institutional pride and a mystique that set it sharply apart from its counterparts in Honduras and El Salvador. The Guatemalan officers were proud to be members of an army that had

[12]See Gleijeses, *Politics and Culture*, p. 20.

[13]Interview with Colonel Héctor Rosales, Guatemala City, Jan. 10, 1985.

[14]Personal interview, Guatemala City, Jan. 6, 1985.

[15]CIA, Directorate of Intelligence, "Guatemala—A Current Appraisal," Oct. 8, 1966, NSFCF: Guatemala, Box 54, LBJL; Hughes (INR Director) to SecState, "Guatemala: A Counter-Insurgency Running Wild?" Oct. 23, 1967, *ibid.*; CIA, Directorate of Intelligence, "The Military and the Right in Guatemala," Nov. 8, 1968, *ibid.*; Amnesty International, *Guatemala: A Government Program of Political Murder* (London, 1981).

[16]CIA, Directorate of Intelligence, "Guatemala—A Current Appraisal," Oct. 8, 1966, p. 5, NSFCF: Guatemala, Box 54, LBJL.

fought alone and defeated the Communist hordes. They were proud to be above the law: as the Intelligence Oversight Board pointed out, the army "acted with total impunity."[17] They were proud of the fear they inspired. "The army is untouchable," a Guatemalan priest lamented. "It is mightier than God. It is everywhere, it sees everything, it knows everything."[18] This pride, this mystique, became as integral to the world of the Guatemalan military as was greed. Officers received subsidized housing and consumer goods, and soft loans; as they rose through the ranks, the perks and opportunities for graft increased. In exchange, they defended the motherland against the enemy within, the Communists, the subversives. Their motherland was Guatemala, but it was also, above all, the army, their one refuge in a world in which all civilians were potential enemies. As they waded through the blood of their compatriots, as they burned and slaughtered, their alienation grew. They grew more powerful, more alone, more hated, more feared, and more fearful of the revenge that might some day overwhelm them.

Since 1986 Guatemala has been, officially, a democracy. Vinicio Cerezo, a Christian Democrat, began his presidency in 1986 amid high hopes, but left four years later in humiliation. His term had been characterized by an orgy of corruption, the mishandling of the economy, and the absence of social reform. It would be unfair, however, to lay all the blame, or even most of it, at Cerezo's door. Guatemala was only, to borrow a line from the CIA, a "guided democracy."[19] Cerezo and his party won at the polls, but they were only the props of the upper class and the army.

How could it have been otherwise? In the culture of fear, only emasculated political parties can exist, just as only stunted vegetation can survive in the tundra. Guatemala had seen the tentative beginnings of

[17]Intelligence Oversight Board, "Report on the Guatemala Review," June 28, 1996, p. 19.

[18]Interview with a Guatemalan priest, Guatemala City, Mar. 20, 1986.

[19]CIA, Office of Current Intelligence, "Guatemalan Communists Take Hard Line as Insurgency Continues," Aug. 6, 1965, p. 8, NSFCF: Guatemala, Box 54, LBJL.

a multiparty system only during the 1944–54 revolution. The over-throw of Arbenz slammed closed the democratic opening. Over the next three decades, the penalty for a troublesome politician was death. Gua-temala, a machista society, increasingly lacked civilian caudillos: civil-ian leaders who challenged the system were killed, or went into exile, or joined the guerrillas. Those politicians who survived accepted the rules that the Guatemalan army determined: competence was acceptable; honesty, suspect; social justice and political democracy, subversive. As the honest and those committed to political democracy and social re-form withdrew from the field, the arena was left to the opportunist, the servile, and the corrupt.

Had there been no guerrillas, there would have been far less blood-shed. Had they not defied the regime, Guatemala would have experi-enced only a fraction of the pain it has known. Does this mean, there-fore, that the guerrillas bear responsibility for the slaughter and the hor-rors perpetrated by the army?

Do the oppressed have the right to fight back? It may be easier to come to grips with this question if one ranges beyond the confines of Guatemala, where left-wing guerrillas fought against a government supported by the United States, and consider also an armed insurrection that evoked widespread sympathy and respect in the United States: the anti-Communist revolt in Hungary in 1956. There is no question that if the Hungarians had not rebelled, the Soviet troops would not have fought or killed. Are the Hungarian rebels responsible, then, for Soviet repression? Do they bear responsibility for the killings committed by the Soviet troops?

Neither in Hungary nor in Guatemala was there any possibility that the change the rebels so desperately sought could have been achieved through peaceful means. The Soviet Union was not going to grant Hun-gary independence, and the Guatemalan upper class was not going to grant the masses justice. As the CIA itself admitted in 1968, the Guate-malan upper class and officer corps were adamantly opposed to "even the most elemental progress and reform" that would alleviate "the mis-erable poverty of most Guatemalans." The ballot box was a sham;

peaceful protest, a death warrant.[20] If Americans believe, as most do, that armed struggle was justified in the thirteen colonies of North America in the 1770's, then it was justified in Guatemala, where the rulers since Jacobo Arbenz have been far more oppressive than the British ever were in North America.

If the guerrillas are not at fault, what about the United States? Does it bear any responsibility for the tragedy of Guatemala?

There is, of course, the original sin of 1954. Just as the Soviet army intervened in Hungary to bring down a reformist government that was moving the country away from the Soviet orbit, so the United States intervened to bring down Jacobo Arbenz, who was moving Guatemala away from the *pax Americana*. Most American commentators now admit, with hindsight, that the intervention was a mistake. Some condemn the Eisenhower administration for acting on behalf of the United Fruit Company. Others, while lamenting the outcome, add an important caveat: America's intentions were pure. A chain of errors—fueled by anti-Communist paranoia, not economic imperialism—led the United States to overthrow Arbenz, but the United States intended no harm to the Guatemalan people. The policymakers who engineered PBSUCCESS were "well-intentioned men," as Latin America expert Robert Pastor has argued.[21] And, as Cullather indicates, if the CIA colluded with members of the Guatemalan upper class to oust Arbenz it was not because it, too, opposed social reform, but because they were the only Guatemalans who were eager to overthrow him. The outcome was tragic, but, as Pastor points out, this was not the Eisenhower administration's intention.

This is a common refrain in American interpretations of U.S. foreign policy: even when the United States has erred, its intentions were pure. The United States always means well. It is the city on the hill.

I agree with Pastor that in overthrowing Arbenz the United States was motivated by anti-Communist paranoia, not economic imperial-

[20] CIA Directorate of Intelligence, "Guatemala after the Military Shake-up," 6, NSFCF: Guatemala, Box 54, LBJL.
"A Discordant Consensus on Democracy," *Diplomatic History*,

ism; that, as José Manuel Fortuny said, "they would have overthrown us even if we had grown no bananas."[22]

I disagree that the men who engineered PBSUCCESS were well-intentioned. Their intentions were as old as international relations: they believed they were acting in the U.S. national interest. Any impact on the Guatemalan people was incidental: if they did not suffer in the process, so much the better, but if they did, *tant pis*. My own study of PBSUCCESS, which has been confirmed by the documents that the CIA has declassified and by Cullather's history, showed that the Eisenhower administration acted with supreme indifference toward the fate of the Guatemalan people. This cannot be described as being well-intentioned. It is, rather, wanton criminal negligence.

In Hungary, after the first months of bloody repression, the regime imposed by the Soviet Union eased up, and by the late 1960's it had become the least repressive of the Soviet bloc. In Guatemala, however, the regime imposed by the United States in 1954 became more repressive as time went by. But is the United States responsible for the regime's crimes?

The United States did not murder Guatemalans, and it did not urge the Guatemalan army to slaughter, rape, or burn. But the United States armed the murderer. The Kennedy, Johnson, Nixon, and Ford administrations supplied and trained the Guatemalan military, and in the 1960's U.S. military advisers helped it fight against the guerrillas. Tenaciously, U.S. officials helped the Guatemalan army overcome its "poor training, indecisiveness, and lack of initiative."[23] The United States did not, of course, want to harm the Guatemalan people; it wanted only to defeat the guerrillas and uphold pro-American stability. The result was tragic for the Guatemalans. And when the stench grew too vile, when the cries of human rights activists grew too loud, U.S. officials tried to shift the blame from the army to the guerrillas or to fictive civilian death squads. The most brazen was the Reagan admini-

[22]Interview with Fortuny, Mexico City, Aug. 16, 1981.
[23]CIA, Directorate of Intelligence, "Guatemala—A Current App 1966, p. 11 quoted, NSFCF: Guatemala, Box 54, LBJL.

stration, and the prize for misstatement belongs to Assistant Secretary of State for Inter-American Affairs Elliott Abrams. On April 4, 1985, Rosario Godoy, a charismatic, 24-year-old leader of Guatemala's only human rights group, disappeared along with her two-year-old son and her younger brother. Their corpses were found in a ravine on the outskirts of Guatemala City. The baby's fingernails had been pulled out. General Mejía Víctores, Ríos Montt's successor, spoke of a car accident. The Archbishop of Guatemala spoke of triple murder. Elliott Abrams came to the general's defense: "So far there is no evidence indicating other than the deaths were due to an accident," he asserted on May 3.[24] The lie was as unnecessary as it was sordid. The general did not need Washington's propaganda: the army had already won; the guerrillas were in retreat.

The army had won without U.S. military aid. In the early 1980's the U.S. Congress resisted Reagan's attempts to resume the military aid Guatemala had spurned in 1977. U.S. aid would have helped, but it was not necessary. The army was strong enough to triumph without it, thanks in large part to American assistance in the 1960's. Furthermore, Israel stepped into the breach, becoming Guatemala's main supplier of arms.[25] But the primary reason the Guatemalan army won was that the guerrillas had been unable to amass enough weapons to arm their supporters. Had it been otherwise, the challenge would have been formidable.

In 1996, after a poignant crusade by Jennifer Harbury, a Harvard-trained lawyer and wife of a slain Guatemalan guerrilla commander, the Clinton administration released a report admitting that the CIA had worked closely with Guatemala's security and intelligence services through the Reagan, Bush, and first Clinton administrations, had funded them to the tune of several million dollars, and had kept a number of Guatemalan officers on its payroll who

[24]For the deaths of Rosario Godoy, her son, and her brother, see: *El Gráfico, El Imparcial, La Razón,* and *La Hora* of Apr. 8, 1985; *Prensa Libre,* Apr. 9, 1985; and Americas Watch, *Guatemala: The Group for Mutual Support, 1984–1985* (New York, 1985), pp. 40–46. For Abrams's comment, see *ibid.,* p. 52.

[25]See Michael McClintock, *The American Connection,* vol. 2: *State Terror and Popular Resistance in Guatemala* (London: Zed Books, 1985), pp. 192–96.

were "alleged to have been involved in significant human rights abuses." Frankly acknowledging the magnitude of the slaughter perpetrated by the Guatemalan army, the report also repeatedly stressed that in providing assistance to the murderous security services, U.S. intentions had been good.[26]

The CIA deserves credit for having released documents about PB-SUCCESS, for having hired someone of Cullather's intellect and integrity to write an internal history of the operation, and for then declassifying it. But for a cleansing to take place there must be the equivalent of a truth commission, one that will shed light on the U.S. role in Guatemala after 1954. "America's relations with Guatemala are a chilling study in cynicism," the *New York Times* noted in 1995. "Americans deserve a truthful accounting of the events of the past 40 years in Guatemala. Guatemalans deserve no less."[27]

This cleansing, however, will not change reality in Guatemala. Guatemala is today a sick society. The tortures, the disappearances, and the killings fester. In a country of ten million, about 150,000 have been slaughtered. Can one imagine the effect on the survivors, on the children of the woman who was raped before she was killed, on those whose father was hacked down and burned alive, or mercifully killed by a machine gun burst, without torture? As of the victims, so of the criminals: can we imagine the scars on those soldiers who perpetrated the atrocities—youths in their late teens, many of them, abducted from their villages to serve in the army and subjected to grueling and dehumanizing military training? The slaughter of the early 1980's tightened the grip of fear over the populace, and the culture of fear, not the democratic opening, remains the fabric of Guatemalan society.

Still, one searches for reasons to hope. Perhaps with the end of the Cold War, the anti-Communist banner, in whose name so many crimes

[26]Intelligence Oversight Board, "Report on the Guatemala Review," June 28, 1996, p. 25 quoted. CIA financial assistance, over $30 million according to press reports, fell under the rubric of "liaison" relationships with foreign intelligence services, which did not require congressional notification and were not affected by the congressional prohibition on military aid to the Guatemalan army (*NYT*: Apr. 2, 1995, p. 12; Apr. 5, p. 6; Apr. 10, p. 8).

[27]*NYT*, May 19, 1995, p. 30

have been perpetrated and so many minds warped, will be lowered. The Guatemalan guerrillas, acknowledging their military defeat, signed a peace agreement in December 1996 in which they relinquished their arms and were welcomed back into the Guatemalan family. Perhaps, at last, the upper class might grant some social concession. Perhaps an honest civilian president will challenge the status quo and support social reform.

These are reasonable hopes, but Guatemala has defied reason since 1954. It still has the most regressive fiscal system and the most unequal land-ownership pattern in Latin America. Its army, victorious on the battlefield, has evolved into an all-powerful mafia, stretching its tentacles into drug-trafficking, kidnapping, and smuggling. And its civilian presidents have shown no inclination to challenge the army and the upper class, to fight for social reform, or to clamp down on corruption. Today Hungary is free. Guatemala is still paying for the American "success."

Piero Gleijeses

Index

Index

In this index an "f" after a number indicates a separate reference on the next page, and an "ff" indicates separate references on the next two pages. A continuous discussion over two or more pages is indicated by a span of page numbers, e.g., "57–59." *Passim* is used for a cluster of references in close but not consecutive sequence.

Abrams, Elliott, xxxiv
Acheson, Dean, 31
Advertising, 40
Afghanistan, viii
Aircraft, viii, 70, 74, 82ff, 98f, 132, 161ff
Air Force (U.S.), 44
Alfhem, 77–80 *passim*, 92, 94, 107, 131, 156f
American Civil Liberties Union, 122
American Federation of Labor, 159
American Financial Corporation, 119
Amnesty International, xxv
Amory, Robert, 44
Amsterdam, 54
Ananda Mahidol, 139
Arana, Carlos, xxvi
Arana, Francisco, 11f, 127, 145f
Arbenz Guzmán, Jacobo, xiii, xxxii, 5, 7, 11ff, 18, 21, 84, 94, 96, 120, 127f, 145–48, 171, 174; betrayal of, xxiv, xxviii, 97, 101; capitulation of, xxix,

xxxi, 102, 110, 157, 159, 162–64; U.S. assessments of, 17, 19f, 37, 60, 143, 145, 169; extralegal authority, 24, 84; Army loyalty to, 42, 47, 84, 89; awareness of plot against him, 53, 55–58, 131; CIA attempts to intimidate, 64, 70; attempts to arm citizenry, 80f; attempts to negotiate, 83, 131; death of, 109
Arbenz, María Villanova, 20, 107
Arévalo, Juan José, xxv, 11–20 *passim*, 127, 146, 148, 167–69
Argentina, 108, 112
Arms: CIA shipments of, 29; embargo, 49, 52f; from the *Alfhem*, 79ff, 107–8
Arzú Irigoyan, Alvaro, 175
Assassination, xix, 137–41, 143
Associated Press, 121

Bananas, *see* United Fruit Company
Bank of Guatemala, 77
Bannell, Marshall, 54

Bannera, 10, 16
Barnes, Tracy, 43f, 72, 76, 83ff, 108ff
Bay of Pigs, xiii, xiv, 5–8 *passim*, 70, 110, 122
Berger, Óscar, 176
Berlin, 15
Bernays, Edward L., 16, 18
Berry, James Lampton, 43f
Bevan, Aneurin, 93
Big Con, The, 40
Bissell, Richard, 44, 46, 72, 74, 89, 97, 100, 110, 121
Black, Eli, 119
Black flights, 59, 130
Boren, David, xi
Bosworth, Stephen, xxviii
Brazil, 92, 111f
British Guiana, 165
Bruce, David, 29, 147
Brutus, Marcus, 139
Burma, 39, 111
Bush, George, xxxiv
Bush, George W., vii, 176

Cabot, John, 32
Caesar, Augustus, 139
Caesar, Julius, 139
Cakchiquels, xxiii
Campesinos, 11, 14, 24f, 42
Canada, 52
Carter, Jimmy, xxvi
Cassius, Gaius, 139
Castillo Armas, Carlos, 5, 12f, 43, 67, 131, 137, 150, 155–63 *passim*, 172; invasion of Guatemala, xxviii, 75f, 87–92, 95, 99f, 132, 162f; CIA relationship with, 18, 28–33 *passim*, 52, 59, 63, 72f, 117, 120, 141; relations with other dissidents, 34, 49, 64; relations with Army, 42, 85, 101; relations with Central American leaders, 48; political philosophy of, 50, 117; use of aircraft, 71, 85–90 *passim*, 99, 107; rebel army, 72, 74, 80, 96; as president, 106, 109, 113–16, 118, 165–67, 169
Castro, Fidel, 5, 110, 113
Catholic Church, 24f, 42, 54, 65, 116, 151, 159, 175

Central Intelligence Agency (CIA), 12; "openness" initiative, xi, xii, xvi, xix, xxxv, 122; History Staff, xii–xvii, 5f; Guatemala City station, xv, 105; destruction of documents, xvii, 105; declassification of documents, xvii, xviii, 175; Historical Review Panel, xviii; post-1954 assessments of Guatemala, xxix, xxx, xxxi; Directorate of Plans (DDP), 8, 26, 39–44 *passim*, 141; assessment of Guatemalan threat, 15, 24, 27; Western Hemisphere Division, 27, 39, 108, 121; Directorate of Intelligence (DDI), 44; plans for Guatemala's future, 61–63; Historical Review Group, 122
Central Intelligence Group, 15
Cerezo, Vinicio, xxx
Chancellor, John, 121
Chicago Tribune, 18, 56
Chile, 40, 76, 108–12 *passim*, 165
China, 15, 39, 71, 143
Chiquimula, 87f, 95–100 *passim*, 109
Chiquita, 119
Church, Frank, 121
Churchill, Winston, 111f
Civil Air Transport (CAT), 45, 71, 98
Clinton, William, xvi, xviii, xxxiv, 143, 165, 175f
Coffee, 9, 41, 52, 113, 170
Columbia Broadcasting System (CBS), 54, 93
Cominform, 141
Comisión para el Esclarecimiento Histórico, 143, 165, 172–75
Comité Anticomunista de Locatorias de los Mercados de Guatemala, 65
Comité Civico Nacional, 34
Comité Estudiantes Universitarios Anti-Comunistas (CEUA), 42, 64–67, 73, 80, 84
Communism, 15, 21, 58, 93, 106, 143ff; nature of the threat, 26–27, 35, 37; international ties to Guatemala, 107
Confederación General de Trabajadores de Guatemala (CGTG), 14
Confederación Nacional Campesina de Guatemala (CNCG), 14

Confederación de Trabajadores de
América Latina, 146, 166
Congress (U.S.), xxxiv, 16, 79, 107,
120, 122
Copán, 87
Corcoran, Thomas G., 16f, 118, 127
Córdova Cerna, Juan, 34, 49, 51
CORONA, xvii
Cortínez, Adolfo Ruíz, 49
Cotton, 170
Covert operations, xiii, 39; PBSUCCESS
as model for, 5, 7, 110
Cuba, 8, 10, 92, 109–12 *passim*
Cuban Missile Crisis, xvi, xvii
Czechoslovakia, 19, 78, 94, 107, 114,
130, 156

Dakar, 78
Dalai Lama, xvii
Defense Dept. (U.S.), ix, 8, 25f, 44, 122
DeLarm, Jerry, 120
Delgado, Jorge Isaac, 53
Del Monte, 118
Denmark, 39
Díaz, Carlos Enrique, 20, 69, 96, 100ff,
132, 157, 162–64
Dominican Republic, 12, 110, 165, 167
Donovan, William, 39
Dostoevsky, Fyodor, 113
Dulles, Allen, 5, 17, 29f, 37, 44, 60, 87,
89, 94, 98, 108f, 112, 119, 121f,
128–31 *passim*, 144–47, 172
Dulles, John Foster, 5, 29, 36f, 39,
52, 58, 79, 92, 111, 113, 119f,
130f, 167

Economic sanctions, 25, 41, 44, 153
Eisenhower, Dwight, xiv, xxxii, 5, 7f,
32, 36ff, 83, 92f, 98, 109, 115, 119f,
167
Eisenhower, John, 121
El Combate, 42, 67
El Rebelde, 42, 67f
El Salvador, viii, xxix, 10, 14, 20, 28,
34, 44, 48, 108, 153; and invasion,
87–90 *passim*
Escuela Claridad, 14
Esquipulas, 88–96 *passim*
Esterline, Jacob, 59

Federal Bureau of Investigation (FBI),
14–15, 72, 122
Flores, Leonardo Castillo, 14
Florida, Honduras, 87
Ford, Gerald, xxxiii
Foreign aid, 20, 114, 158
Fortune, 118
Fortuny, José Manuel, xxxiii, 8, 14, 20,
22, 54, 64, 83, 97, 102f, 109, 129
France, 82, 94, 109
Freedom of Information Act, 122

Gálvez, Juan Manuel, 29f, 48f, 79f
Gates, Robert, xi, xii, 122
Geneva Conference, 93
Germany, vii, 52, 78, 93, 111
Gleijeses, Piero, xiii
Godoy, Rosario, xxxiv
Good Neighbor policy, 31
Grace, W. R., and Company, 10
Great Britain, xxxii, 82, 93f, 111
Greece, 45, 163
Gruson, Sydney, 54, 94f, 130
Gualán, 89f, 95f, 101, 109, 132
Guardia Civil, 12, 28, 47, 82
Guatemala: documents on, xiii–xix; history of, xxiii–xxxi, 9–14; Revolution
of 1944, 11, 20, 25, 60f, 102, 116,
144f, 164; nationalism in, 15, 106;
state radio and press, 22, 25, 77; as
testing ground, 35, 37; Constitution,
64; Constituent Assembly, 166
— Army of, 9–13 *passim*, 34, 80f, 109,
145ff, 166, 174; coup against Arbenz, xxv, 98, 100f, 163; power after
1954, xxviii–xxx, 168–70; U.S. assistance to, 17, 176; threatened by land
reform, 24, 53; in PBSUCCESS plan,
42, 47, 63,160; CIA pressure on ("K-program"), 68–73 *passim*, 82, 84,
89, 98, 159f; encounter with rebels,
88, 97, 99; involvement in drug trafficking, 176
Guatemala City, 9, 58, 81, 83, 89, 103–
7 *passim*, 157
Guatemala Human Rights Commission,
176
Guerrillas, xxxi, xxxii, 168
Guevara, Ernesto "Che," 113

Gulick, Lewis, 121
Gutiérrez, Víctor Manuel, 14, 20–24
    passim, 109, 131, 166

Haines, Gerald, xiv, 137
Haiti, 167
Hammarsskjold, Dag, 111
Haney, Albert, 45–46, 57, 60ff, 66, 70,
    73f, 81, 84, 95–98 *passim*, 105, 117;
    "facts of life" cable, 68–69; two-
    string strategy, 85–89 *passim*
Harbury, Jennifer, xxxiv
HARDROCK/BAKER, ix, 82, 131
Hedden, Stuart, 146
Helms, Richard, 121
Herring, George C., xviii
Hirsch, Richard, 151
Hiss, Alger, xi
Hitler, Adolf, 140
Hobbing, Enno, 102ff
Holland, Henry F., 59, 81, 92ff, 108,
    114f, 130
Honduras, xxix, 13, 28, 32, 34, 42–48
    passim, 75, 92, 97, 137, 153–57 *pas-
    sim*, 171; aid to PBSUCCESS, 79,
    169
Hugo, Victor, 113
Human rights groups, 176
Hungary, xxxi–xxxvi
Hunt, E. Howard, 110, 121

Immerman, Richard, xiii
Indians, xxiii, xxvii, 9f, 116, 170, 173
Indochina, *see* Viet Nam
Indonesia, xii, 9, 110
Institut de Anthrópólogia y História, 18
Intelligence Oversight Board, xxviii,
    xxx
International Monetary Fund (IMF), 114
Investa, 78
Ipala, 100
Iran, viii, ix, xii, xvii, 7, 38–43 *passim*,
    63, 93, 117, 122
Iraq, viii
Israel, xxxiv
Italy, 107

James, Daniel, 112
James, William, 161

Japan, viii, 22, 93
JMARC, *see* Bay of Pigs
Johnson, Lyndon, xxvi, xxxiii
Joyce, Robert P., 146
Justice Department, 19
Jutiapa, 87f, 92

Kennedy, John F., xii, xxxiii, 123
KGB, xi
King, Joseph Caldwell (J. C.), 27–33
    passim, 39–44 *passim*, 55, 61, 71,
    109, 129f, 146, 154f
Kinzer, Stephen, 122
Kirkpatrick Report, xiv
Korea and Korean War, 9, 19, 26
Labor unions, 10–12, 14, 18f, 25, 63,
    79f, 106, 115, 144f, 151, 159; mobi-
    lized against invasion, 83, 85, 100,
    131
Ladinos, xxiii, 173
Lahey, Edwin N., 162
Land reform (Decree 900), xxiv, 20–27,
    35, 42, 48, 53, 61, 92, 103, 109, 117,
    128, 143f, 148–50, 167, 172
Lantaff, Paul, 79
La Union, 90
Leddy, John M., 34
Leddy, Raymond, 43
Le Monde, 111
Linares, José Bernabé, 113
LINCOLN, 45–52 *passim*, 60, 66, 69,
    73, 129, 132, 172
Linebarger, Paul, 40
Lobe, Jim, 176
Lodge, Henry Cabot, 92f
Long, Huey, 139

MacDonald, Charnaud, 157
Macuelizo, 87
Mafia, 113
Mann, Thomas C., 17, 29, 33, 114,
    127f, 146
Mao Tse-tung, xxvii
Marines (U.S.), 80, 96f, 167, 172
Marks, Frederick, 72
Martínez, Alfonso, 20, 53f, 77, 80, 130,
    143
Matamoros, 12, 132
Mayans, *see* Indians

Mazatenango, 12
McAuliffe, Mary, xiv, xvii
McCarthy, Joseph, 27, 45
McCone, John, 120
McCormack, John, 79
McDonald, J. Kenneth, xii, xiii, xiv, xvii, xviii
Méndez Montenegro, Julio César, xxv, xxvi, xxix, 168–71
Mendoza Azurdia, Rodolfo, 83, 131
Mercador, Ramón, 139
Mexico, 28, 49, 112, 153, 167; as asylum for Guatemalans, 104, 108f, 166
Mexico City, 18, 53, 94f, 111, 128
Miami, Florida, 70, 75, 97, 171
Military advisers (U.S.), 68f
Miller, Edward G., 29ff, 146
Monzón, Elfego, 48, 70, 99, 101f, 112; urged to lead revolt, 84–92 *passim*, 97, 161; in junta, 102f, 132
Morton, Thruston B., 120
Mossadeq, Mohammad, ix, 38f

Napalm, 83
Narcotics, xxxvi
National Broadcasting Corporation (NBC), 56
National Intelligence Estimate (NIE), 25, 34, 144, 168
National Security Council (NSC), 15, 19, 35, 38, 107, 115, 129
Navy (U.S.), 32, 44, 80, 82, 131, 156
Network in Solidarity with the People of Guatemala, 176
New Deal, 148
New Leader, The, 112
New Look, 36f
New Orleans, 30
Newsweek, 18, 122
New York Times, xviii, xix, xxv, xxxv, 18, 54, 56, 79, 94, 130, 167
Nicaragua, 12, 32, 34, 45, 50, 57, 70, 92, 130, 153, 167, 171
Nitze, Paul, 33
Nixon, Richard M., xxxiii, 109
North, Oliver, xv
Novotoný, Antonín, 54
NSC 162/2, *see* New Look

Nuclear weapons, 15
Nueva Ocotepeque, 87

Office of Policy Coordination, 17
Office of Strategic Services, 39
Office of Survey Information, xiv
Oklahoma Press Association, xi
Opa Locka, Florida, *see* LINCOLN
Operations Coordinating Board, 38, 151
Organización Regional Interamericana de Trabajadores, 159
Organization of American Historians, viii
Organization of American States (OAS), 31, 40–44 *passim*, 52, 92, 111, 123, 153f, 171; Caracas conference, 56, 58, 69, 83, 130
Osorio, Oscar, 48f, 103

Panama, 53, 75, 167
Panama Canal Zone, 32, 52
Pan American Airways, 10, 75, 129
Pan-American Highway, 14
Pan-Americanism, 58
Partido Acción Revolucionaria (PAR), 11, 14, 80
Partido Guatemalteco del Trabajo (PGT), 14, 20–25, 47, 53f, 58, 65, 83, 103, 108f, 115, 117, 129, 146, 149, 158, 164–67; ties to international communism, 26, 78, 166
Passarelli, Ortiz, 116
Pastor, Robert, xxxii
PBFORTUNE, 29–37 *passim*, 50, 129, 137
PBHISTORY, 106, 132
PBSUCCESS, plans for, 38, 40–51, 60, 150–56; security breaches, 59, 93f, 119–23; backlash against, 105, 111f; disclosures on, 119–23
Pellecer, Carlos, 20, 22, 166
Peralta, Enrique, 169
Perón, Juan, and Perónism, 15, 50
Peurifoy, John, 26, 45, 59, 69, 85, 94, 97, 101ff, 112, 129, 156f, 163f
Philippines, xii
Phillips, David Atlee, xv, 76, 81, 109f, 121f

Pike, Otis, 121
Pravda, 93
Press (Guatemalan), 151, 160
Press (U.S.), 18, 56, 79, 94, 162–64
Psychological Strategy Board, 40
Psychological warfare (propaganda),
  viii, xxiv, 7, 32, 40, 61–73 *passim*,
  79, 106, 150; philosophy of, 66, 74
Puerto Barrios, 9, 77–81 *passim*, 87,
  131; battle at, 90, 95f, 101, 109, 132,
  156
Puerto Cabesas, 70
Puerto Cortés, 78

Quezaltenango, 12, 161
Quezaltepeque, 87, 100

Radio Internacional, 65
Radio propaganda, xv, 40f, 75f, 80, 88,
  98, 101, 105, 131f, 156–57, 162
Radio Universal, 67
Railroads, 10, 81, 95, 99
Reader's Digest, 56
Reagan, Ronald, xxvii, xxviii, xxxiii,
  xxxiv, 165, 172
Regime change, vii
Rhodesia, 52
Rio Pact, 20, 31, 82
Ríos Montt, Efraín, xxviii, xxxiv
Rivera, Diego, 112
Robert F. Kennedy Memorial Center for
  Human Rights, 176
Roettinger, Philip C., 111, 165, 171
Roosevelt, Franklin D., 31, 148
Roosevelt, Kermit, 39, 46
Ross, Thomas B., 120
Rossell y Arrellana, Mariano, 65, 130
Rumsfeld, Donald, 176

Sabotage, 88, 131, 154, 157
St. Petersburg, Florida, 71
Salamá uprising, 33–37 *passim*, 42, 54,
  119, 129
Sánchez, José Angel, 80, 101f, 132, 164
San Miguel Correderos, 90
San Salvador, 102
Saturday Evening Post, 56
Schlesinger, Stephen, 122
Schneider, Ronald M., 107

Schoenfeld, Rudolf E., 151
Secrecy, xii, xiii, 122
Shaffer, Robert, ix
SHERWOOD, *see* Radio propaganda
Silva Girón, César Augusto, 90
Simmons, Carlos, 33
Smith, Richard Harris, 122
Smith, Walter Bedell, 27–33 *passim*, 37,
  45, 118
Solarium talks, 35
Somoza, Anastazio, 12, 22, 28–33 *pas-
  sim*, 45, 48f; assistance to PBSUC-
  CESS, 70, 83, 171
Somoza, Tacho, 30
Soviet Union, xi, xvi, xxxi, xxxii, xxxiii,
  9, 15, 26, 57, 106, 108, 112, 148, 163
Spain, 9
Springfjord, 99, 111
Stabank, 77
Stalin, Josef, 22, 93, 107
State Department, xviii, xxvii, 8, 14–20
  passim, 24, 26, 79, 103, 122, 146f;
  FRUS series, viii, ix, 143; oversight
  of operations, 29–33 *passim*, 81,
  158; concerns about deniability, 30f,
  94, 111f, 144; policy planning staff,
  33; apprehensions about Arbenz, 34;
  Bureau of Inter-American Affairs, 35;
  and diplomatic isolation of Guate-
  mala, 44, 52; attempts to stop *Alf-
  hem*, 77f
Stone, Oliver, xii
Student groups, *see* Comité Estudiantes
  Universitarios Anti-Comunistas
Suez crisis, 112
Sulzberger, Arthur Hays, 94
Switzerland, 54, 109, 130
Szczecin, 78

Taiwan, 22, 93
Team-A Team-B Experiment, xvi
Tegucigalpa, 82
Tenet, George, xix
Terrorism, vii
Tibet, xvii
Time, 18
Times (of London), 111
Times of India, 93
Tiquisate, 10, 16, 18, 23, 127ff

Tofte, Hans, 39, 41
Toriello, Guillermo, 57f, 92, 94, 100,
  130, 163f
TPAJAX, 38f, 43, 46
Tranger, George, 47, 66f, 70, 84
Tropical Radio, 119
Trujillo, Rafael, 12, 28
Truman, Harry S., 14, 19, 27f, 37, 40
Truth and Reconciliation Commission,
  see Comisión para el Esclarecimiento
  Histórico
Turnbull, Walter, 18, 128

Ubico, Jorge, 9, 15, 34, 51, 113
Union Bank of Switzerland, 77
United Brands, 118f
United Fruit Company, xiii, xxxii, 8, 10,
  15f, 18, 22, 34, 79, 92, 127f, 144ff,
  158, 172; antitrust action against, 19,
  118; and Decree 900, 23, 130, 149f;
  as asset, 25, 35, 51; CIA plans for,
  62f; as propaganda liability, 93, 118;
  fate after PBSUCCESS, 118–19, 164
United Nations, 31, 92, 98, 115
United States Information Agency
  (USIA), 93, 115f
Uruguay, 109

Vaughan, Harry, 28
Venezuela, 10

VENONA, xvii
Víctores, Mejía, xxxiv
Viet Nam, viii, xi, xxix, 92, 110, 117
Villegas, Perfecto, 161

Washington Office on Latin America,
  176
Washington Post, 79, 162–64
Weiss, Carl, 139
Welles, Orson, 76
Whelan, Thomas, 45
Willauer, Whiting, 45, 59, 120f
Winchell, Walter, 56
Wise, David, 120
Wisner, Frank, 17, 32f, 44, 55, 59, 77f,
  85, 89, 92, 100, 102, 108f, 114, 129f,
  157; "shift of gears" cable, 103–6
  passim, 132
Woolsey, R. James, xvi
World Bank, 22, 63
World Federation of Trade Union, 146,
  166
World War II, vii, 10
Wulfsbrook, 78

Ydígoras Fuentes, Miguel, xxiv, 12, 49,
  51, 64, 116, 120, 169
Yugoslavia, 39

Zacapa, 87–100 *passim*, 163

CPSIA information can be obtained
at www.ICGtesting.com
Printed in the USA
JSHW022330290123
36987JS00001B/1